Heroes Who Changed the World

Scandinavia Publishing House
Drejervej 15,3rd floor DK-Copenhagen NV Denmark
www.scanpublishing.dk info@scanpublishing.dk

Artdirection and design by Ben Alex
Produced by Scandinavia Publishing House

Printed in China
ISBN 9788771323979

HEROES
WHO CHANGED THE WORLD

SCANDINAVIA

INTRODUCTION

Today's parents and teachers are desperate to get positive role models in front of their kids. They demand quality reading packed with fun and an easy-to-digest feast of learning.

Here is the biography series that fulfill these demands. 10 HEROES WHO CHANGED THE WORLD is different because it doesn't just tell about people and values — it shows them — in a way kids' spirits grab ahold of and want to imitate.

This is value-building, character-shaping reading just right for today's 10-14-year-olds. Here are the great heroes — men and women who shaped our faith and times in the tradition of Biblical standards. In the process, these people changed the world.

The Heroes project was accomplished during a rough time in my own personal life, but it sure had its rewards. To study the lives of these great men and women changed my life — and I know it can change yours and your child's, too.

Ben Alex

CONTENTS

has been called the greatest Christian visionary and scholar of the 19th century. With no academic education he taught himself more than twenty languages, translated the Bible into forty-three Asian languages and dialects, became a distinguished botanist and laid the foundation for the modern Protestant missions movement. His life's motto, "Expect great things, attempt great things," has inspired millions of people around the world.

has been an inspiring role model to millions of men and women who wanted to make a difference in the world. Her life is an amazing account of one woman's determination to follow her lonely calling, despite all the odds against her. And as with all great heroes, Florence's character was formed in early childhood.

was the son of a wealthy Italian merchant. As a young man he renounced his inheritance in order to follow Christ and live in poverty for the rest of his life. Francis is one of the greatest role models for following Christ ever to challenge the Christian Church - and a beautiful example of trust and earthy faith.

was one of the most reknowned Christian martyrs during Hitler's Third Reich. A brilliant theologian, pastor, writer and ecumenical leader, Bonhoeffer joined the German Resistance as it attempted to overthrow Hitler. After two years of imprisonment, Bonhoeffer was finally executed at Flossenbtirg concentration camp, only a few weeks before the Allies arrived. His life is a rare example of determination, faith and courage.

JUSTICE PAGE 385

Martin Luther King, Jr.

led the non-violent Civil Rights Movement in America with such conviction that he became known as the drum major for his people. Those who followed him during his lifetime learned the same lesson we can learn from his legacy today - "the few" speaking God's truth will always prevail against "the many" believing a lie.

THE EARLY CHURCH PAGE 433

St. Augustine

is the foremost Christian theologian after Paul. More than anyone else, he has promoted a better understanding of the doctrines of the Christian faith. His writings provide the central pillars of Western civilization. Augustine's tumultuous life is a remarkable example of how God is found by those who honestly seek Him.

HEROES
WHO CHANGED THE WORLD

EXPLORATION
REFORMATION
PRAYER
SERVANTHOOD
MISSIONS
COMPASSION
SPIRITUALITY
DISCIPLESHIP
JUSTICE
THE EARLY CHURCH

Stories by
Ben Alex
Sharon Jones, Marlee Alex, Caroline Higgins
Illustrations by
Giuseppe Rava, Musio Cosimo, Andrea Jula

SCANDINAVIA

For my friend Jens Kargaard,
a modern–day Livingstone in the primitive
bush country of South Africa.

David Livingstone

THE MISSIONARY WHO "DISCOVERED" AFRICA

1813—1873

Great men and women are not in need of our praise.
We are the ones in need of getting to know them.

By Ben Alex

Illustrations by Giuseppe Rava

INTO AFRICA

We're going on a trip. It'll be a long, hard trip, probably the toughest trip you'll ever make. So pack your things — and don't forget your hiking boots, insect repellant and sunblock. We're going to Africa.

To get to the place where our trip begins we'll take an airplane across the Sahara desert down to the equator. From there we'll turn south, drop over the mountains, across **Lake Edward** and continue until we hit a blue lake stretching south as far as the eye can see: **Lake Tanganyika**.

Look over to your left! On the distant eastern shore you'll see the town of **Ujiji**; and further away, the deep jungles of Burundi and Tanzania.

To the West is the country of Zaire. As we descend, you'll see zebra and antelope, a lonely herd of giraffes or elephants. Our plane sweeps over a grove of bent trees, then hits the ground with a bump, rolls down the narrow runway and comes to a halt. As we step out we are met by a breeze that feels as hot as air from a giant hairdryer.

MEET DR. LIVINGSTONE

It's a bright, sultry summer afternoon. From the east, a dozen natives wind their way slowly through the yellow grass. The Africans wear nothing but loincloths. They carry heavy packs on their heads. The sun glistens off their

sweaty backs. A tall white man limps in front of them. His face is lined with wrinkles, his brown hair streaked with grey. His beard and moustache are nearly white.

Though he seems exhausted and in pain, the man motions impatiently at his carriers that they should move faster. Finally, he points with his walking stick towards the soft grass under a tall **mvula** tree. There the group unloads its burdens and drops down into the grass.

The white man pulls out a metal-backed notebook, along with ink and pen from his travel bag, then sits down and sighs. "So many difficulties have been put in my way," he writes, "I'm doubting whether God is with me . . . ."

He drops the notebook onto his lap and opens a well-worn Bible: "All power is given unto me in heaven and on earth: go ye, therefore, and teach all nations... and lo, I am with you always, even unto the end of the world."

This man is the Scottish missionary, doctor and explorer, **David Livingstone**. He is heading toward the end of his African adventure. Let's retrace his footsteps — and peek inside his journals. Along the way we will discover why David Livingstone is called the greatest explorer of the nineteenth century.

THE MASSACRE AT NYANGWE, 1871

On the following morning David Livingstone's African caravan reached the banks of the Lualaba river and market town of **Nyangwe**. Women in colorful clothes arranged their baskets of fish and displayed trays of sweet potatoes and corn. It was market day, and Dr. Livingstone's crew were stocking provisions before continuing their treck north along the river.

Africa Before Livingstone

When Livingstone arrived in South Africa in 1841, the map of the "dark African continent" was unlike our maps today except for the coastline. Portuguese explorers had accurately drawn that 350 years earlier: Bartolomeu Dias sailed along the western coast, reaching the Cape of Good Hope (1488). Ten years later, Vasco da Gama rounded the Cape and explored the eastern coastline, surprised to find wealthy Arab trading posts there. (These later became slave stations. By Livingstone's birth, an estimated 100,000 African slaves were being exported yearly to Arab countries, America and Brazil.)

Yet although the coastal regions and the lower streams of Africa's four great rivers — the Nile, the Niger, the Congo, and the Zambesi — had been mapped by Europeans, beyond them were enormous spaces marked "Unexplored" on maps of the 1800s. It was believed that the interior of Africa was one vast desert

This map shows Central Africa as it was known in 1841 when Livingstone arrived.

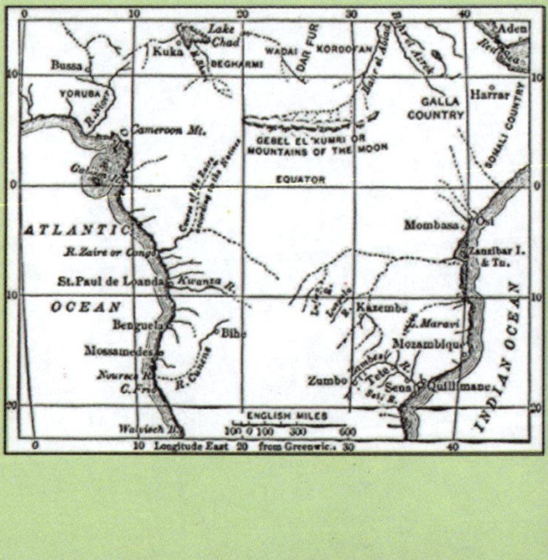

All the hustle and bustle made Livingstone cheerful, even though he was suffering from several tropical diseases. Four years earlier he had set out to solve an ancient mystery: Where did the great **Nile**, the world's longest river, begin? Explorers had wondered about the source of the Nile for thousands of years, yet no one had found it. The interior part of Africa had never been explored; no highways or railroads crossed the thick, impassable jungle. The only way through it was by riverboat.

If Livingstone could find the Nile's source and trace the river up to **Lake Victoria** in the north, then the interior of this dark continent would become open to European trade and colonization — and most importantly, to missionaries. Then the good news of the Gospel could be brought to the millions of African people who had never even heard of Jesus!

Nyangwe was the last place Livingstone could buy food before the difficult journey northwards along the Lualaba river. Livingstone felt optimistic as he bargained with the women at the market. He was convinced the Lualaba river would lead him to the Nile. In a few weeks he would be able to put the upper Nile on the map!

Then something happened which drastically changed his plans.

An African suddenly ran out of the forest into town, pointing at clouds of black smoke behind the trees.

"Slave traders!" he shouted. "Fire in our villages!"

Livingstone spun around just in time to see a gang of Arab men in white robes storming through the marketplace. The Arabs stopped and shot into the crowd. Children screamed and ran. Baskets and buckets were knocked over.

landscape. No European had ever been further north of the South African colony than the edge of the great Kalahari desert, where Dutch settlers, called Boers, moved after the English took over their colony and abolished slave labor on their farms.

Dr. David Livingstone, in 1849, was the first European to cross that desert and plunge into unexplored Central Africa.

"Africa is like a chest," he said. "The top and bottom drawers have been pulled open. But the center drawer is locked tight."

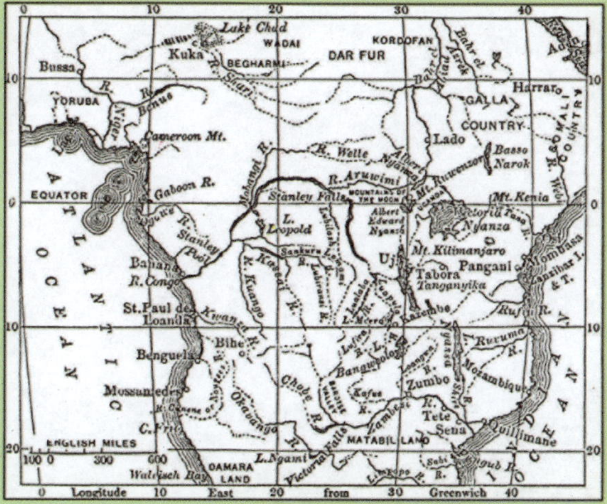

Central Africa as known shortly after Livingstone's death.

Vegetables and fruit rolled onto the ground or splattered as they fell. Some Africans ran for the river and jumped into overloaded canoes; many were shot in the back by Arabs as others paddled madly with hands and arms to get away. The canoes turned over, and many people were swept away by the current. Their heads disappeared one by one under the water. Those left unharmed were hunted down and captured by the Arabs; then marched off to a slave station in Ujiji.

Livingstone was in shock. Around him lay wounded children, and from the river the cries of drowning people echoed through the village. More than three hundred were dead.

Later that day, Livingstone counted the clouds of smoke from different villages on fire around Nyangwe: seventeen. "Like being in Hell," he wrote in his journal. "I'm sick at heart! This place is a den of the worst kind of hunters!"

Never before — not even in times of tribal warfare — had women and children been attacked like this on their way to market. The slave traders were plunderers and murderers.

LOST IN THE JUNGLE

That night Livingstone was restless and could not sleep. He called **Susi**, his African servant.

"Tomorrow," he said, "we'll start out north along the Lualaba. It'll be a long and hard journey. Susi, what do you think our chances are?"

"Not good, **Bwana**," answered Susi. "Many carriers have deserted us. Bwana is sick. We have no medicine since the carrier bearing the medicine chest ran away in the forest. Chances not good, Bwana."

"What disturbs me," nodded Livingstone, "is that I cannot trust the Arabs anymore. In the past, the slave traders were kind to me. They helped us against hostile tribes on the trail. But after what happened at the market today, I will not accept another favor from them! I'm wondering if we should turn around and go back to Ujiji."

"How far to Ujiji?" asked Susi.

"Five hundred miles," replied Livingstone. "In Ujiji we can hire new carriers and pick up medicine. By the time we get there I'm sure the supplies I ordered up from the coast will have arrived."

Early next morning, Livingstone and his little caravan walked back along the same trail they had just travelled. Susi was watching the doctor's face, marred by pain with every step he took.

"Please rest!" said Susi as he gently helped Livingstone to lean against a tree before he took off his master's shoes and cleaned the huge sores on his feet.

The journey back to Ujiji took more than three months. All the while Livingstone became weaker, suffering from pneumonia with its fever, while his feet were covered with terrible sores. Finally, the caravan reached its destination — only to find that the medicine and supplies had been stolen!

Now all Livingstone could do was wait.

Tropical Diseases

Because Livingstone was a physician he was able to cure many deadly diseases among the Africans and thus earning their respect and protection. He was also able to cure himself from tropical illnesses. During his 32 years in Africa he suffered from malaria (fatal disease with violent fever caused by parasites in mosquitoes), dysentery (exhausting bowel disease that causes the body to lose too much fluid), ulcers (painful sores on his feet that "often lame permanently if they do not kill") and pneumonia (infectious lung disease).

The drugs that helped Livingstone survive were Quinine and Calomel. The photo shows some of the medicines and tools that Stanley took to him in 1872. Susi and Chuma, Livingstone's faithful servants, brought them back to England after Livingstone's death.

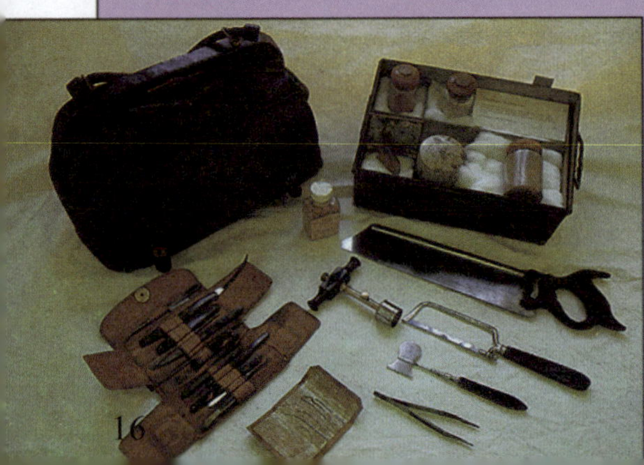

Some of Dr. Livingstone's medical tools

"DR. LIVINGSTONE, I PRESUME?"

But a miracle was on its way: A long, winding caravan was at that very moment heading toward Ujiji with 192 African carriers and more than six tons of supplies: medicine, food, kettles, cloth, blankets, tents — even a bathtub! One carrier bore the American flag. Beside him tramped a tall white man, leading the others. This was **Henry Morton Stanley**, a young reporter for the **New York Herald**, the world's largest sensationalistic newspaper.

"There are rumors Dr. Livingstone is dead," Stanley's boss had told him. "Nobody has heard any news from the famous explorer for years. He may be lost in the jungle. If you can find him it'll make sensational headlines!"

Stanley headed straight for Ujiji. "A white man was recently seen here," he was told. **Could it have been Dr. Livingstone?**

When Lake Tanganyika came into Stanley's sight at noon, he and his men marched into Ujiji firing guns to announce their arrival.

Livingstone was lying inside a straw house reading the Bible, his only medicine, when he heard the shots.

Susi rushed in. "Bwana, big caravan

is coming down mountain!" he cried.

Livingstone staggered outside into the sunlight. The whole village was in an uproar. Through the trees he caught a glimpse of horses and an endless band of carriers loaded with bales and boxes. This was no merchant caravan!

Moments later, a tall young man in sun helmet and white tropical suit walked straight towards him, stopped, snatched off his helmet and said, **"Dr. Livingstone, I presume?"**

Livingstone smiled and held out his hand. "Welcome to Ujiji!"

"I can't believe it!" exclaimed the young American. "I have walked a thousand miles — and I've found you!"

"Found me?" asked Livingstone puzzled. "Did you think I was lost?"

Dr. Livingstone, so glad to be "found" by Stanley, was thrilled with the abundance of supplies which had been brought to him. "What a miracle," he thought. "God has shown his favor by sending this good Samaritan to me!"

Livingstone enjoyed Stanley's company and his provisions — cookies, jelly, smoked herring and Dutch cheese. Stanley also brought news from the world: The opening of the Suez Canal in 1869, the election of America's new president, General Grant, the laying of the Atlantic telegraph cable between Ireland and Newfoundland.

Stanley asked Livingstone a thousand questions for his article about the explorer. But Livingstone, when warned that Stanley was only interested in making a fortune by selling the story to newspapers around the world, just smiled:

"If so, he's heartily welcome, for it's a great deal more than I could ever make out of myself!"

In the months which followed, the two men explored the northern end of Lake Tanganyika together. Livingstone told Stanley about his earlier travels from **Capetown** in South Africa across the **Kalahari** desert to the Atlantic ocean in the west and the mouth of the **Zambesi** river in the east. He told about his feelings when he first discovered "the smoke that thunders"—the great **Victoria Falls**. He told how terrified he was when a lion once jumped on him, grabbed his left shoulder in its mouth, shook him like a cat shakes a mouse and pinned him to the ground. He told about the hostile **Chiboque** tribe to the southwest who would have killed him and his men with their arrows had he not turned his back to show he was not afraid of them.

One evening, the two men were sitting around the camp fire. The quiet around them was pierced only by the chatter of monkeys in a nearby **mango** tree.

Livingstone's Earlier Travels

The London Mission Society appointed David Livingstone to help Robert Moffat at Kuruman mission station 700 miles north of Cape Town. As soon as he arrived in 1841, Livingstone began to look north towards "the smoke of a thousand villages," where no missionary had ever been. Two years later, another mission station was built at Mabotsa, 250 miles northeast of Kuruman. The next station was built at Kolobeng, 40 miles north of Mabotsa, where Livingstone made his first and only convert, the Bakwena chief Sechele.

In 1849, Livingstone pushed

further north, across the barren Kalahari desert, to discover Lake Ngami. Here the natives told about a "land full of rivers" further north. It was at this point that Livingstone decided his task was to chart the "river highways" of Central Africa rather than build mission stations.

On his next trip north, Livingstone discovered the upper Zambesi, a mighty river 1,000 miles long and 3/4 mile across. Anxious to follow the river east and west, he wondered, Could this be "God's highway" to the hidden peoples in the interior of Africa?

Livingstone's search northwest took him to Luanda on the Atlantic Ocean coast and back straight across Central Africa to Quelimane at the Indian Ocean, a trip that took 20 months and crossed 4,000 miles of unexplored savannah and jungle. Livingstone was the first European to walk across Central Africa — an accomplishment that earned him the National Geographic Society's gold medal and a hero's welcome back in England.

But Livingstone wasn't satisfied. He wanted to prove that the Zambesi was a waterway accessible by steamboat. In 1858 he led an expedition of English scientists up the river to the Kebrabasa Rapids. The rapids stopped the steamer and Livingstone had to give up his Zambesi plan.

Instead he turned to the Nile. When he set out to find the source of the Upper Nile, it was his last chance to track a waterway to the interior of Africa. He died in the attempt.

Four years after Livingstone's death, Henry Stanley traced the White Nile to its source some 8,000 feet up in the mountains above Lake Victoria. By then though, the idea of a riverway to Central Africa had become outdated in favor of land roads and railways.

Livingstone's steamboat "Ma-Robert" on the Zambesi

"Dr. Livingstone, you seem different from other missionaries I've met," said Stanley. "Are you a missionary or an adventurer?"

"Both," answered Livingstone. "Missionaries should always be adventurous." Then he added: "To be honest, I suppose the Mission Society at home thinks I'm not a very successful missionary. After more than 30 years here I have only one convert . . . and not a good one either."

"What do you mean?" asked Stanley.

"**Sechele** was a tribal chief at **Kolobeng**," continued Livingstone. "I stayed with him before crossing the Kalahari desert. He was impressed with my medicine that cured his people, and he listened with interest when I told him about God. One day Sechele said:

'Doctor, I want you to change my heart — right now! It is proud and angry. Please give me some medicine for my heart!' I told him that no medicine can change one's heart — only the love of Christ. Eventually, although he became a Christian, he would not give up his many wives."

"Give up his wives?" asked Stanley.

Livingstone looked into the dying fire, then said slowly: "I'm sure about the truth of the Gospel, but I'm uncertain about these customs."

Stanley listened to Livingstone,

impressed with his modesty and respect for the African people. Stanley's fascination for the explorer turned into a deep admiration. In his newspaper story published in the New York Herald, Stanley described Livingstone as a hero, almost a saint, in terms of praising his achievements and character.

"For four months and four days," wrote Stanley, "I lived with Livingstone in the same house, same boat, or same tent, and I could find no fault in him."

Stanley's article made headlines around the world. Having "discovered" the discoverer, he became almost as famous.

But Livingstone ignored fame. He felt it was important to direct the world's attention to the cruel slave trade in Africa. And Stanley's article served this cause. Governments in Europe began to recognize the horrors of the slave trade and its long-term consequences for Africa: it was a barrier to peaceful trade and the spreading of the Christian faith.

Livingstone's Family

Almost four years after Livingstone came to Africa he married Robert Moffat's daughter Mary at Kuruman. Mary followed her husband on his travels for seven years and shared his many hardships. During those years they had five children (one died six weeks old).

Mary's health suffered severely, and Livingstone decided to send his family home to England before he set out on his first great journey across Africa. He didn't see them again until he came back to England for a visit four years later.

In 1862 Mary joined her husband on the Zambesi expedition. Four months later she died from malaria and was buried on the bank of the Zambesi. Her death was a terrible blow to Livingstone. Another blow came when Livingstone learned that his oldest son Robert had crossed the Atlantic Ocean and enlisted in the Union Army during the American Civil War—under a false name because he didn't want to "bring further dishonor to the family name." Robert died in a prisoner-of-war camp in South Carolina in 1864.

When Livingstone became older he realized that he had spent too little time with his family. But then it was too late. His children hardly knew him — and they were off on their own.

At a visit in England, 1857. From left to right: Oswell, Livingstone, Thomas, Agnes, Mary and Robert. One child died at birth; another child, Anna Mary, was born the following year.

A STRANGE DISEASE

Africa was on the verge of civil war. Neighboring tribes raided each other's villages to capture people for the traveling slave merchants: mostly Arabs and the Swahili (Africans from the coast). The hunters plunged deeper and deeper into Africa to expand their business, lining up Africans, putting them into iron collars or into "taming sticks" (forked tree branches laid over the slaves' shoulders which closed around their throats with a metal bar). They then drove them to **Zanzibar** from where the slaves were shipped to Arab countries. An estimated 12,000 slaves were exported from Zanzibar every year, despite the British Navy ships in the Indian Ocean trying to stop the slave boats.

Livingstone was helpless against the armed slave traders. The most he could do was aid the abandoned slaves he found along his way. Once he found a woman tied by the neck to a tree, too exhausted to walk on. The Arabs had left her in the scorching sun to die. Another time the doctor saw a three-year-old left behind as the slave hunters dragged her mother away. Later he found a twelve-year-old boy, left to suffer on the slave trail. Before he died, the

boy whispered, "I have pain in my heart."

Dr. Livingstone knew this was a kind of pain he could not cure with any medicine. That night he wrote in his journal: "The strangest disease I have seen in this country is broken-heartedness. This disease attacks free men who have been made slaves . . . it really seems to be brokenhearts of which they die."

Livingstone decided that his most important work would be to heal the broken hearts of the Africans. To do this the slave trade had to be stopped. Before persuading the British government to make a greater effort in capturing slave ships, he would have to change their attitude towards the Africans.

For this he needed Stanley's help. In the spring of 1872, Stanley walked the 1,000 miles from Ujiji back to the coast. Livingstone followed him 300 miles of the way. At **Unyanyembe**, Livingstone said goodbye and handed Stanley his sealed journals and a stack of letters for the British government and his friends back in England.

The two men never saw each other again. Livingstone went back to Ujiji to prepare for his final quest in search of the Nile's source. Stanley returned to England, and then New York, eager to tell the world about the little boy who had grown up and become the greatest missionary and explorer of his day.

"The Smoke That Thunders"

On his expedition along the Zambesi river towards the Indian Ocean, Livingstone discovered Mosi-oa-tunya or "the smoke that thunders" — the world's greatest waterfall. He renamed it after Victoria, the reigning queen of England.

Victoria Falls is 350 feet deep. 500,000 cubic meters of water pour over the edge of the falls every day. The clouds of mist and vapor rise 300 feet into the air and can be seen ten miles away. From a little island in the Zambesi, on the very lip of the falls, Livingstone watched this spectacular scenery (which today is counted one of the seven natural wonders of the world) and gave thanks to God. The falls had never before been seen by European eyes. But "scenes so lovely must have been gazed upon by angels in their flight," he wrote.

Livingstone carved his initials and "1855" in a tree on that little island.

NO TIME FOR PLAY

It all began when David Livingstone was born at **Blantyre** near Glasgow, Scotland, on March 19th 1813. When he was ten, he started to work at the Blantyre cotton mill where his father and grandfather had worked. His job was to piece broken threads back together on the spinning machine. His work day began at 6 in the morning and ended at 8 at night. In those days there were no laws against children working, no unions to protect the workers' interests, and no limits on how long a work day could be.

It was terribly hot in the factory and sometimes hard for David and his two brothers to stay awake during their long working hours. David often dreamed about an escape, but he realized the only way was through education. He wanted to be a missionary to a faraway country where no one had been before. He wanted to be a scientist, too. His father had told him about the great need for a whole new kind of missionary: medical preachers who could teach the Word of God as well as heal sickness. David decided to become a missionary doctor.

"Aye lad! Are you dreaming again?"

Caught daydreaming in the factory, David turned around — just in time to get a bucket of cold water in his face.

"Thatta keep ye awaik for a lang time!" grinned the foreman.

As soon as the foreman was out of sight, David pulled out his Latin grammar book and propped it on top of the spinning machine. He took a long look in the book, then walked down the wheels to inspect the thread, his lips moving to repeat what he'd just read.

Every evening at 8, the children who

worked at the Blantyre cotton mill gathered in an adjoining classroom for two hours of school. Most were too tired to learn; but not David. He eagerly prepared for his future by reading every book he could get hold of — especially those about science and nature.

At 10 p.m. David hurried home for five hours of sleep before he would have to be at work again. His family lived in a tiny one-room apartment with a fireplace and two beds, all provided by the mill. This is where David slept alongside his two brothers, two sisters and parents until he was 23 years old.

On Sundays no one worked. After church, David and his brother **Charles** loved to explore the countryside, gathering rocks, plants and insects. One Sunday they came to a quarry where someone was loading rocks into a wheelbarrel.

"Look, Charles!" said David as he picked up a rock. "There are seashells in this stone."

"Seashells?" wondered Charles. "Why are there seashells here when the ocean is fifty miles away?"

The man loading the rocks answered, "When the good Lord made the rocks, he made those shells and put them there!"

David laughed and said, "Aye Charles, there's science for you!"

Charles turned around. "Why are you laughing, Davy? Those science

books have turned your head.

See what that has done to your religion! Don't you still believe that God created the world?"

"Oh yes," answered David and put the rock into his pocket, "but the quarryman skipped the real explanation. The shells in the rock prove that a long time ago, the sea covered this area. When it receded, the sand grew hard — and the shells were trapped inside the rock. To accept that, Charles, is not to deny God created the world. It only confirms there is logic and order in all his creation!"

By the time David turned 23 he had saved enough money to quit the mill and go to school in the city. His father walked him to Glasgow eight miles away and helped him find a tiny room in a poor area called Rotten Row.

MISSIONARY AT LAST

Four years later, Livingstone passed his final medical exams. The **London Missionary Society** appointed a minister who would teach him to preach. One evening when he entered the pulpit at Stanford Rivers, Livingstone forgot his memorized sermon. "Friends . . . I have forgotten all I had to say!" he stammered and rushed out.

But shortly before his missionary training was completed, Livingstone listened to the preaching of a successful missionary on leave from South Africa, **Robert Moffat**. After the meeting, Livingstone told Moffat he was soon to be a medical missionary, but did not know where to go.

"Mr. Moffat," he asked politely, "do you think I would do for Africa?"

Moffat's answer shaped the vision that would guide Livingstone for the next 33 years: "Yes," said Moffat, "if you don't settle, but advance to unknown territory. In the morning sun, on the vast plain to the north of my station, I have seen the smoke of a thousand villages where no missionary has ever been!"

In November 1840, Livingstone was licensed as a physician — although he nearly failed because of an argument with his professors about how to use the stethoscope. The next morning he boarded a steamer for London, then the sailing ship George, heading for Cape Town, South Africa.

PRESSING ON

Thirty-two years later — at Unyanyembe where Stanley had left him that last time — Livingstone sensed he'd come close to the end of his journey. While waiting the five months for new carriers, he read and observed everything around him: the African children's games, the tribal customs, and the geological structure of the land.

The doctor's plan was simple. As soon as the carriers showed up he would press southwest around the southern tip of Lake Tanganyika and onto the copper mines of **Katanga**. "Only eight days' journey from there are the great springs you're looking for," the natives told him. He would follow the Lualaba river north, hoping to find it emptied into the Nile. Then he would retire and return to England.

The Mysterious Nile

The Nile river is the longest river in the world (2,160 miles). Along its lower course rose one of the earliest civilizations some 8,000 years ago. But the river's upper course remained unknown to Europeans for thousands of years.

Since the days of the Egyptian pharaohs, explorers and geographers had speculated about the location of the Nile's source. No one knew for sure. The Greek historian Herodotus, in the 5th century BC, told about two mysterious hills in Africa's interior with sharp conical tops. Between them, he believed, lay the fountains of the Nile. The Egyptian geographer Ptolemy, in the 2nd century AD, claimed that the Nile rose from two great lakes at the foot of the "Mountains of the Moon" south of the equator. These ancient theories went unchallenged until the 18th century.

Yet Livingstone never returned. For a long time he had been continually sick and he suffered from internal bleeding. "I'm ill with bowels," he wrote, "having eaten nothing for eight days." The journal entries became shorter each day. The rainy season set in. His men had to carry him through floods and swamps thick with papyrus and lotus plants while searching for dry ground.

One night the caravan made camp beside a hill of fierce safari ants, known for their painful bite. Livingstone wanted to prove that the ants would not bite unless they were provoked. He let the ants swarm over his foot. Soon his whole body was covered. It took his men two hours to get the biting ants off of him.

All winter Livingstone pressed on, advancing only a mile a day. Determined to reach his goal, though, he wrote, "I encourage myself in the

In 1770, the Scottish explorer James Bruce traced the origin of the river's northern branch (the Blue Nile) to the highlands of Ethiopia. Still a much longer branch (the White Nile) was believed to rise far to the south.

In 1858 the British explorer John Speke discovered Lake Victoria which he believed was the source of the White Nile. Eight years later, when Livingstone set out on his last journey, he was determined to prove that Speke was wrong. Livingstone believed that the Nile rose further southwest, by the copper mines of Katanga. He died on his way there.

After Livingstone's death, his friend Henry Stanley continued the search around Lake Tanganyika and Lake Victoria. Stanley once and for all settled the ancient mystery. John Speke had been right: Lake Victoria was the fountainhead of the White Nile.

Stanley circumsailing Lake Victoria

Lord my God, and go forward."

By April, no longer able to go forward, Livingstone had his men make a stretcher and carry him as he groaned from the pain. When they reached the village of Chief **Chitambo**, they knew it was no use carrying their leader any further. **Chuma** and Susi, the two faithful men who had been with him so long, built a large hut and brought him his most precious possessions: his Bible, geographical instruments, rifle, medicine chest and metal-backed notebook. Finally on Sunday, April 27th 1873, David Livingstone wrote his last entry: "Knocked up quite . . . . We are on the

The holy Bible

banks of River Molilamo."

Three days later, Livingstone was drifting deliriously in and out of sleep. At 11 p.m., noise woke the doctor and he called for Susi.

"Are our men making that noise?" he asked faintly.

"No," said Susi, "the villagers are scaring a buffalo away from their fields."

The doctor was drifting. "Is this the Luapula river?" he asked.

"No, not yet," replied Susi.

Then the doctor asked in Swahili: **"Siku ngapi kuenda Luapula?"** (How

many days to the Luapula?)

"Na zani ziku tatu, Bwana!" (I think three days, master!)

"Oh dear, dear," sighed the doctor in great pain.

The next morning before dawn, on May 1st 1873, Susi found the doctor kneeling by the side of his bed, body stretched forward and head buried in his hands. Susi went forward and gently put his hand on the doctor's cheek. It was almost cold.

Dr. David Livingstone was dead.

THE FINAL JOURNEY HOME

Chuma and Susi carried their dead leader outside. The local villagers of Chitambo mourned the doctor's death, waving bows and spears. For two hours drumming and wailing filled the air. Then **Farjala**, the doctor's assistant who had observed once how he opened up a body to determine the cause of death, cut Livingstone's chest, drew out the heart and intestines and buried them in a tin box under an African mvula tree.

Jacob, a former slave freed by Livingstone and trained by missionaries, read the burial service from the doctor's prayer book — determined to show the respect he would show any great African chief. Then the Africans rubbed the body with salt and anointed it with brandy from the medicine chest in order to prepare it for travel back to Livingstone's own people.

For two weeks the body was left to dry in the sun, then it was covered with an animal skin and fitted into a cylinder of bark from a myonga tree. Finally it

was wrapped in sailcloth, painted with tar and lashed on poles. The party set out for the coast at Zanzibar 1,550 miles away. Nine months later they arrived and were welcomed by 700 freed slaves who had come down to say goodbye to the missionary who showed them the love of the Christian God.

Eleven months after his death, the remains of the famous explorer finally arrived in England to receive a hero's funeral in Westminster Abbey. He was mourned by the entire country.

But Livingstone's faithful servants back in Africa also mourned. His heart was buried in African soil, at the roots of a fine mvula tree.

SUCCESS AT LAST

That dark morning at Chitambo, when Livingstone buried his head in his hands and died, he must have believed he had failed. Not only were the geographical questions he had struggled with still unanswered; the mission work he had come to establish had failed, and the Arab slave trade had not been stopped.

Livingstone's journals

If only he could have known that within five years of his death all three problems would be solved — all due to his persistent pioneering work! The Lualaba river was traced to the **River Congo** by his friend **Verney Cameron**. The source of the Nile was confirmed to be Lake Victoria by his friend Stanley. New mission societies were started and stations popped up all over Central Africa. And in 1876 the slave market at Zanzibar was effectively shut down, partly due to another friend, **John Kirk**.

Livingstone's journals and letters provide detailed knowledge of the plants, rocks, insects and animals of Africa — as well as its people and their tribal customs. The vast blank areas which had until then been marked "Unexplored" was filled in by Livingstone with highlands, valleys, lakes, mountains, forests and hundreds of rivers.

Africa after Livingstone

Livingstone never showed interest in the political development of the land he was exploring; he never hoisted a flag or claimed any land in the name of the British government. Livingstone assumed Africa belonged to the Africans. Yet the "scramble for Africa" was a tragic result of his pioneering work.

After Livingstone's death, his friend Henry Morton Stanley was hired by King Leopold II of Belgium to explore "the Congo

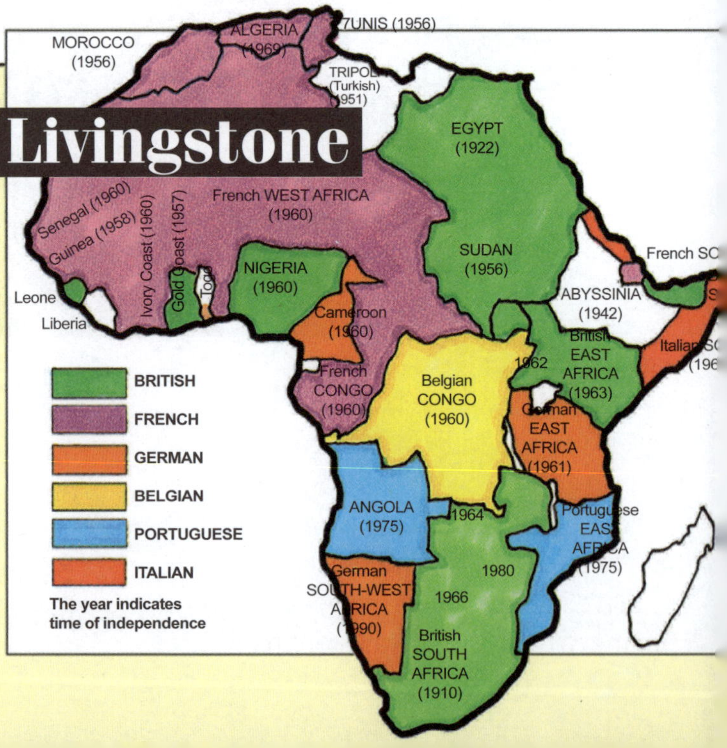

What set Livingstone apart from other explorers of his time was not just his many impressive discoveries, but a rare sympathy and understanding towards the African people whose languages and customs he had learned. When Livingstone died, a new attitude in white Europe was born — respect for the African people and a growing willingness to treat them as equals.

Livingstone paid a high price for his dream of setting Africa free. He gave up a career among his own people and exchanged comfort and conveniences for hardships and sickness, even to the point of feeling abandoned by God. Yet Livingstone accomplished more through his apparent failure than most men accomplish with their success.

"Westminster Abbey had opened her doors to men who have played larger and greater parts in the history of mankind," wrote a London newspaper on the day of his funeral, "but the feeling amongst many this afternoon was, that seldom has been admitted one more worthy — one more unselfish in his devotion to duty — one whose ruling desire was to benefit his kind and advance the sum of knowledge and civilization — than the brave, modest, self-sacrificing, African explorer."

region's possibilities for development." In reality, the king was looking for a colony—and since Stanley was looking for an investor for his next expedition, he accepted the royal match.

While Stanley marched through the vast Congo Basin between Lake Tanganyika and the Atlantic coast, King Leopold founded the "International African Association" of scientists and geographers. In practice, it was a disguise for the king's personal economical and political interests in Africa. Leopold succeeded in securing the Congo Basin for himself.

In 1885, at a Berlin meeting between fourteen European powers, Africa was carved into European colonies: France took the northwestern part; Belgium a slice of the western part; Britain and Germany part of the east. After World War I, the German territories were given up to the others.

The "scramble" was a smash-and-grab enterprise with no rules except diplomatic rhetoric — and with no regard for the wishes of African chiefs who had been ruling the land for centuries.

Along with colonization came civilization and its promised blessings of economic development, hygiene, trade, railways, missionaries, education, and the abolition of the slave trade. Within a few years Africa was being pulled from the stone age into the industrial age — and it's hard to say whether Africa's own peoples gained or lost in the process. Today, as the African countries are becoming independent from their European colonizers, they are struggling for identity and democracy.

"I go back to Africa to try to open a path for commerce and Christianity; do you carry out the work which I have begun! I leave it with you!"
(Livingstone, Cambridge University address, 1857)

Main Events in Livingstone's Life

1813 David Livingstone is born on March 19 at Blantyre, Scotland.

1823 Livingstone starts working in Blantyre Cotton Mill.

1836 Livingstone enlists at the university in Glasgow.

1840 After his medical exam and missionary training Livingstone sails for South Africa.

1841 Livingstone arrives at Kuruman mission station.
Henry Stanley is born in Wales.

1843 Livingstone builds frontier station at Mabotsa.

1845 Livingstone marries Mary Moffat.

1849 Livingstone crosses the Kalahari desert.

1851 Livingstone discovers the upper Zambesi and Victoria Falls.

1853-56 Livingstone crosses Africa between Luanda (Angola) and Quelimane (Mozambique).

1856-58 Livingstone visits England and is received as a hero.

1858-63 The Zambesi expedition fails.

1862 Mary Livingstone dies at the Zambesi.

1864 Livingstone visits England for the last time. His son Robert dies in the American Civil War.

1865 Livingstone goes back to Africa to find the source of the Nile river.

1871 Livingstone is "found" by Stanley.

1873 Livingstone dies at Chitambo on May 1.

1874 Livingstone is buried in Westminster Abbey, London.

BOOK RESOURCES

David Livingstone, Missionary Travels and Researches in South Africa (1857)
David and Charles Livingstone, Narrative of an Expedition to the Zambesi and its Tributaries (1865)
David Livingstone, The Last Journals of David Livingstone in Central Africa (1874)
Jack Simmons, Livingstone and Africa (1955)
Jeanette Eaton, David Livingstone (1947)
Richard Humble, The Travels of Livingstone (1991)
East Africa (Time/Life 1987)
Susan Clinton, The World's Great Explorers: Henry Stanley and David Livingstone (1990)
Thomas Pakenham, The Scramble for Africa (1991)

Martin Luther

THE GERMAN MONK WHO CHANGED THE CHURCH

1483 —1546

Great men and women are not in need of our praise.
We are the ones in need of getting to know them.

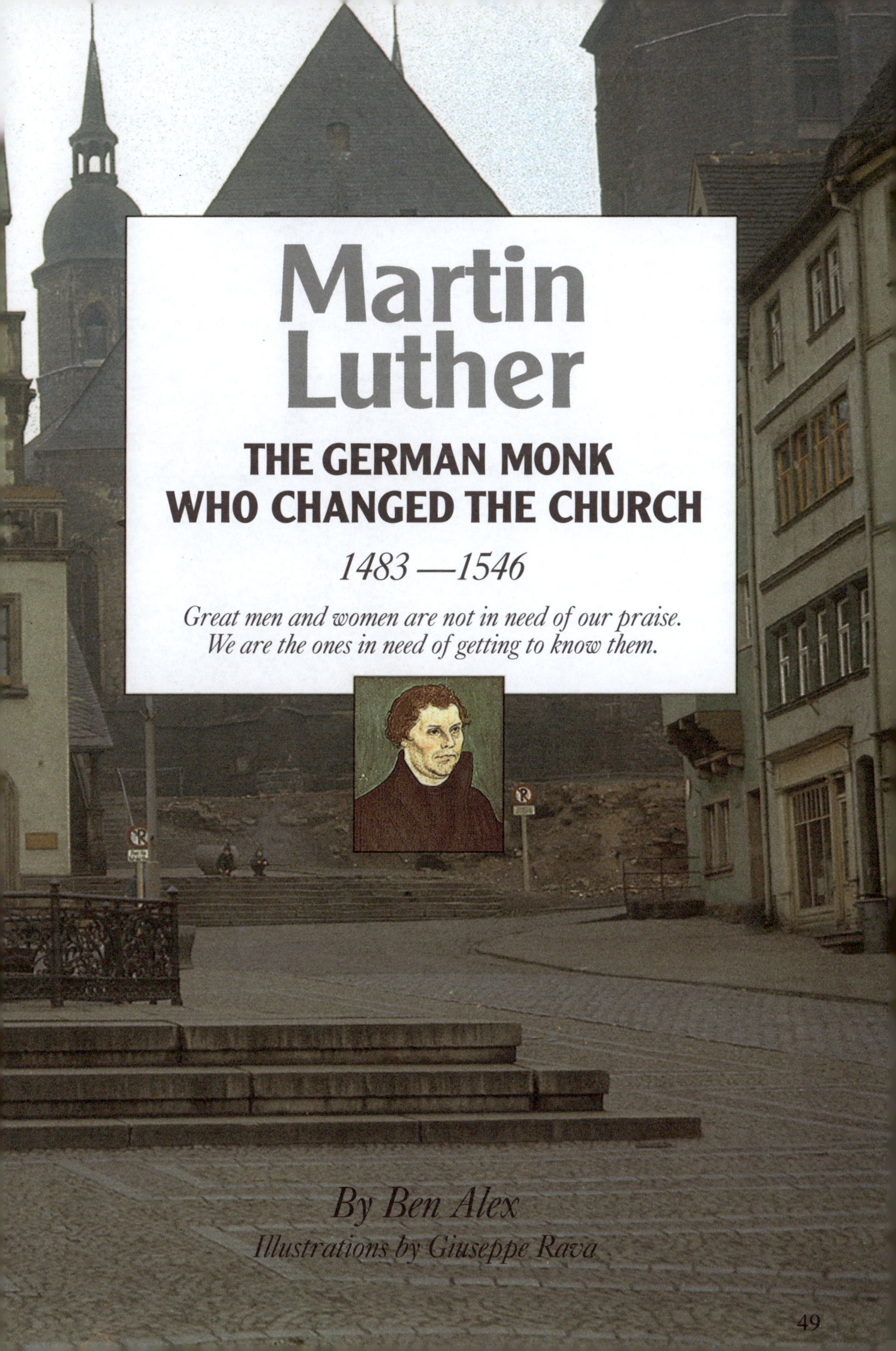

By Ben Alex

Illustrations by Giuseppe Rava

A FRIGHTENED BOY

Five hundred years ago, a simple country boy sat in the pew between his parents in a small church in Mansfeld, Germany. The boy was short but sturdy, with lively, dark eyes peeking out beneath ruffled hair. Like his parents and other peasants and miners in Europe, he was dressed in simple, homespun clothes.

Martin watched as the priest at the altar turned around and faced the congregation, silver plate and silver cup in hand. Martin thought the priest looked like the awesome angel of the Lord, and he was glad to stay in the pew as his parents and other parishioners walked down the aisle to receive Holy Communion as a sacrifice for their sins.

"Hoc est corpus Christi—this is the body of Christ," said the priest as he handed out little flat wafers to the congregation kneeling at the altar. But to Martin, it seemed more like he'd said, "Hocus pocus." The whole scene seemed like a magic trick to Martin's 12-year-old mind. Somehow the priest had managed to turn the wafer into a

piece of Christ's body! Martin wondered what it would look like and taste like as the priest put the bread into his mother's mouth. What did it do to her when she swallowed it?

Martin looked up at the high altar and shuddered. Above it he could see the triangle with the eye of God in the middle—the disapproving eye he could never escape. What kind of God was this? Why had He sacrificed His own Son Jesus and sent pieces of His Body around the world so people could swallow them Sunday after Sunday at Mass? If God had treated His own beloved Son in this horrible way, how would He treat someone like Martin, who had done so many bad things that his parents and teachers had to cane him several times a week?

Martin thought he hated God. He was afraid of Him, too. Martin was confused. He didn't know what to think. The only thing he knew for sure was that he was a wicked person who needed someone to help him escape hell and reach heaven. God was stern and remote — at least that's what he imagined. Jesus, God's Son, was the righteous Judge of all people; Martin didn't think he could count on mercy from Him either. Then there was Mary, Jesus' mother. She seemed too pious and holy for Martin. His only hope seemed to be the saints — especially St. Anne, the mother of Mary. She was the patroness of miners, and Martin's father was a miner. Maybe St. Anne would put in a good word for him at the judgment throne of God.

Martin looked up at the paintings on the church wall and shrugged again. There were monks — bishops even — being tortured by monsters and vampires in purgatory. There were people being dragged off to hell by devils with claws and pitchforks. There were saints being beheaded with the sword for their firm faith in God. On the ceiling was painted a picture of Christ on a rainbow, surrounded by angels with trumpets. From Christ's right ear grew a lily, from his left ear a sword. Martin knew that the lily meant grace and forgiveness; the sword, judgment and damnation. How could Martin earn the lily and avoid the sword? He thought about it all during the Church service.

The late Middle Ages was a time of discovery and adventure, but people's minds were controlled by superstition and fear of evil.

Europe Changes

Martin Luther grew up in the period of great change between the Middle Ages and what we now call the Renaissance. For over a thousand years Europe had been dominated by what had been a wealthy Catholic Church. Anyone who spoke against the teaching and policies of the Church risked being burned at the stake. Among peasants of that time, the only hope for a reasonably good life was to obey what Church leaders said and patiently wait for heaven.

But at the time of Luther's birth in 1483, the Church had serious problems. It was nearly bankrupt. Its power was crumbling. Emperors, princes and nobles were securing the land and influence which had once belonged to the Church. Universities sprang up, breaking the

Church's monopoly on education. New ideas about life began to take shape as artists like Leonardo da Vinci and Michelangelo, and scholars and scientists like Erasmus of Rotterdam and Copernicus showed there were other ways of thinking.

Adventurers explored the earth beyond the boundaries set by the Church centuries before. When Luther was five years old, the Portuguese rounded the southern tip of Africa for the first time (1488) and opened up the sea clear to the Orient. When Luther was nine, Christopher Columbus crossed the Atlantic Ocean and discovered the continent known as North America. These discoveries and others made it plain that the Church had been wrong about many scientific questions. The earth was not flat, after all. Neither was it the center of the universe, as the Church had taught people to believe.

New knowledge about the world spread quickly due to the first mass media invention in history: Gutenberg's printing press (around 1450).

But young Luther was not impressed by the newest artistic or scientific ideas or the latest inventions. He had grown up among simple folk, fighting poverty and sickness just like them. He had a quick mind and curious nature, and he believed firmly in the traditional authority of the Church. Gradually, his personal study of God's Word changed the way he thought about the Church. His beliefs and opinions were published widely via the printing press and began to influence the culture of the day. Without knowing it, Martin Luther changed the history of the Church and its impact throughout the world.

PRINCE, EMPEROR AND POPE

Once outside, after Mass, Martin felt better. The green hills of Thuringia were blooming with flowers. He could smell the moist earth and feel the sun on his back. A lark fluttered above, singing a song for spring. Swallows flew north from faraway Africa to the blue skies of Scandinavia. A fawn watched him curiously from a distance.

"Sir, look!" cried Martin to his father as he pointed to the castle outside Mansfeld. At that moment the heavy iron gate was opening and out rode a knight dressed in a velvet jacket and plumed hat, riding a black horse. Three servants followed. They wore crimson-colored vests with purple trim and yellow-striped hose. The horses' silver trappings jingled.

"Take off your hat, Martin!" warned his father. "It's the Count of Mansfeld."

The count and his men galloped by, startling a nearby rabbit. Then they disappeared over a hill. In passing, the count shouted, "Guten Tag, Hans Luder!" Martin's father felt proud and waved. Martin felt proud too.

"You know the count, sir?" he asked admiringly.

"Yes," smiled his father. Then he added, "And you'll know him too, if you follow in my footsteps. You may even become an overseer of the count's copper mines!"

"Sir, who is more important than the count?" wondered Martin. "The emperor?"

"No," answered his father, "the count

is under the authority of Prince Frederick, Elector of Saxony, and the prince is under Emperor Maximilian, lord of the Holy Roman Empire. The country of Germany is part of that empire."

"Is the pope over the emperor then?"

"No. The pope is the great lord of the Church. The emperor is lord of the world."

"We must obey both the emperor and the pope, is that right?" questioned Martin.

"Yes," nodded Hans. "Any disobedience to the pope means excommunication from the Church and eternity in hell. Disobedience to the emperor means punishment and sometimes death. Just look over there!" Hans pointed.

Martin shuddered at the sight of the gallows. In one of them still hung the lifeless body of a peasant. Martin remembered the stocks in the marketplace, where he'd often seen people being held for days.

"That's why a child must learn to obey his parents," said Martin's mother. "If not, the count may come and take you to the dungeons."

A STRANGE BEGGAR

Martin was almost 14 when his father came home one day from the smelting furnace in the mines and said, "Son, you're a smart lad. I've been thinking you ought to have a good education and become a learned man instead of a miner. I want you to become a lawyer so you can support your mother and me in our old age."

Martin beamed as his father added, "It's time we sent you to a better school. I've arranged for you to spend the next term at the Franciscan school in Magdeburg."

A week later Martin waved goodbye to his parents and his younger brothers and sisters and set out for Magdeburg, forty miles north of Mansfeld. With him was his friend Johann.

Martin loved his new school. The teachers were not as harsh as his teachers in Mansfeld, and he soon advanced in his studies. His teachers noticed his thirst for learning.

One day after school, when Martin and Johann went door to door to beg for food — as was customary at the Latin school in Magdeburg — they noticed a lonely beggar staggering down the street. The beggar carried a bag of food on his back. He looked like moving bones — a bent skeleton in a monk's robe.

Martin stopped. "Who's that?" he exclaimed.

Luther's Early Life

Luther's birthplace in Eisleben

"I'm the son of a peasant," Luther liked to say. Luther's great-grandfather, grandfather and father, Hans Luder, were all farmers. Hans did not inherit his family's farm, however, because custom dictated the youngest son should have it. So Hans went to the city to seek his fortune in the copper mines. He became a hardworking miner, prospered and bought two mines of his own. He was a well-to-do middle-class citizen by the time his son Martin became a monk.

Hans and Margaretha, Luther's mother, had at least five children (Martin was the oldest). The couple disciplined their children for the smallest offences. Once, Martin's mother caned him "until the blood came" for taking a nut without asking. Another time his father beat him so he ran away and "felt ugly toward him." "Although they meant well," Luther

"Aye, that's William of Anhalt," said a passerby. "William was once a wealthy prince, but he gave everything up to seek God and become a monk. He's a very saintly man. He fasts and prays whenever he's not begging food for his fellow monks."

Martin stared after the monk as he turned down another street. Then he said to Johann, "I wish I were holy. Maybe God would love me if I were as holy as Prince William."

said later, "it was discipline like this that finally drove me to the monastery." There, he found the balance between strictness and grace he was seeking.

Some biographers suggest Luther's arguments against the Catholic Church may have been linked to the harsh punishment he received from his stern parents. However, there is every reason to believe Martin also received from Hans and Margaretha the love necessary to foster self-esteem, which enabled him to break with the authority of the Church.

Luther's parents, Hans and Margaretha Luder. Painted by Luther's friend, Lucas Granach.

HAPPY DAYS IN EISENACH

A year went by. Martin's father sent him to a better school further from home. At first Martin was sad to leave his friends at Magdeburg. But in Eisenach he found new friends — and didn't have to beg for his supper. His father could now afford to pay tuition as well as a small allowance, and he had arranged for relatives to look after his son occasionally.

The Latin school at St. George's Church in Eisenach was no ordinary school. The students learned, not out of fear of punishment as in the other schools, but for love of knowledge. The school principal, Master Trebonius, would remove his scholar's cap in the classroom and address the students as "sirs." And he required his teachers to do the same.

"The students on these benches," he would say, "are the future mayors, chancellors, doctors and rulers of Germany."

Martin blossomed in this new environment. By now he had mastered the difficult Latin language, while also making exceptional progress in other lan-

guages and literature. At a party in honor of a visiting professor, Master Trebonius chose Martin to make the official welcome speech — in Latin.

"Keep an eye on this lad," whispered the professor to Trebonius during the speech. "Prepare him well for the university. He will go far in life."

Frau Cotta, a merry, wealthy woman, had given Martin free room and board in return for helping her little son with his homework. Musicians, artists and pious priests were regular visitors at the Cotta house, and Martin basked in their conversations. He learned to play the lute and studied various musical disciplines.

After three years in Eisenach, Martin walked north to visit his parents in Mansfeld. Once outside Eisenach, he turned and took one last look at its beauty along the Elbe river, with the castle of Wartburg towering above it.

"This is my favorite place," he thought, "and always will be, even if I should live a hundred years!"

HIGH GOALS FOR MARTIN

Hans and Margaretha Luder were thrilled to see their oldest son again. How tall he'd grown! How deep his voice had become! How smart he seemed! Hans couldn't help returning the respect he'd always demanded from Martin.

"Sir," Hans said with pride in his voice, "you certainly look like a real scholar!" Then he handed Martin a present he had long wanted to give him: a complete set of law books called **Corpus Juris Civilis**. As he watched the look of surprise on his son's face, he added, "You'll need them. Martin, I want you to go to the university at Erfurt!"

"And another thing," said his mother from behind, "you'll need a good and able wife. We've already been talking to a wealthy family . . . ."

THE CROWN OF LEARNING

Erfurt was a beautiful and prosperous city fifty miles south of Mansfeld. The forest sloped down into gentle hills covered with orchards and vineyards, while green-blue-yellow fields of indigo, flax and saffronon grew on the other side of the city. In the midst of this beautiful German landscape rose the walls and steeples of the many-spired city.

To walk through the city gate was to enter the promised land of the highest education on offer at that time. The university at Erfurt made other universities in Germany seem like elementary

schools. After four years of further study, Martin, nicknamed "The Philosopher" by his many friends, had received a Master of Arts degree, ranking second out of a class of seventeen.

"A few more years of hard study," he thought as he and the other graduates rode through the crowds of cheering citizens, "and I'll be a prominent lawyer with the whole world at my feet! Mother and Father will be so proud of me!"

But then something happened which would alter Martin's promising career forever, and bring to ruin the high hopes of his parents.

A TERRIBLE THUNDERSTORM

One sultry July afternoon in 1505, as 21-year-old Martin was walking back to Erfurt after a ten-day visit with his parents, he was overwhelmed by childhood fears of God and death. There had been a series of dark events in his life. The Black Plague had struck Erfurt. Shortly before, a close friend had died from typhoid fever along with many other people, all behind doors painted with black crosses. Martin himself had nearly died following an accident with his sword. Now, on his way back to his law studies, he felt terrified as thoughts of God's anger and punishment coarsed through his mind.

Such fears were common to people in the Middle Ages, provoked partly by the Roman Catholic Church, where Martin had received his religious training. In order to control the lay people, the clergy stirred the fear of hell in them as a way of driving them to the sacraments of the Church. The sacraments and confession raised hope for God's forgiveness through penance. The Church's teaching on purgatory as a place between heaven and hell with temporary torment for those not bad enough for hell, nor good enough for heaven, nurtured new fear of death. The

Church helped overcome this fear by promising to reduce time in purgatory if people gave money to the Church and prayed to the saints.

The picture of the beggar prince from his Magdeburg days flashed through Martin's mind. How could he become holy and earn the mercy of God? How could he be rid of his sin and sure of going to heaven — not purgatory, when he died?

Suddenly Martin was interrupted in

his thoughts. The blue sky had turned black with clouds. Torrents of rain began pouring down. A lightning bolt hit a nearby tree and split it in half. Terror filled Martin's eyes as he sought shelter from the thunderstorm. Another bolt knocked him to the ground. He thought it must be the bolt of wrath from an angry God! Martin raised his head from the mud and cried out, "Saint Anne! Help me! If you spare me, I promise I shall become a godly monk!"

MARTIN BECOMES A MONK

Martin did survive that storm. Back in Erfurt, he kept his vow. Two weeks after the thunderstorm he left the university for the monastery. His friends all tried to talk him out of the plan, but in vain. Martin had already given away his Corpus Juris books and written a letter to his father, explaining his decision to give up a worldly career. Martin's mind was set. He would become a monk by making the threefold vow of poverty, chastity and obedience to God and the Catholic Church!

On the morning of July 17th, 1505, the gates of the Augustinian monastery in Erfurt closed behind him. That same day he was received as a novice into the order, at a ceremony in the chapel.

"Do you know what your decision means?" asked the prior from the altar. Then he quickly added, "This means poverty, rough clothing, a scant diet and the shame of begging! It means dying to yourself, abstinence from worldly desires, vigils by night and labors by day, daily confessions, constant prayer, and the loneliness of monastery life! Are you willing to take such burdens upon yourself?"

"Yes, with God's help," answered Martin, "as He gives me strength."

Then the crown of Martin's head was shaved into the tonsure of a holy man. He was stripped of his fine student's clothing in front of the friars and given the hair shirt and simple robe of a monk.

SEEKING GOD IN A MONK'S CELL

Life in the monastery was more difficult than Martin had expected. Not only was he given the hardest labor to perform, he also had to deal with the suspicion and jealousy of friars less educated and less zealous than himself. But Brother Martin threw himself wholeheartedly into the pious lifestyle of the strict monastery. He starved himself and spent hours lying on the floor in his cell, arms stretched out in the shape of a cross. By night he threw off his allotted blankets and froze himself to sleep. Every morning at 2 a.m. he got up to say his first prayers. Day and night he brooded over past sins and spent hours confessing them to the prior. But in spite of his determination to please God, the self-tormenting monk did not gain peace in his heart.

"I was a good monk, and I kept the rule of my order so strictly that I may say that if ever a monk got to heaven by his monkery it was I."—Luther

One day, when the rector of the Augustinian order, Dr. Staupitz, was visiting the monastery, he took the zealous friar for a walk in the garden.

"Brother Martin," began Staupitz, "you're making religion too difficult. You can't impress God by trying to become perfect. All you must do is love Him."

"Love Him?" exclaimed Martin. "Father, how can I love a God who's angry with me?"

The old rector stopped and put a hand on Martin's shoulder. "God is not angry with you," he gently said, "it's you who are angry with God! You're trying to find sins in yourself instead of trusting that God loved you first. He proved it by sending Jesus to die for your sins!" Then he added, "Brother Martin, I have a new task for you. Instead of tormenting yourself with the confession of your sins, I want you to teach at the university in Erfurt . . . and I want you to become a priest!"

"A priest?" gasped Martin.

"Yes," repeated Staupitz, "a priest who will preach for others and administer the sacraments of the Church."

"No!" protested Martin. "I am too sinful. I could never do that! I think I should die!"

"Well," replied the old man with a twinkle in his eye, "do you suppose God will wait until heaven to make use of clever men like you?"

MARTIN BECOMES A PRIEST

Martin studied harder than ever to prepare for the priesthood. He learned the liturgy of the Church by heart. He spent many hours reading the large Bible on the stand in the dining hall until he was finally given a red leather Bible of his own. This gift meant a hundred times more to him than the law books he had received from his father.

On April 3rd, 1507, Martin was ordained as a priest. A month later he was to say his first Mass. Yet, he still remained as unsure of his heavenly Father's acceptance as he was of his earthly father's.

For Hans Luder had not seen his son since he had become a monk almost two years earlier. Now old Hans was sitting in the monastery chapel watching the ceremony.

Martin performed his duties at the

altar and faced the congregation of honored guests and distinguished scholars, cup and plate in hand. He seemed calm. But no one could know that in his head a tiny voice whispered, "Martin, you'll never make it! You're not worthy to be a priest. This is blasphemy! How are you going to transform the bread and wine into the Body of Christ? Instead you'll drop it on the floor! You'll desecrate God's Gift with obscene words! Look, your father is watching you. He'll never accept you!"

Martin raised his head and brushed the voice of doubt aside. He noticed a gentle smile on Dr. Staupitz' face. Then he distributed the bread to the altar guests. As his father opened his mouth to receive the Body of Christ, Martin looked him in the eye and smiled. He knew he was doing something important beyond his father's opinion of him.

"**Hoc est corpus Christi**," he said and placed the bread on the tip of Hans Luder's tongue.

Later, at the celebration in the dining hall, Martin greeted his father, hoping for a word of encouragement. But old Hans was grave and quiet.

"Father," said Martin, "today I'm a priest! Why didn't you want this? Life here is so quiet and godly!"

Hans Luder had long tried to suppress his disappointment in his son's decision. Martin's innocent question was too much, though, and old anger welled up inside him. In front of all those monks and educated guests Hans burst out, "You learned scholar, haven't you read the Bible enough to know you are to honor your father and mother? See what you've done! You've left your parents to look after themselves in their old age!"

"But father," replied Martin with a confidence that surprised even him, "the Bible also tells us to forsake our father and mother and follow Christ. You know He called me through a thunderstorm to become a monk!"

"God grant it wasn't the devil!" snarled Hans Luder.

Luther's First Doubts

While Martin Luther was a priest in Erfurt, Germany, his supervisor sent him on a business trip to Rome. Luther was excited to be chosen for the trip. He could hardly wait to see the places held sacred by the Church, especially the new St. Peter's basilica and the Scala Santa stairs, believed to be the stairs Jesus climbed on His way to crucifixion.

Outside the city, Luther fell on his knees and exclaimed, "Hail, Holy Rome, you glorious city where the blood of the martyrs was spilled!"

But Rome was not as holy as Luther had expected. During his four-week stay he was shocked by the poor morals, language and behavior of Church officials. He heard stories about the rich luxury in the pope's court, all paid for with money taken from poor farmers. He heard jokes making fun of the sacraments, told by priests who were supposed to love and honor God. Even the monks openly ridiculed the saints respected by Luther.

But even in Rome, Martin Luther did not lose his faith in the Church. He prayed in Roman chapels where relics of the martyrs and saints were displayed. He climbed the stairs of Scala Santa on his knees, saying the Lord's Prayer on every step and believing, as he'd been taught, that a soul would be released from purgatory when he was done. But when Luther arrived at the top step, he was suddenly overcome by doubt. He turned to a friend and said, "Who knows if this is really true?"

This flash of doubt in Church authority stayed with Luther all the way home to Erfurt. He began to study God's Word more eagerly than ever and eventually came to realize no one is able to receive eternal life for himself — or for anybody else — by doing good works.

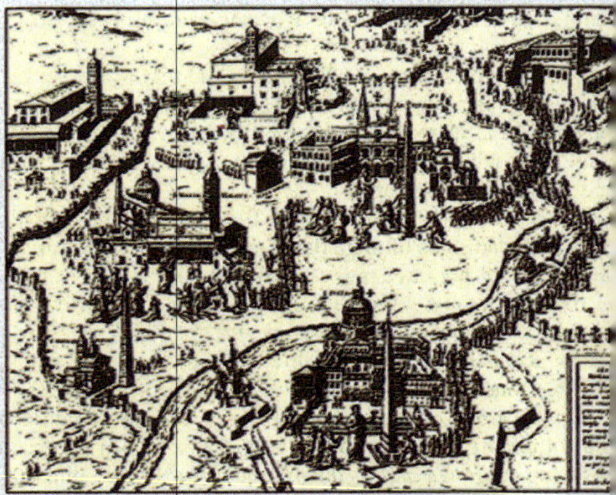

LUTHER THE LEADER

Time proved old Hans wrong. Six years after Martin had said his first Mass, he became Dr. Martinus Lutherus, a respected Doctor of Theology, subprior in the monastery, district-vicar of the order, after Dr. Staupitz, and a popular professor at the new university in Wittenberg.

Compared with beautiful Erfurt, Wittenberg was an insignificant village of 2,000 people. Situated on a barren sand dune along the Elbe river, it seemed on the edge of civilization. But the elector of Saxony, Prince Frederick the Wise, had his residence here — and Frederick had big plans for his hometown.

First, Frederick wanted to make Wittenberg the most prestigious center of learning and education in Germany. For this purpose he needed a modern university with brilliant professors. Second, he wanted to turn Wittenberg into a famous place of worship for pilgrims. His remarkable collection of relics, or sacred objects, was exhibited at the castle church and drew pilgrims from all over; more than 5,000 relics, including a twig from Moses' burning bush, a thorn from the crown of Christ and a tooth from the holy church father, St. Jerome. Pilgrims who saw the relics and paid a coin to the Church were given an indulgence — a piece of paper signed by the pope guaranteeing forgiveness of sins and reduction of time for loved ones in purgatory. A successful pilgrimage to Wittenberg could reduce purgatory time by 1,443 years.

Martin Luther was a frequent preacher in the castle church. But he didn't like the way people worshiped the relics and saints in order to gain forgiveness of their sins. He wished they could worship God and repent of their sins, rather than looking to pay their way out of it!

The people of Wittenberg liked Luther. Here was an honest man, they felt, who went right to the heart of things — practical, not theoretical like

most other preachers. He didn't try to impress the educated. He cared for the common man, and bravely spoke out against Church abuse of people's sincere devotion and religious fears.

As a university professor, Luther was admired for his straightforward teaching methods. Though Latin was the required classroom language, Luther often used common German phrases — just as we use slang today — in order to bring the Bible to life in the hearts of his students. Once, a colleague exclaimed, "This man will completely revolutionize the teaching of theology!"

THE DARK NIGHT OF THE SOUL

Even as a university professor, however, Luther still struggled with the fearsome God of his childhood. Night after night, as Wittenberg slept, he continued to sit at the heavy wooden table in the tower of the Black Cloister, the monastery where he lived. In front of him the light of a candle flickered across the pages of a worn Bible.

"God, how can I know You?" he whispered into the darkness. "How can I love You?"

"Ha," he seemed to hear a voice mocking him, "what are you praying for? Just see how quiet it is around you. Do you think God hears your prayers and would pay attention to a sinner like you?"

Luther's eyes sought the candle, then fell on the section in the Book of Psalms he was preparing for the next morning's lecture. Suddenly a sentence jumped out at him, "My God, my God, why hast thou forsaken me?"

Wasn't this the cry of Christ on the cross? What could this mean? Could it mean that Jesus, the Son of God, had once felt abandoned and forsaken by God, also? Had Jesus suffered torment

"I felt myself to be reborn and to have gone through open doors into paradise."
—Luther

and abandonment? Was it because of sin? No. Jesus was without sin. Why then? Luther wondered.

The answer came like a flash of light into Luther's dark soul: Jesus had taken upon Himself the sufferings of sinners! On the cross He had carried the sins of the world!

A heavy load fell from Luther's mind. In an instant the burden of sin and condemnation lifted. A smile crept over the shadows of his face as he turned to the words from St. Paul's letter to the Romans that had puzzled him for so long, "The righteous shall live by faith."

Those words had made him tremble with fear in the past, for he was far from righteous. Now, in the light of the cross, Luther realized Jesus had suffered the punishment for his sin so that he could receive the righteousness of Jesus as a free gift. God had declared him righteous and without sin in Jesus. To trust God for this was to live by faith!

That night, in the cloister tower in Wittenberg, Luther felt at peace because he knew that a God who gives His own Son as a sacrifice for sin is not an angry, but a loving God.

Luther had found the lily of grace.

TETZEL'S TRUNK

There were rumors in town. Pope Leo X, the head of the Catholic Church, had pronounced a special jubilee year. By offering a generous contribution to the Church during this year of jubilee, people could purchase an indulgence, or letter of credit, signed by the pope himself. An indulgence letter promised immediate forgiveness of past sins and reduction of time for loved ones in purgatory.

Ordinarily people would have been excited because this meant they could secure the afterlife for themselves and their families. But people were becoming increasingly angry. They thought the pope and the German archbishop had invented the idea in order to raise money to pay off their debts and finish the new St. Peter's Cathedral in Rome. Yet no one dared speak out against them.

The pope's messengers traveled throughout Europe, carrying letters of indulgence. The most well-known messenger, the monk Johann Tetzel, approached a town not far from Wittenberg. He entered the town in a spectacular religious parade, preceded by the cross with the pope's coat of arms, and the bull of indulgence on a gold-embroidered velvet cushion.

The cross was planted in the marketplace. Tetzel preached a masterful sermon that played on the fears of the common people:

"Now, listen to the voices of your dear dead relatives and friends! They

"Christ did not command the preaching of indulgences but of the gospel."
—Luther

are begging you, 'Pity us! Pity us! We're in terrible torment! Only you can save us. All it takes is your small contribution!' Why don't you help them? Open your ears! Hear parents cry to their children, 'We gave birth to you, we nourished you and raised you! We left you our inheritance! Why are you so cruel that you won't save us now? Will you leave us here in flames forever? Will you really delay our entry to heaven?'"

After the sermon Tetzel opened his money trunk with a little chant:

> "Once the coin into the coffer clings,
> The soul from purgatory heavenward springs!"

People flocked around Tetzel's trunk. Some of Luther's parishioners were among those who threw in coins to receive the pope's official letters of indulgence.

Die 95 Thesen

LUTHER GOES PUBLIC

When one of these letters was shown to Luther, he thundered, "This peddler thinks he can bargain with God's forgiveness!" Luther stamped on the letter. "This indulgence thing has gone too far. It has to be stopped!" Then he turned and disappeared into his study.

On the Eve of All Saints, October 31st, 1517, Luther marched out of the Black Cloister gate towards the castle church. In his hands he held a poster, a hammer and some nails. He was spotted by a couple of university students who then followed him. The professor stopped in front of the heavy church door, the town's official bulletin board. Then he nailed the poster to the door and marched back towards the Augustinian monastery.

"Look," said the one student as he glanced at the poster, "Dr. Luther is protesting against indulgences!"

"Goodness," answered the other, "he has written 95 arguments in Latin!"

"Prince Frederick won't like this!" continued the first. "All Saints' Day is the only day of the year the prince has permission to sell indulgences in Wittenberg. Now Luther is protesting against this business."

"And the prince needs money to run the university. Luther is in trouble!"

"But he's right, isn't he? Isn't it scandalous that people are taught they can be saved by paying money to the prince and the pope?"

"You can say that again! Dr. Luther says it's an abuse of God's grace."

The Poster on the Church Door

The 95 theses were Luther's reasons for questioning the Church's trafficking in indulgences. The poster was printed by a local man who kept a copy for himself. Within two weeks the theses were reprinted and distributed throughout Germany, without Luther's permission. Within another two weeks they had been translated and were being read all over Europe.

Six months later, Luther wrote to Pope Leo X, "It is a mystery to me how my theses were spread to so many places. They were meant only for local academic debate."

Little did Luther know they would eventually become the declaration of independence for the reformation movement that broke with the Catholic Church.

The following are some of Luther's theses:

- When our Lord and Master, Jesus Christ, says "Repent," He means the entire life of the faithful should be a repentance.

- They preach human folly who pretend that as soon as a coin in the coffer clings, the soul from purgatory heavenward springs.

- Those who suppose that on account of their letters of indulgence they are sure of salvation will be eternally damned along with their teachers.

- Christians should be taught that whoever sees a person in need and, instead of helping him, uses his money for an indulgence, obtains not an indulgence of the pope but the displeasure of God.

- Christians should be taught that the pope ought and would give his own goods to the poor . . . even if he had to sell St. Peter's Cathedral to do it.

- Let them set their trust on entering heaven through many tribulations rather than some false security and peace.

The Wittenberg Castle Church

ORDERED TO ROME

Pope Leo put the books back on his secretary's desk and said, "These writings by Martinus Luther sound like the words of a drunk German monk!"

Pope Leo did not like what he had read. He did not like Church authority to be questioned, because that was to question his own authority as head of it.

Emperor Maximilian, head of the Holy Roman Empire which covered most of Europe, did not like Luther's writings either. He felt Luther might incite a revolution against the government. Besides, Maximilian needed the Church's moral support. "We must stop this monk immediately," he wrote Pope Leo, "before the German people and princes follow him."

Pope Leo had an official document drafted, making it a law that people show absolute loyalty to the teachings of the Church. This made Luther's writings a criminal offense. It stated, "Anyone who questions the teaching of the Church and the pope in all matters of faith is a heretic."

When Luther learned about Leo's document, he became furious. He realized Church authorities were only interested in protecting themselves, not in seeking the truth or looking to God for help. Luther had hoped for a worthy debate that would stop the indulgence trade. Instead, he had become trapped in a political power game and been declared a heretic.

A letter with the pope's seal arrived at Luther's door. Luther was ordered to appear before a court in Rome within sixty days. He was being charged with heresy and disobedience.

Immediately, Luther wrote a letter to his protector, Prince Frederick. Frederick admired and favored Luther because of the publicity Luther had attracted to Wittenberg. In the letter, Luther asked

"I have great hope, that as Christ was rejected by the Jews and received by the Gentiles, so this true theology, rejected by opinionated old men, will pass over to the younger generation."

—Luther

Frederick to promise not to allow any trial to take place outside of Germany. This would make it too easy for Luther's enemies to have him killed. If a hearing could be arranged on German soil, Luther wanted a promise of safe conduct from Emperor Maximilian himself.

A hearing was arranged in Augsburg. But Luther left for that place with a troubled heart. What would happen to him? How could he be sure he was right and everyone else wrong? With the pope, the emperor and the archbishop against him, he could hardly escape the guilty verdict, and would inevitably be burned at the stake.

"Now I must die!" he thought. "What a disgrace I shall be to my parents!"

LUTHER REFUSES TO RECANT

Cardinal Cajetan, the pope's representative in Augsburg, expected only a brief interview with Luther. The cardinal was instructed not to discuss any of the issues raised by the so-called obstinate monk.

"My son," said the cardinal in a fatherly tone, "all I want you to do is say revoco — I recant!"

"Father," answered Luther humbly but firmly, "I didn't come all the way to Augsburg to do what I could just as well have done in Wittenberg. Please inform me of my errors."

Cajetan paused. He noticed the innocent look the question had left on Luther's face. Then he took a deep breath and overstepped his instructions. The discussion which followed lasted three days.

"Your main error," he began, "is that you deny a person will receive God's forgiveness in Christ by buying indulgences from the Church. This is against the teaching of the Church."

"But not against God's Word!" retorted Luther. "The Bible doesn't even mention indulgences. It states clearly that only by faith in Jesus Christ can we receive God's forgiveness."

"Your next error," continued Cajetan unmoved, "is that you deny the word of the pope is above the Bible."

"Yes. The Word of God is above any pope and any Church," exclaimed Luther.

"Let me remind you, my son, that the Bible has to be correctly interpreted. His Holiness, the pope, is the

God-appointed interpreter."

"I say," spoke Luther, "that any humble Christian armed with the Word of God is a better interpreter than the pope."

"Will you also deny that the pope is Christ's representative on earth?"

"If the pope abuses Scripture as in the case of indulgences — then yes! Indulgences are only a scheme meant to raise money!"

The next day Luther handed Cajetan a written statement that explained his view in detail.

"Thank you, I shall forward your letter to Rome," said the cardinal. Then he

added, "But now it's time to recant. Just say revoco. That's all."

"I refuse to recant," declared Luther, "unless you convince me that I am wrong according to Scripture or with reason."

The cardinal's face grew red with rage. "Do you realize," he thundered, "I have orders to put you in chains and take you to Rome for trial if you do not recant! Don't appear before me again until you're ready to recant!"

Luther knew the verdict of Rome would be execution. He left Augsburg as fast as he could, and not through the city gate either, but through a hole in the city wall. Luther was running for his life.

"Cajetan was no more fit to handle the case than an ass is fit to play on a harp."
—Luther

Understanding Luther's Enemies

Johann Tetzel was a short, fiery preacher of the Dominican order who was especially good at selling indulgences throughout Germany. In 1517, when the pope and the German archbishop needed extra money, Tetzel saw his chance to make use of his talents. In many German towns he preached his "indulgence gospel" of the forgiveness of sins: no repentance required, just money in Tetzel's trunk.

After being exposed by Luther as a crook, Tetzel was still granted the title of "Doctor of Theology" with the right to publish his writings. Immediately he fired off 106 theses against Luther. But contrary to his opponent, Tetzel was a poor theologian and thinker. He eventually lost the pope's favor.

The indulgence peddler retired to a monastery in Leipzig and was further disfavored for his luxurious lifestyle. He had two children out of wedlock, and the retirement income he had established for himself was said to be ten times higher than the Leipzig mayor's. Tetzel died a broken man, only two years after his lucrative career had begun. Before his death Luther wrote him: "Don't be too discouraged! You were not the one who started this madness."

POPE LEO X came from a prominent Italian family that managed to buy him status as a cardinal by the time he was thirteen. Twenty-five years later (1513) he was elected pontiff of the Roman Catholic Church.

Pope Leo was a sociable, pleasure-loving and careless leader. On his coronation alone

A TRIUMPHANT MARCH

Though on the run, Luther was a target Pope Leo wouldn't want to miss. When he spoke openly against the teaching of the Church, Luther had defied "His Holiness" himself. Luther was causing a national uprising in Germany that Leo knew might divide the Church and the entire empire.

Pope Leo was watching Luther's every move from Rome. When he heard that Luther had defended a heretic, executed a hundred years before, he had the evidence he was looking for: Luther himself was a heretic!

Leo signed a document that threatened to excommunicate Luther from the Church unless he confessed his "errors" within 60 days. Luther replied

"This will be my recantation at Worms, 'I declare that the pope is the enemy of Christ and the apostle of the devil.'"

—Luther

by burning the bull, the document declaring him to be a heretic, together with the constitution of the Church. He even called the pope "Antichrist," enemy of Jesus.

This added fuel to the fire being

he spent 100,000 ducats — one seventh of the reserve in the papal treasury. His ambition to finish St. Peter's Cathedral in Rome would cost over a million ducats. After a few years Leo had exhausted his financial resources and was in serious trouble. New cash flow was needed.

In order to get money, Leo created thousands of new church offices and filled them with wealthy people in return for financial bribes. The Church was fast becoming a secular institution lacking spirituality.

Another important source of income was the sale of indulgences. Indulgences had been sold since the Crusades three hundred years earlier. Leo turned the practice into big business. He hoped to get enough money to start another crusade against the Muslim Turks.

Luther's attack on the indulgence trade was a threat to Leo's lifestyle. Leo's condemnation of Luther in 1520 was based on ulterior motives, rather than spiritual ones. However, Leo was forced to send out a document, Cum Postquam (1518), that complied with Luther's views and corrected the worst abuses.

In 1521, after having won a battle with the French, Leo celebrated his triumph with a great banquet. That night he caught a cold and soon afterwards died.

At his funeral, half-burned candles borrowed from another funeral were used because the papacy was so deeply in debt. During his seven years in office, Leo had spent five million ducats.

JOHANN ECK was a fellow professor at the university of Ingolstadt and a good friend of Luther until the indulgence controversy broke out. From that time on Eck organized the opposition against Luther.

prepared for Luther in Rome. But Luther had slowly come to realize he was giving voice to the longings of an entire nation. There was no turning back. If he recanted now he would go against the Bible and his conscience — and that would make him a heretic in the eyes of God. Luther could only preach and write on, refusing to go to Rome, hoping for a fair hearing under the Roman emperor and resting his case with Almighty God.

Twenty-year-old Charles, the new emperor who followed Maximilian, had just been elected by Germany's seven princes, of whom Luther's protector, Frederick the Wise, was the most influential. Frederick convinced Charles that Luther deserved at least a trial. If the emperor's council found Luther guilty of heresy, Frederick promised to be the first to condemn him.

The occasion for a trial came in 1521 during the emperor's first national Council in Worms, Germany. Luther was granted safe conduct and escorted by the emperor's herald and guard on the long journey from Wittenberg.

Everywhere people flocked into the streets to see Luther and encourage him. At Leipzig he was honored by the town council and given gifts. At Erfurt he was greeted with music and speeches. The professors and students at his old university lined up to honor him.

After two weeks of triumphant traveling, Luther finally arrived in Worms. His arrival was announced by the town trumpeter. Luther turned to the friends

In 1519, George, the duke of Saxony, arranged a public debate between Eck and Luther. Eck was a professional debater who wanted to corner his former friend. The debate lasted eighteen days, and Eck managed to convince the audience that Luther was a heretic like John Hus, a reformer from Bohemia who had been burned at the stake one hundred years earlier.

The papal document, or bull, that condemned Luther as a heretic in 1520 was most likely drafted by Eck. Luther called it "the work of that man of lies, hypocrisy, errors, heresy — that monster Johann Eck." Still, Eck did not succeed in destroying Luther.

CHARLES I of Spain was elected Holy Roman Emperor in 1519, at age nineteen. His empire covered most of Europe. Though Charles had many enemies (including France, the pope and the Turks), his most urgent problem was the Protestant uprising that threatened to split apart his empire.

After the Council at Worms (1521), Charles banned Luther with the words, "A single monk who goes against the Christianity of a thousand years must be wrong."

But Charles never pursued his decision to destroy Luther. Other political problems preoccupied him until he finally lost control of his territories. The Protestant princes forced him to accept their right to determine the religion of their own countries.

Charles abdicated the throne in 1556 and retired to a monastery. In his hour of death his last word was, "Jesus."

who were with him and said, "Now I've had my triumphant Palm Sunday. What comes next may be my Calvary."

The hearing was scheduled for 4 p.m. the following day.

BEFORE THE EMPEROR

Luther entered the hall in the palace and stood before the emperor, who sat on his throne. Around him were princes, noblemen, bishops and distinguished officials from many states and cities throughout Germany. The contrast between the richly clothed medieval dignitaries and the simple monk in a coarse robe, confidently challenging the religious system of his day, marked the beginning of modern times.

"Martin Luther," began an official, pointing at a pile of books in the middle of the room, "have you written these?"

Luther did not answer.

The official read the titles out loud and asked again, "Have you written these books?"

"Yes," answered Luther, "and I have written others, too."

"Is there anything in your books," questioned the official, "that you want to recant?"

Luther was confused. What was this? He had come to Worms in the hope that he would be asked about his views, but all he was being asked was Cajetan's old question. Had the council already judged him?

"This," he stammered, "touches God and His Word — and the salvation of souls. Please give me time to think it over."

Next day, when Luther was finally led into the hall, the dark room was lit with candles. The official repeated the question from the previous day. Did Luther regret anything in the books he had written? The emperor and the princes leaned forward anxiously. Prince Frederick looked pale. The pope's ambassador had a face of stone. Luther took a deep breath and said with a clear voice,

"There are three kinds of books in the pile. The first kind deal with faith and life so simply that no one will object to them. I cannot retract any of those, of course.

"The second kind of books," he continued, "attack the pope and his teach-

ing. I cannot withdraw those either, since I won't support tyranny.

"Finally there are books attacking others. I may have been harsh in my judgments, but cannot renounce any of these without encouraging the ungodliness these men represent.

"I ask you to show me my errors. If you do, I'll be the first to throw my books into the fire."

"Martin," objected the official, "how can you assume you are right and the Church wrong for a thousand years? Please answer my question simply: Do you or do you not renounce your books and the errors in them?"

Luther's answer has become a classic one, "Unless I'm convinced on the grounds of Scripture or by plain reason, I cannot and will not recant. My conscience is captive to the Word of God. It's neither safe nor wise to act against one's conscience." Then he bowed his head and said in a low voice, "Here I stand. I can do no other. God help me! Amen."

Three Important Books by Luther

DE CAPTIVITATE
BABYLONICA
ECCLESIAE,
Praeludium Martini
Lutheri.

Vuittembergae.
1520

More books have been written about Martin Luther than any other individual in history — except for Jesus Christ.

Luther himself wrote many books and pamphlets (about 60,000 pages!). His enemies did what they could to ban and burn his books, but the success of the Reformation was greatly due to these books. Still Luther said, "I wish all my books would disappear and the Holy Scriptures alone be read."

Three of the reformer's early books are most important to the Reformation:

An den Christlichenn
Adel teutscher Nation:
von des Christlichen
standes besserung:
D. Martinus
Luther.

Durch yhn selbs ge-
mehret und corrigiert.

Vuittemberg.

- **ADDRESS TO THE CHRISTIAN NOBILITY** (1520). Luther encouraged the German leaders to take on the responsibility of reform since the Roman Catholic Church barricaded itself against change.
- **THE BABYLONIAN CAPTIVITY OF THE CHURCH** (1520). The title refers to the exile of the Jews in Babylon (586 BC). Luther claimed the people of God in his own day were led away from Scripture and held captive by the pope and the papal system. Luther also reduced the traditional seven sacraments to two: Baptism and Communion. He denied that the bread and the wine are transformed into the actual Body and Blood of Jesus and suggested that lay people receive the wine as well as the bread.
- **ON THE FREEDOM OF A CHRISTIAN** (1520). This powerful book turned the repressive medieval view of man upside down. Luther's main idea was that true freedom has two sides: A Christian is lord of all, subject to no one, and a Christian is a dutiful servant of all, subject to everyone. Luther said this book "contains, in a nutshell, the whole of the Christian life."

Von der Freyheyt
eynis Christen
menschen.

Martinus Luther.

Vuittembergae.
Anno Domini
1520.

KIDNAPPED!

Several days passed while the officials tried to negotiate with Luther. But he would not change his mind. Finally he was allowed to go home before his period of safe conduct ran out. The emperor forbade him to preach or write new books until a decision had been reached.

Luther obeyed — almost. On his way northeast towards Wittenberg he did accept a few invitations to preach, one of which was in Eisenach, where he had spent the happiest years of his childhood.

It was late afternoon by the time Luther and his few companions had left Eisenach and were making their way down a lonely road through the dark woods. Suddenly, a group of armed horsemen came out of nowhere and forced the wagon to stop.

"Which of you is Martin Luther?" demanded one of the horsemen. The wagon driver panicked and pointed at Martin. The men dragged Luther from the wagon and mounted him on a horse. Then they disappeared with him the same way they had come. Luther's companions fled on foot.

Soon rumors of Luther's kidnapping spread throughout Germany and beyond. Some thought he'd been taken

Biblia Hebraica
NOVU-M TESTAMENTUM Graece

to Rome to be burned. Others said he'd been killed in the forest by the emperor's men. Everyone knew the emperor had sided with the pope and declared Luther an outlaw. This meant anyone could kill him without being charged for murder. Luther's friends were shocked. One of them, the artist Albrecht Durer, wrote from The Netherlands, "O God, if he is dead, who will then explain to us the gospel? If we lose this man who has written more clearly than any other in centuries, may God raise up another."

"I wish my name may be passed over in silence, and that people will call themselves not Lutheran but Christian."
—Luther

"PRISONER" AT WARTBURG

But Luther was perfectly safe. From the forest he had been taken to Wartburg, one of Prince Frederick's castles. The kidnapping scene had in fact been arranged by Frederick himself.

For the next ten months Luther was held "prisoner" at Wartburg. He was given a beautiful room with a retractable stairway, fine meals and clothes fit for a knight.

Knight Jorg, as Luther was now called, had plenty of time to think about the movement he had started. With its leader condemned both by Church and state, it looked as though his mission had failed. Could the movement go on without him? How could he best make sure it took a just and peaceful course? He wanted a reformation of the Church, not a bloody revolution. The German peasants were restless and could very well turn his cause into civil war.

"I would rather burn on live coals than rot here without being able to do anything," he thought — overwhelmed by discouragement and depression.

Then he sat down and began to write. The next ten months were to be the most productive in his life. The twelve books he wrote at Wartburg contain the pastoral consequences of his theology. He also translated the New Testament from Greek into German in only eleven weeks. This translation, Luther's gift to his beloved people, helped form a common German language.

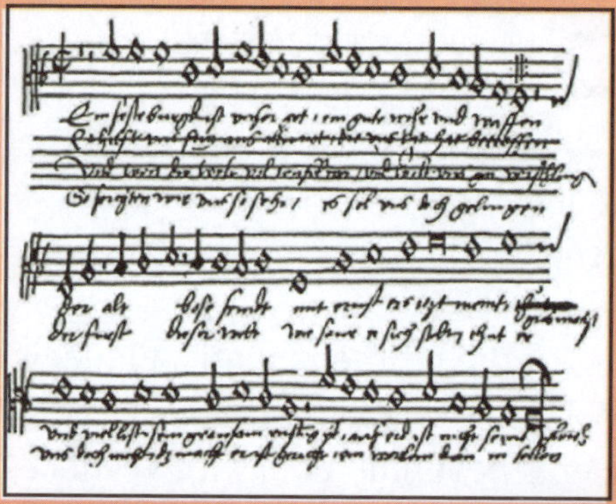

"A Mighty Fortress"

In 1527, when the Black Plague struck Wittenberg, Luther became seriously ill. Depressed, he wrote his friend, Philip Melanchton, "I spent more than a week in death and in hell. Completely abandoned by Christ, I struggled with depression and blasphemy against God. But through the prayers of the saints, God began to have mercy on me and pulled my soul from the inferno below."

In the midst of his depression, Luther wrote and composed the powerful hymn, A Mighty Fortress, about the faithfulness of God. Verses 1 and 3 read:

A mighty fortress is our God,
A bulwark never failing;
Our helper He, amid the flood
Of mortal ills prevailing.
For still our ancient foe
Does seek to work us woe;
His craft and power are great,
And, armed with cruel hate,
On earth is not his equal.

And though this world, with devils filled
Should threaten to undo us,
We will not fear, for God has willed
His truth to triumph through us.
The prince of darkness grim —
We tremble not for him;
His rage we can endure,
For lo! his doom is sure,
One little word shall fell him.

LUTHER'S LATER YEARS

After Wartburg, Luther lived another 25 years, although he remained banned by the emperor and the pope. Under his leadership, the Reformation Church, nicknamed the

Protestants, grew healthy and strong. By his death in 1546, the movement had spread to all the countries of northern Europe and set the stage for a nationalism that refuted the emperor and the Catholic Church.

At the core of the Protestant Church's beliefs was the absolute authority of the Bible and faith in Jesus Christ as the only Way of salvation. Instead of the hierarchy of pope, cardinals, bishops and priests, the

Luther's Wife Katie

"I believe in marriage," said Luther repeatedly. He encouraged the monks and nuns who fled the cloisters because of his teaching to get married.

Katharina von Bora and eight other nuns showed up on Luther's doorstep one day, smuggled out of their Cistercian convent on a wagon with barrels of beer and herring. Luther felt responsible for their future and found husbands for seven of them. When only Katharina was left, she refused to marry anyone but Luther or one of his close friends.

Two years later, in 1525, Luther and Katie were married in the Wittenberg church. She was 26. He was 42. The prince gave them the Black Cloister, Luther's former monastery, for a home. The house was always full of people who needed spiritual or physical help. The dinner table usually had 20-30 people seated around it.

Katie was an excellent wife with common sense in practical matters that her husband often lacked. Luther was fond of her and called her "my lord." Together they had six children and adopted four.

Protestant Church claimed the "priesthood of all believers," or every Christian's right and responsibility to minister to other Christians, interpret the Scriptures and represent Christ among unbelievers. The Church, or at least part of it, had finally come back to the teachings of the first-century Church.

Luther's death occurred while on a business trip to Eisleben, where he had been born and baptized. On February 17th, 1546, at age 63, he went to bed with chest pains. At 1 a.m. he cried, "Oh Lord God, the pain is unbearable!" As companions rushed into the chamber they heard their leader repeat words from the Gospel of John, "For God so loved the world that He gave His only Son . . . ."

> "I don't want people to fight on the side of the gospel with force and killing. The world is to be won over with the Word of God."
>
> —Luther

"Reverend Father," a friend broke in, "do you stand firm in Christ and the teachings you've preached?"

"Yes," answered Luther in a faint voice. Then he was dead.

Today, more than 450 years after his death, Martin Luther is considered by many, to be the most important church teacher since the apostle Paul.

Main Events in Luther's Life

1483	10 Dec.	Born in Eisleben.
1484	June	Family moves to Mansfeld.
1497	Easter	Latin school in Magdeburg.
1498		St. George's school in Eisenach.
1501	May	University of Erfurt.
1502	29 Dec.	Receives Bachelor of Arts degree.
1503	16 April	Seriously wounded by sword.
1505	7 Jan.	Receives Master of Arts degree.
	20 May	Begins law studies.
	2 July	Thunderstorm and vow.
	17 July	Enters Augustinian monastery in Erfurt.
1507	3 April	Ordained priest.
	2 May	First Mass.
1508	Winter	Teaches philosophy at Wittenberg.
1510	Nov.	Pilgrimage to Rome.
1511	April	Returns to Erfurt.
1512	19 Oct.	Transfers to Wittenberg. Doctor of Theology.
1513-1516		Lectures on Psalms, Romans and Galatians.
1517	31 Oct.	Posts the 95 theses.
1518	5 Aug.	Maximilian warns Pope Leo.
	7 Aug.	Summoned to Rome.
	8 Aug.	Appeal to Frederick.
	12 Oct.	Hearing before Cajetan at Augsburg.
	20 Oct.	Flight from Augsburg.
1519	July	The Leipzig debate with Dr. Eck.
1520	15 June	Pope's bull. Luther has 60 days to recant.
	12 Nov.	Luther's books burned at Cologne.
	10 Dec.	Luther burns Pope's bull at Wittenberg.
1521	3 Jan.	Excommunicated from the Church.
1521	16 April	Arrives at Council in Worms.
	26 April	Leaves Worms.
	4 May	Arrives at Wartburg.
	Dec.	Begins translation of the New Testament.
1522	6 March	Returns to Wittenberg.
1525	5 May	Death of Frederick the Wise.
	June	Peasant uprising crushed.
	13 June	Marriage to Katharina von Bora.
1527	Aug.	Sick and depressed. "A Mighty Fortress."
1530	June	Diet of Augsburg.
1534		Completes German Bible.
1546	18 Feb.	Dies in Eisleben.

BOOK RESOURCES

Here I Stand: A Life of Martin Luther, by Ronald Bainton (Abingdon, 1977).

Martin Luther,by Mike Fearon (Bethany, 1986).

Luther the Reformer, by James Kittelson (Augsburg, 1986).

Martin Luther: The Man and His Work, by Arthur McGiffert (Century, 1911).

Martin Luther, by McNeer and Ward (Abingdon, 1953).

Luther: His Life and Work, by Gerhard Ritter (Harper & Row, 1963).

Christian History, Issue 34, 1992: Martin Luther: The Early Years.

Hudson Taylor

THE MISSIONARY WHO WON A NATION BY PRAYER

1832 — 1905

*Great men and women are not in need of our praise.
We are the ones in need of getting to know them*

By Marlee Alex

Illustrations by Giuseppe Rava

STORM AT SEA

A tall, thin figure stood at the rail of a wooden ship looking toward the open water. I can't wait to get to China, the young man thought. Shivers of excitement ran down his spine. Lord, put the wind at our backs. Move this ship on toward the East. In the wind I can almost hear the cries of the Chinese people. They've never heard the Word of God or the name of Jesus. I'm going into the interior of that huge empire and will be the first Protestant missionary to bring them the message of salvation. Blow wind, go on and blow us toward China.

The morning wore on, and as the man stood by the railing and paced the deck, the sea grew rougher. His prayers for a safe voyage seemed to have been lost in the foam of the wild waves. Finally he fought his way to the captain on the bridge. Waves towered over the crew of men working the rigging on deck. Cold water smashed against the bow with hurricane force, nearly splintering the timbers and threatening to drag the sailors into the ocean depths.

"How far have we come from the coast?" he shouted above the crash of the sea.

Captain Morris was fighting with the sail and listening for any sign or sound that the wood was cracking. His ship, called the Dumfries, leaned at an incline down toward the black-gray water, then rebounded and clipped along the sea's surface at lightning speed. "Not far," Morris shouted back. "This is the worst storm I've ever seen. We're heading toward a rocky beach wall. I can't turn her!"

The young man crawled below, slamming into the walls and furniture in his cabin as the ship rocked back and forth. He fished out a pen from the desk, and clearly scribbled his name – **HUDSON TAYLOR** — into a notebook, then fastened this securely inside his pocket. Perhaps this way when they find

my body, they can identify it for my parents, Taylor thought. He wrestled with his fear and was already grieving the loss of his dream — to bring the gospel of Jesus Christ to those living in the interior of China.

Years of preparation buried at sea, he thought. All I've worked for, gone. He climbed back up to the slippery deck.

There, Hudson saw right away that the ship, rocking and plunging in the wilderness of water, was already within two ship's lengths of a jagged rock near the shore. Captain Morris was heaving at the sail like a wild man. Taylor grabbed hold of a thick rope and held on. Will I never see China, he thought. Will this be the end of my dream? In the bone-chilling chaos he relived the history of that dream and brought to mind childhood memories of his home in Barnsley, England . . .

CHILDHOOD MEMORIES

"You're late again, Hudson!" his father, James Taylor, exclaimed.

The five-year-old boy shuddered as he climbed into his place at the table between his two sisters. He knew that being late for meals was never tolerated. But Mr. Taylor merely said, "It won't happen again, will it son?"

"No, father," Hudson replied.

"Now, let us thank God for this food. Then after lunch Hudson, you and I will go and work an hour at the pharmacy, then begin our Latin lessons before tea. You'll have it ready, my dear Amelia?"

There were times when Hudson grew tired of his parents' stringent rules, but he still adored his father and mother. Through them he found security and love beyond the orderliness they demanded.

Hudson's home was full of warmth: the tidy parlor with its glowing oil lamps, crumpets and shortbread at the tea table, his father's head bowed over breakfast during long periods of prayer. Prayers always seemed to last far longer than Hudson's young, restless little body could endure. But in his father's shop, where pharmaceutical bottles of every color and description covered the shelves, Hudson's imagination was given full play. He liked watching his father mix, pound and wrap the different medicines for his customers.

During the afternoons Hudson's sisters, young Amelia and Louisa, sat beside him in home school, their eyebrows wrinkled as they studied languages, history and arithmetic. But the best times of all were during winter evenings by the coal fire. The voices of his parents and their friends would drone on and on over the chink of china tea cups and saucers. As a boy, Hudson often drifted into sleep while listening to the adults talk about theology, politics and ministry within the Methodist church.

"Learn to love your Bible above all," Hudson's father frequently told him. "God cannot fail." Often he would lead his son to the tall bookcase with glass doors. Mr. Taylor would pull down one book after another, sometimes from a collection about the country of China. "Who invented gunpowder?" he would ask. "The compass? Paper? The art of printing? Which people of the earth live in an ancient empire over one hundred times the size of England?"

Hudson knew the answer every time. "The Chinese," he would say.

Now 21 years old, Hudson knelt on the deck of the heaving ship, and cried out to God for survival and safe passage to that nation he so longed to see. Strengthened by his memories, he remembered the moment God had actually called him to China . . . .

HUDSON RECEIVES A CALLING

"Your dad's a right old religious fanatic!" one boy said to Hudson.

Hudson opened the Barnsley Bank books and began to add up the numbers and record the accounts. Although only 15, he was already living on his own and earning a living.

"All Christians are hypocrites," his friends continued. "You've got your own life to live, Hudson. Why go on with your father's old-fashioned God?"

Hudson pretended not to mind. But he was thinking, It's true, Dad's prayers and all that church language does seem so ridiculous! I'm so sick of it.

Yet Hudson could not free himself from the tug of God. He finally made his decision and told the boys, "I'll believe what I want to. God is the wisest course. He cannot fail."

In his own mind though, Hudson

was afraid he might just be repeating his father's words. It's not my faith or my choice, he thought to himself. Besides, church is a bore and I don't have to go there now that I'm not living at home anymore.

Hudson brooded, unsure of where he fit in. On the other hand he wanted adventure and challenge, yet he felt unhappy whenever he imitated the other boys and went along with their pranks.

One afternoon when he was 17, Hudson wandered into his father's library, hoping to find a way to fill an empty afternoon. He picked up a gospel tract that appealed to him with the promise of an amusing story. I'll skip the sermon, he thought. I've heard them all a thousand times. But Hudson was wrong. The simple truth in the message of the story captured his attention. He didn't need the sermon, God was speaking to him personally, calling him to a lifetime of faith.

"Lord, I accept Jesus as my Savior," Hudson prayed that day. As months passed, certainty and vision replaced the confusion and turmoil he had felt.

But Hudson wasn't content just to go to church and be a Christian in name. He longed to do something daring. Something that had never been done before. "I will go anywhere, do anything, suffer anything for You, Lord," he prayed. "Please give me the assurance of what You want me to do."

As he prayed, he could almost feel God's presence. It was as if God was saying, "Your prayer is answered, your conditions accepted. I will call you to a rugged life that will be hard on your body and make you trust in Me, not any man."

Hudson believed God was calling him to China, the land that his father and mother loved to talk so much about. He decided to begin preparing immediately for missionary service. Hudson began to exercise his body and to evangelize among the poor in the worst areas of his own hometown. He visited the alleyways and marketplaces, passing out gospel tracts and preaching from the Bible. The more he spoke to others about Jesus, the more he felt at the center of God's will. But every day, he longed more and more to evangelize among the people who had never even heard the name of Jesus and where, in the interior of the country, there was not a single Protestant missionary to bring them the Good News.

Hudson knew China was closed to foreigners at that time and that the Taiping Rebellion, a kind of civil war, was in full swing. But these obstacles only made him that much more determined. He began to dream of the impossible. I will go, he thought. I will be the first to come with the message of salvation to the millions living deep in the heart of China.

Hudson took a job as a physician's assistant, hoping to use medicine and its practice as a way of getting inside China. In order to prepare himself for the cultural challenges of that land, he decided to move out of his own comfortable home and go live among the poor. He rented a cold, barely furnished apartment and gave up the diet he was used to. Refusing to live well while his neighbors suffered, he existed on only oatmeal or rice, a biscuit and herring, or a few apples a day. In his free time he visited the poor, bringing medicine, comfort from the Scriptures or prayers.

China's Political History

Caption: The Chinese Wall

China is a country with a rich cultural heritage, stretching back to the dawn of civilization. After centuries of turmoil and fighting among local rulers, China rose out of prehistoric times as an empire of thirty six states, or provinces. The first emperor, Qin Shihuang (259-210 B.C.) built the famous Great Wall as a defense against the nomadic tribes to the north, and laid the foundation for what later became the world's greatest civilization during the next centuries.

Early in the thirteenth century China was overthrown by the Mongol empire and trade with Europe was promoted for the first time. The most famous European to visit China was the explorer Marco Polo, who returned to Europe and told about this highly civilized, rich country in the East. The Mongols were eventually driven out and the Ming Dynasty ruled China for 300 years until the Manchus invaded northern China in 1644. During the Manchu rule China opened up to European and American trade and influence.

In 1840 a Manchu official

burned a shipload of British-owned opium intended to be sold in China. War broke out between the two countries. England won and forced China to open some of its ports to European trade. The Europeans began to support the Manchu rulers against the Chinese peasants because the Manchus favored European business interests. The peasants revolted and the Taiping Rebellion broke out. The revolt was put down. But the Manchu Dynasty was weakened and in 1911 Chinese revolutionaries finally overthrew the imperial government and established a republic.

However, the Chinese people were not trained for democracy. Over the following years the country suffered under local military chiefs, or warlords, who fought each other for power. An exhausting war with Japan broke out in 1931 and continued until it became part of World War II. China then joined the Allies against Germany, Italy and Japan.

When the war was over, the Communists managed to take control of China, and in September 1949 a new Communist government was set up in Beijing, establishing the People's Republic of China, with Chairman Mao Zedong as its head. China is still ruled by Communists today.

Caption: Mao Zedong proclaims the Communist Republic of China

THE LESSONS OF FAITH

One day the physician who employed Hudson forgot to pay him his wages. In fact, the man was so forgetful he had often asked Hudson to remind him to pay his wages every week. But Hudson had been wondering what more he could do to make sure he'd be ready to face life as a missionary. He decided to use his employer's forgetfulness as an occasion to trust God. I won't remind Dr. Hardey, he thought. I will just pray about money for my rent and food and train myself to put my expectations in the Lord instead of man.

Hudson discovered that putting his faith to the test was not an easy thing. One Sunday evening when Hudson had nothing but one coin left, a poor man approached him and asked if he would come to his home and pray with his wife, who was dying. Hudson asked the man why he had not called his own priest.

"I did," said the man, "but he wouldn't come without payment and we haven't a cent to our name. My children are starving."

Hudson thought of the coin in his pocket, the only money he had. He thought of the last bowl of porridge and piece of bread waiting for him at his lodging. "How is it you have allowed your family to reach such a desperate state?" Hudson asked. "You should have called the civil authorities for help."

To himself Hudson thought, If only I had two coins, I'd give the man one of them. The two men continued walking through the night, down into a courtyard, then up a tiny flight of stairs and into a wretched room. There Hudson saw five children sitting on the ground, their cheeks and temples sunken with hunger. Lying on the floor beside them was their mother with a tiny infant at her side. Hudson noticed that instead of crying, the baby was as if in exhausted pain. If only I had an extra coin, he thought. I would be happy to give it to them so they could buy food for the children.

"Don't be discouraged," Hudson said to the family. "You have a loving Father in Heaven who knows your needs."

But within him, Hudson heard a voice. "Hypocrite!" the voice said, "You tell these people to trust God, yet you are not willing to trust Him yourself without that money in your pocket!"

Hudson began to feel he was the one in need of comfort and help. "Let's pray together, shall we?" he asked.

But again, the voice spoke to his heart: "Are you mocking God, Hudson? Give that coin away!"

Hudson finished his prayer, looked into the eyes of the children, put his hand into his pocket and took out the coin, giving it to their grateful father. Then he went home with a heart full of joy to what he imagined would be his last meal for many days.

The next morning, though, Hudson received a letter with a blurred postmark. He didn't recognize the handwriting. When he opened the envelope, out fell a coin that was worth four times as much as the one he had given away. There was no letter and Hudson never did find out where it came from. It was just enough money to tide him over until his rent was due.

Two weeks later, Hudson got on his knees again and prayed that God would supply the money he needed for his landlady. Hudson did not want her to suffer on behalf of his decision to live by faith. When Dr. Hardey delayed paying him yet again, Hudson prayed until he felt sure that God would meet his need some other way. He remained in his room, praying and thanking God for the answer in faith.

Late that evening, Dr. Hardey came up the stairs to Hudson's apartment, laughing heartily. "Here, take this money," he told Hudson. "A former patient just arrived at my door and paid his bill in full. He must be crazy to come so late with money on a Sunday! Keep whatever I owe you."

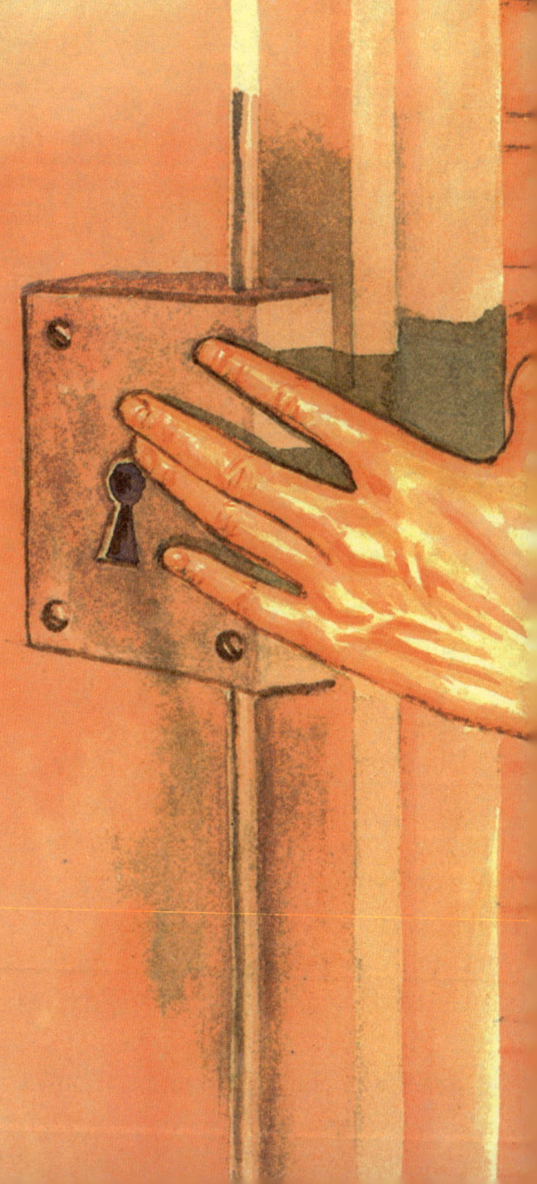

THE GOLDEN OPPORTUNITY

During the following years Hudson became more and more determined to move closer to his dream of going to China. He turned down offers of money toward his studies, showing he cared more about getting a stronger faith than getting a strong education. He chose to live on brown bread and water. "I want to practice what I preach," he wrote in his journal. "My goal is to move men and women to God through prayer alone." Besides, time is running out, he thought. If I wait until I've become a doctor to sail for China, millions will have perished without knowing Jesus. I must pray for an opportunity soon.

Then one day, the opportunity Hudson had been waiting for happened. Leaders of the rebellion in China had gotten the upper hand in the war and were showing an openness to western ideas. Hudson heard they wanted Christian teachers in Shanghai and knew his golden moment had arrived. It may be now or never, the door is open and I must go through it, he determined.

Although Hudson had no medical degree, university training or papers of ordination, he did have the enthusiasm and courage of ten men as he made plans to sail away. With the promise of financial sponsorship from the Chinese Evangelization Society in London, Hudson stored away medicines and doctor's instruments alongside Chinese Bibles and books, wrapping everything carefully for the four-month voyage. With bags and boxes in tow, he left his family on the dock in Liverpool, England and turned his vision toward the East.

Now, only a few days later, trapped in the unpredictable storms of the Irish Sea, Hudson found himself praying against shipwreck. Even as he begged God to watch over them, the Dumfries veered away from the jagged off-shore rock and turned back toward the open water. Straight on it sped for days on end — all the way to the Bay of Biscay, around the Cape of Good Hope, heading past Australia and onward, right into the East China Sea.

Hudson's Way to China

LIFE IN SHANGHAI

When the Dumfries finally docked on an island near the coast of China, Hudson waved goodbye to the crew. He jumped down from the deck onto a small pilot boat headed upriver toward Shanghai. The river's current was steady and serene compared with the slap-dashing sensation of the ocean. Hudson settled back and surveyed his belongings. He had enough supplies to start a medical dispensary, plenty of ink and paper for writing, lots of books and a few clothes.

Stepping ashore at Shanghai, Hudson headed in the direction of a distant English flag. The solid earth seemed to rock beneath his feet and his heart pounded wildly. China, at last! The red, white and blue Union Jack flying above the British consulate meant the promise of people who would help him settle in Shanghai. He expected to draw money there from the account of his sponsors, the Chinese Evangelization Society (C.E.S) and pick up a letter of welcome and instruction.

But the only welcome for Hudson was the sound of gunfire and cannon

blasts. Shanghai was completely occupied by soldiers — the rebellion forces — and surrounded by the imperial army of China. Wounded and dead soldiers lay moaning in the streets. Hudson had to step around them. He paused to allow one group to pass — soldiers hauling captives along the stone streets by their hair. They were going to a place of execution. The doomed men cried out in pain and grapped wildly for Hudson's legs as they were being dragged off.

And so Hudson discovered that the country he had waited so long to see was being torn apart by civil war. In the days that followed there would often be political riots in the city. The Chinese mistrusted people from the West. These things made it hard for the missionaries to cut a path into the interior of the country. Little did Hudson know that the war would drag on for another eleven years, hindering his work every step of the way.

On that first day at the consulate, Hudson found no letter of instruction, no money available to him, no contact person with the C.E.S. mission. Turning aside, he faced the glare of battle going on outside city walls. There was no housing other than shacks and when food was available, it was old and stale and terribly expensive.

Burned- and bombed-out houses lined the walls of the city of Shanghai. Starving children, orphans and beggars shuffled along the alleyways, despite the freezing temperatures. Hungry women stared at him from hovels. Infants lay naked in their arms, sucking desperately at their mothers' empty breasts. An occasional shrill cry from a child shattered the daylight, turning Hudson's bright expectations to darkness. His vision turned to grim determination. Hudson wanted to help these people and bring them hope. He shuddered in the damp, chill air and walked away from the consulate.

After some time, Hudson met a British doctor in a Shanghai hospital

who offered him shelter in his own home. Hudson felt grateful, but frustrated. He ached to get his own place where Bible studies could be held and where he could start a school for the children. Hudson barely knew where to begin. But begin, he did.

Hudson visited shops and offices, made friends with local business people, visited homes where disease and starvation had made entire families sick. He studied Mandarin, the language spoken by most Chinese and got to know other missionaries living in Shanghai.

One evening a woman was shuffling along the street and saw Hudson giving out booklets about Jesus. The woman reached for a booklet, bowed and began to leave. Hudson noticed her feet were so tiny that she could hardly walk. They were the size of a toddler's feet, crippled and deformed. He had seen many women with feet just like hers.

Just then from a house nearby, he heard women's voices crying out, "Stop, stop, please have mercy." The woman on the street pulled a scarf over her head and hurried on. Hudson felt helpless and sad. He wished he could do something to help the women he had just heard and other women in China, as well. Hudson knew many baby girls were crippled on purpose by their families as a sign of wealth. When they grew up, they could barely walk. He understood just how dreadfully most women were treated. They were considered possessions of men, were not allowed to go to school, were sometimes sold as slaves and were often tortured into doing what men wanted them to do. Hudson went home and turned his sadness into prayer for China.

Not long afterwards, Hudson came face to face with the powerful Chinese drug trade. Walking near the harbor, he noticed a large quantity of boxes containing opium being loaded onto the dock. He learned from other westerners in Shanghai that thousands of pounds of opium were imported into China yearly and used to keep people poor and ignorant through addiction. Wealthy men grew richer from the trade. And the poor were dying. Hudson had always known the powers of darkness and evil cut deep in China. Now he began to realize just how treacherous and dangerous the work was to which God had called him.

Hudson also witnessed the horror of the "coolie traffic" and his heart broke with sadness. One morning he noticed Chinese men being loaded on board a ship by the hundreds. Some were

bound and blindfolded, others appeared to go willingly, but once on board, became confused. The men were refused the right to get off the ship. Hudson heard the crack of whips and moans of pain from men inside the ship's hold. He learned the men were being sent to far-off places to do menial, back-breaking labor and that many would die on the way, while those who did survive the inhumane treatment would never return to China.

Hudson renewed his determination to pray for the Chinese people even as he renewed his abandonment to God. He knew there were millions of people sold into slavery from the interior of China. He vowed to be their messenger of salvation. He vowed to challenge other young people in England to respond to the incredible needs in China and bring the freedom of Christ to Chinese people beyond the coastline.

THE DREAM TO REACH INLAND CHINA

Hudson studied the areas on his map north, south and west of Shanghai. These were large, heavily populated regions, linked by an intricate web of waterways. Junks, or small sailboats were readily available to navigate these channels, although Hudson knew travel would be slow and primitive.

Yet the day did come when he could load hundreds of New Testaments and thousands of leaflets about the gospel onto a junk and take off through the narrow watery passageways. He passed out tracts wherever the boat stopped and took time to explain the message to people for whom it was strange and unbelievable. He realized, also, how odd he must look to these people in his tattered western clothes, fair hair and blue eyes. Most of them stared and gawked at him. Sometimes they ran from him. Other times, they threatened to kill him.

On one trip with a friend, he offered free medical care to the people he met. He soon learned that the potions, pills and powders in his medicine chest fascinated the Chinese and opened a door for his preaching about the salvation God offers through Jesus. Day in and day out, Hudson traveled the waterways leading into the interior of China. This was the land of his dreams. Regardless of how dangerous the trips sometimes were, he felt fulfilled and joyful.

One day after many trips, Hudson had an idea. Why not live permanently on a boat? he wondered. Many Chinese

Christianity

do it? Why not live as closely to their lifestyle as possible? I don't want them to notice me because I am a foreigner, but to listen to the stories I have to tell from the Bible. That way I can avoid the suspicions of many who believe I am a spy for the rebellion in China and I can become better friends with the Chinese wherever I go.

Hudson knew of no other missionaries who had dared to think like this or dared to dress like the Chinese. Though he was certain to be criticized by othe westerners, he decided that the acceptance of the Chinese people was more important than that of fellow missionaries. Hudson ordered a pair of wide, short trousers and a silk jacket from a Chinese tailor. He was fitted for a pair of turned-up shoes by a shoemaker. Then he dyed his hair black with the help of a barber and purchased a long braided pigtail hairpiece to wear until his own hair grew long. The next day he appeared dressed as a typical Chinese teacher, a man who would be respected for his education.

Hudson sailed for Chongming where more than one million Chinese lived. The people of Chongming received him with great enthusiasm and curiosity. One of them offered him a room in the attic of a Buddhist temple. Hudson began treating sick people and holding church meetings. It was a confirmation to him that the real work in the interior of China had begun.

Despite this early success, Hudson was later forced to return to Shanghai to live. There he continued the inland ministry through frequent trips. Yet on

ina

Christianity came to China during the late Middle Ages. But not until today, 600 years later, is it bearing fruit – thanks to Hudson Taylor and many other faithful missionaries who shared the Gospel with the Chinese.

When the atheistic Communists took over in 1949, all western missionaries were thrown out of China, leaving behind an estimated 900,000 Chinese believers, who were then harassed and persecuted by Communist officials. During the Cultural Revolution (1966-1970) pastors were imprisoned, churches and temples were closed, and religion banned.

But religion survived in the hearts of the Chinese people, and the government eventually allowed Christians to meet in the government-regulated "open" churches. Yet many Christians preferred to worship without being registered and controlled by the government. Underground "house churches" sprang up all over the country. These churches – mainly growing in the rural areas where eighty per cent of the population lives – are self-supporting and self-propagating. A typical house church has 100-300 members who meet in homes at unusual hours so as to avoid harassment by the police. Most members do not even have a Bible. All they have are handwritten copies of Scripture verses. But they are happy and thankful for having been found worthy to suffer for Christ.

Today, an estimated forty million believers meet in house churches, while only six million are affiliated with the official Church.

Caption: Believers worshipping in house church

each trip, obstacle after obstacle was placed in his way. His path to the heart of China was blocked again and again by the civil war, diplomatic bureaucracy between Britain and China, threats to his life and the destruction of his medical supplies and books.

One day on a journey by ship from Shanghai to Ningbo, Hudson took along a Chinese man named Peter who had been educated in England. They had become friends and Hudson often talked to Peter about God. Late that afternoon, Hudson heard a splash and a shout. Peter had fallen overboard and the boatman was pointing to the dark place in the water where he had disappeared.

Hudson jumped over the side of the ship and swam back to the spot, searching desperately in the murky water for Peter. When he saw some nearby fishermen with a dragnet he shouted, "Come and bring that net here! A man is drowning!"

"Not right now," they shouted back. "We're busy fishing. Maybe later."

"I'll pay you well!" answered

Hudson. "Don't wait until it is too late!"

"We won't come for less than thirty coins," the fishermen replied.

"I'll give you everything I have. But hurry!"

Finally, the fishermen brought the net over and within a few minutes hauled Peter to the surface. Hudson tried to revive him, but failed. The loss of time caused by the fishermen's indifference had cost Peter his life.

Hudson was heartsick. They could easily have saved him. But they were too busy. What about the millions of Chinese men dying every day because Christians are distracted by other things? Hudson wondered. Isn't the soul more valuable than the body? I will preach the gospel every day to as many as I can reach.

Though provisions from England were slow in coming and Hudson often had to go without food, booklets or medicine, he preached at every opportunity and created ways of interesting people in the gospel. Through every problem, he learned to rest in God, growing daily in love for the Chinese people, even as he had loved Peter.

HUDSON'S LOVE STORY

Months later, hostilities arose between England and China. War broke out between the two countries. Hudson was detained at the town of Ningbo due to the nearby sea battles. While living there, he became acquainted with two young women who were sisters, orphaned as children, now helping to run the first-ever school for girls in China. The girls' parents had been among the earliest missionaries in the country.

The eldest sister, Maria, also participated in neighborhood evangelism. Because of her vision and compassion for the Chinese people and her gentle spirit, Hudson fell in love with Maria. Their friendship blossomed until circumstances of war forced an end to it: A plot to massacre all foreigners was discovered in Ningbo and Hudson was chosen to escort families with small children safely back to Shanghai.

Before leaving, Hudson agonized over whether or not to ask for Maria's hand in marriage. What do I have to offer a wife? he asked himself. I can give her no security whatsoever. My funding comes from a weak and disorganized mission society. I've never been able to depend on them. My life is dangerous and physically hard. Why, I haven't even a home or a bed to call my own. I'm always moving about and often criticized by the other missionaries because of my Chinese dress. No, I cannot ask Maria to marry me.

Back in Shanghai, Hudson was almost too busy to miss Maria. Because of the fighting, thousands of homeless refugees poured into the city from outlying districts. Many lived in cemeteries where they took shelter by breaking into the low, arched tombs. Others crowded into ruined buildings. Hudson went on daily rounds to these places, caring for the sick, starving and freezing people. Because of the deteriorating financial situation of the C.E.S., he decided to end his connection with them completely. He took on the status of an independent missionary, trusting in God alone for the food, shelter and provisions he would need. This was unheard of among the missionaries of his time, but Hudson was willing to endure their criticism for the sake of what God had called him to do in China.

In spite of the chaos in Shanghai and the burdens of his work there, Hudson could still not get his mind off the lovely Maria. And back in Ningbo, Maria could not get her mind off Hudson. She was attracted by his commitment to the Chinese people and his willingness to be dependent on God alone. She admired the manner in which he had adopted the Chinese dress and his vision of taking the gospel to the interior of China. But Maria was not allowed to communicate with Hudson, so she took all her dreams and desires to God.

At last Hudson sent a letter to Maria declaring his desire to marry her. Maria took the letter to her guardian who responded, "What? How dare that poor unconnected nobody ask for your hand in marriage? The proposal must be refused at once!" Then she forced poor Maria to write the refusal in her own hand. Maria believed she would never see Hudson again.

But in the spring, Hudson returned

to Ningbo on business. Maria's guardian criticized his clothing and scorned his radical dependence on himself and God. She refused to allow him to see Maria. Then a friend of Maria's quietly arranged for a secret meeting between the two young people. Maria and Hudson shared their feelings for each other and agreed to seek God on the matter of marriage.

Hudson told Maria, "If we marry, our life will be difficult. Even now my finances are dwindling to almost nothing. And my calling is dangerous. I'm going to take the gospel further and further into the interior of China."

"Have you forgotten?" Maria replied. "I was left an orphan in a far-off land. God has been my Father all these years; do you think I shall be afraid to trust Him now?"

With confidence in a shared vision, Hudson asked Maria to write for permission to marry from her uncle back in England. Four months later, a letter arrived granting permission. Maria's uncle had been assured from mission associates in London that Hudson was a missionary of unusual promise.

Hudson's marriage with Maria seemed destined to bring closer their mutual vision of reaching inland China, despite the political storms raging around them. The summer of their wedding the Treaty of Tianjin opened the way for foreigners to all interior provinces. The Taylors rejoiced, but decided that next year to stay in Ningbo, rather than move on. This was because the hospital and dispensary there looked set to close when the resident physician lost his wife and returned to England with their children. Hudson and Maria accepted the challenge of running the hospital.

Hudson, not sponsored by any medical or missionary society, knew they would have to pray for the funds needed to keep the hospital running. The situation was not new to Hudson. He had been living by faith alone for years and he believed God was with them. Finally, the day came when the last bag of rice had been opened and was disappearing fast as the patients received their daily meal.

Hudson looked at the few grains of rice in the hospital kitchen and said, "The Lord's time for helping us must be close at hand."

Before the end of that day the Taylors had received a check enclosed with a letter from a man they'd never met. "I've inherited a great deal of money," the letter said. "And I prayed about what God would have me do with it. I'm sending it to you in case you may have need of it and will send more if you allow."

"Suppose," Hudson said to Maria, "we had turned down the challenge to take over the hospital because of lack of finances? Or because of lack of faith?"

"Now we can go on helping people here and sharing the gospel with them," Maria added.

Hudson and Maria threw themselves into the hospital work. But the stress and strain of the project, as well as having to look after their new baby, took its toll on their health and spirits. There was simply too much to do and not enough people to help. They worked hard for six years as patients continued to flood the wards. At last, the endless needs of helpless people finally became too much to bear. Hudson became sick and grew weak. Maria was caring for him and their daughter while performing the administrative duties of the hospital. She was desperate for help. And no help came.

Faced with the impossibility of all she and Hudson were attempting, the day finally came when she closed the door to the Ningbo hospital, giving the large iron key an extra twist. Then she joined Hudson and Gracie on board a ship, and the family headed back to England. Hudson and Maria had come to realize that they must dream a new dream. They talked of stirring interest in British young people to consider service in China. Maria looked forward to a period of rest for herself and hoped

Hudson could recover completely from his illness. They envisioned a time when they would return to their beloved China with plenty of workers to share their vision of reaching the interior.

But doctors in England told Hudson he would never again be strong enough for missionary service. They warned him to slow down and stay put. Year after year they treated him and watched for his health to improve. But Hudson did not listen to his doctors. He was determined to help the Chinese even from his room, which overlooked a dreary street on London's east side.

Hudson worked on a revision of the Chinese New Testament that could be understood by less educated people. He wrote articles about China from his bed and whenever possible, he called meetings and preached to the English people about the great need in China. Determined to return one day himself, he resumed his medical studies so he would be better prepared to help the Chinese people.

Maria was also busy, giving birth to a son every other year during their stay in England. And she was making the difficult adjustment to what was for her, a strange culture. Maria longed for her childhood home of China and an opportunity to serve its people. Both she and Hudson were homesick for the country they loved half a world away. Their apartment, the British Isles and traditions there, all seemed too small for their vision and dreams.

Hudson was discouraged that men and women were not responding to the call of need in China. The flurry of interest stirred by his arrival in London had now died down. "God has put me on a shelf," he said to Maria.

But every day Hudson studied a map of China and prayed for inland areas by name and the people he knew who had responded to the gospel message in each place. Hudson compiled facts about the size and population of every province. One day he got a letter from a mission society in England: "The number of Protestant missionaries in

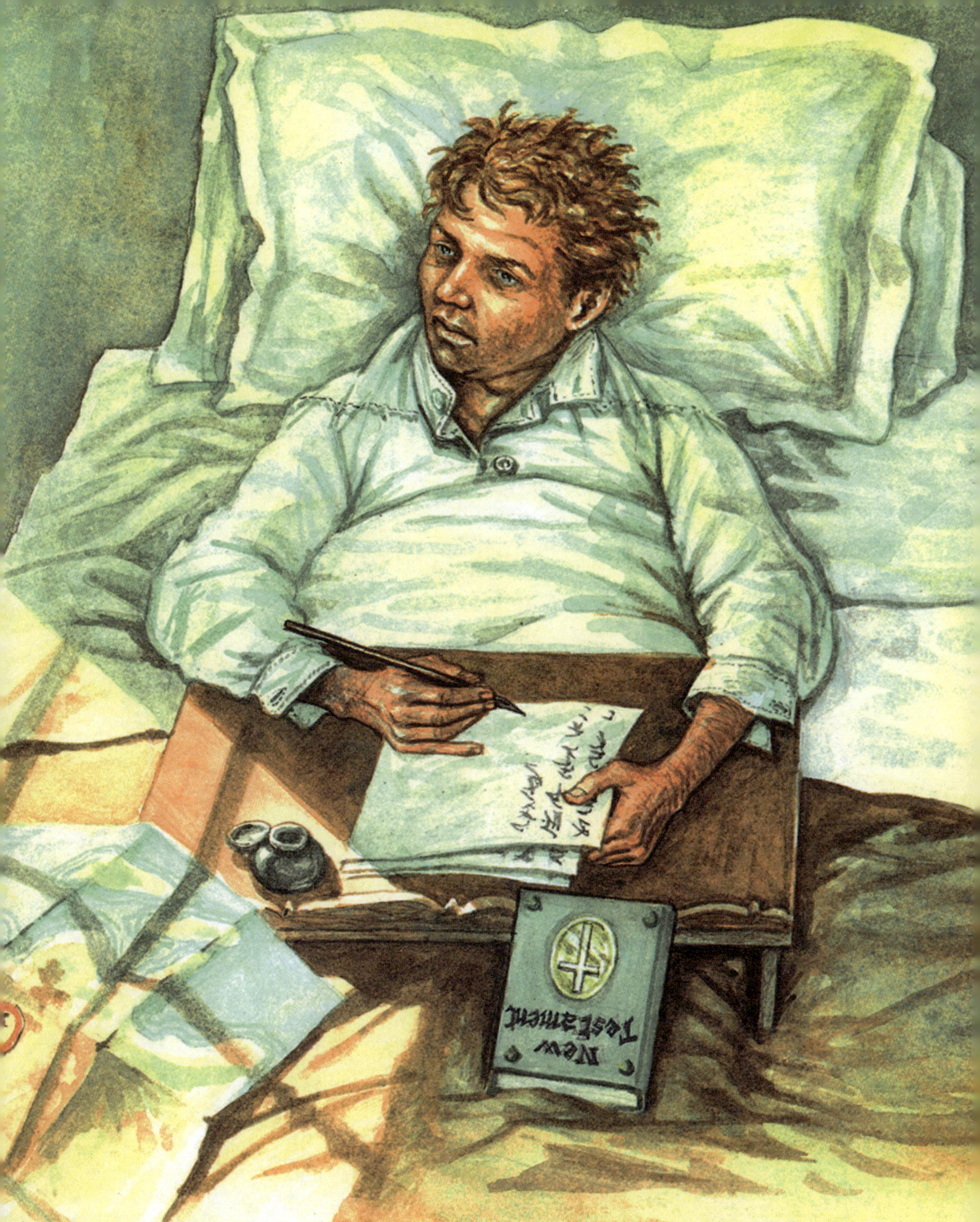

China has been reduced from 115 to 91 in recent months," it reported. Hudson grieved at the loss of workers. People are perishing daily and we in England are allowing it to happen, he thought. We are too busy attending to our own affairs to be concerned about men drowning in a sea of spiritual darkness. Then he thought of his friend Peter. Hudson became so sad, he ceased to write in his journal for seven weeks. He just sat alone and prayed and cried.

Finally, one day Hudson took a walk on the beach. He felt alone, exhausted and thoroughly spent from his grief. As the waves beat the shoreline, he stopped speaking to God and started listening.

"Seek from Me the needed workers," the Lord told him. "Stop trying to do it all yourself. Pray for the spiritual life of

the Church so that out of it, young people will respond. Trust Me."

"But Lord," Hudson replied, "What if new workers come, but fail? We need at least twenty-four, two for each of the eleven provinces without a missionary and two for Mongolia. But I can't offer them any security at all — only danger and life on the brink of starvation. What if they break down under the burden? What if they can't endure the political problems? What if they are not up to it?"

"The power," said God, "by which I call men and women will also be the power by which I keep them."

"Then, Lord, take the burden off my back," Hudson cried. "I'll leave it up to You."

A NEW ADVENTURE IN FAITH

Two days later Hudson went to the London and County Bank and opened an account for what he entitled the China Inland Mission (C.I.M.). He deposited ten pounds sterling into the account — every cent he and Maria owned. This would be the start of a new kind of mission society where workers had to trust God alone for food and provision.

"There will be no salaries for outgoing missionaries," he and Maria agreed. "We can afford to have as little as the Lord chooses to give. We will wear native dress and head inland."

Hudson knew the idea of an organization requiring missionaries to go without secure funding and to dress like the native people was a radical idea. He knew he would be considered fanatical and rebellious by many churches and mission boards.

"My past experience of God's faithfulness gives me the courage to proceed," Hudson told startled church members who questioned the wisdom of his idea. "I've survived storms at sea, civil war battles, political uprisings and sickness. But from the response of the Chinese people, I know we have a covenant-keeping God."

"That brash upstart!" said one minister when he read of Hudson's idea. "This new mission might take away men or money from already existing organizations! What good will it do in the kingdom of God — robbing Peter to pay Paul?"

Hudson responded to this criticism even before he had heard of it. He established standards that allowed C.I.M. to accept workers not accepted by other missions, particularly those who hadn't completed university training. No one would be recruited or asked to join the mission.

"We will depend on God alone to prompt those whom He wants to volunteer," Hudson announced. "And we will not appeal for money! In this way we will not divert money from other organizations."

"It is a foolhardy business," snapped Hudson's critics. "It's an impossible idea. You will be forgotten and soon find yourself without even the necessities of life!"

"God is moving," Hudson told them. "Are we willing to move with Him?"

REBIRTH OF A DREAM

Two small boys grasped the hands of their older sister and crossed the gangplank onto a huge ship. As the mast creaked in the breeze they looked up at their mother for assurance. Maria carried their baby brother in one arm and a suitcase in the other. "It's all right boys," she said. "Let's get up on top and then we can see the water." Maria and her oldest child, Gracie, saw the anxiety in the boys' eyes and Gracie squeezed their fingers in hers while Maria prodded them with gentle words.

Hudson followed the family on board the Lammermuir with sixteen missionaries behind them. Volunteer missionaries had responded to the call of the China Inland Mission and had been training and studying Chinese together for months. The excitement and anticipation on their faces was a source of great joy to Hudson. These are God's chosen workers, he thought. And I trust Him to send the final eight workers soon.

The party was ready for the four-month voyage. Maria and Hudson had plenty of help with the children as the young missionaries pitched in with schooling and practical care. After a few weeks at sea, the children settled down and began to enjoy the shifts in the wind and the rocking of the ship. Even though they were heading off to an unknown land, they were secure in the protection of parents who had taught them to trust God and love Him.

When the Lammermuir finally reached the China Sea, there was great excitement on board as they neared

their destination. Soon they would have real beds, fresh food and be able to walk and run for miles if they wanted. With cramped legs, they stood on deck one night hoping to catch their first sight of land. Suddenly, the air changed, the wind picked up and the sky opened, drenching the ship with rain. Taking refuge in their cabins below, the Taylor family and their friends knelt and prayed.

Day after day, the ship was battered by one typhoon after another. Rain and sleet kept the decks wet. The storms blew the vessel off course and threatened to destroy it. For twelve days, the crew and passengers fought fear, nausea and discouragement. Then one morning, they saw the coast of China. Just as they began to rejoice, another typhoon came along and blew the ship in the opposite direction. It was as if the ship could take no more. The jibs and staysails gave way. The decks were swept by a violent sea. Soon one entire side of the ship had rolled under water. The jibboom broke, followed by the foretop and masts. They swung in the wind like broken arms on a worn-out doll. Tubs, buckets, cask and timbers floated all around the little ship.

The captain ordered everyone to put on life belts. "The ship can scarcely hold together for another two hours," he said. "We're going under."

Hudson kissed his children in their cabin below, left them in the care of Maria and climbed on deck to join the crew. He found them taking refuge in the forecastle with revolvers, intending to use them on themselves if washed into the sea.

"Please, don't use force," Hudson pleaded. "We must try everything to stay afloat. We must keep working. God will bring us through this, but the navigation depends on you."

All who could, climbed up on deck. Men and women together took turns manning the pumps. They pulled what was left of the damaged sails, working day after day, night after night to keep the ship from the sea. It was an exhausted and ragged group of missionaries who finally landed in a mangled vessel on the coast of China one week later.

When the other Shanghai missionaries saw them, one man chided, "Hudson Taylor is back. And he's

brought six unmarried ladies with him. Imagine bringing unmarried English women to China!"

"Yes, and they say he plans to send them inland!" said another.

"In Chinese dress, no less!" said someone else. "Is this Taylor some sort of madman?"

"Where will they stay?" another wondered. "I've heard they have no financial support from England. How will they stay alive? They don't even

have a place to sleep tonight."

The ragged party immediately boarded houseboats to travel into China's interior toward Hangzhou. They were in search of permanent headquarters for their mission. The nights were bitterly cold and several people became ill. Maria stayed on board the boat and cared for them while Hudson explored the city of Hangzhou for a place to stay and to plan the next step of going further inland.

Before the end of a year in Hangzhou, tragedy struck the small party of missionaries. Winter came and went, and summer arrived with its stifling 103 degree heat. As a result, tempers flared and fighting broke out among the members of the China Inland Mission. Several in the group criticized the dress standards, while others complained about Hudson's leadership style. Worst of all, one day Hudson and Maria's only daughter became sick. Within a few desperate hours, little Gracie was dead.

"She was the sunshine of our lives," Hudson wrote to his sister back in England. "I'll never forget the day we buried her — those little white hands folded on her bosom, holding a single flower. It is too sad."

But Hudson and Maria were determined to pursue their vision. They decided to work harder than ever and put their sadness behind them. They went out preaching and helped the sick as far as they could go up the waterways of inland China. Within a few months, members of the C.I.M. were establishing churches in cities twenty-four days' journey from each other.

The Taylors accepted as part of mission life that wherever they went, there was the possibility of riots against them. In Hangzhou the people who had first welcomed the missionaries now hated them. They passed out papers saying the foreigners who preached "the religion of Jesus" had committed horrible crimes.

One night an angry mob of Chinese people gathered outside the door of the C.I.M., accusing the Taylors of kidnapping Chinese children.

"Revenge!" cried the mob. "Attack! Destroy the foreigners! Take their medicines. Burn their books!"

Hudson crept away in the darkness and raced to the governor's house for help. He slipped through the gates, but was kept waiting as he listened to the rioters' shouts back at the house. He knew Maria and the children were defenseless in the hands of the angry mob. "God must protect us," he prayed. "Lord, You are the only defense we can count on now or ever." And Hudson's family was protected.

HUDSON'S DREAM COMES TRUE

For many years Hudson and Maria continued to work from town to town. There were more riots. Some of the missionaries wanted to give up. Others criticized Hudson for the way he led the mission. It was never easy to find enough food or medicine. The Taylors had to nurse each other and their sons through sickness, loneliness and fear. At one point, before the hot summer season started, they decided to send their three older children back to safety in England because the boys had been so ill and weak.

Then tragedy struck again when shortly before the children were set to sail, one of the boys died. The hardest thing Maria ever did was put the other two on the ship, not knowing whether they would ever see each other again. Although she was determined to do the best for them and for the ministry, stay-

ing behind in China without her children nearly broke Maria's heart. Weakened by that, Maria fell ill with cholera. She was pregnant at the time and her newborn son died shortly after being born. Maria's strength was gone and she died soon afterwards in her husband's arms.

Hudson buried Maria and their infant son beside Gracie and her younger brother. It was a crushing blow. Still, he determined that the work must go on in spite of the pain, and the crippling effect Maria's death had on the ministry. "Perhaps God will give new life out of this death," he hoped.

There were still nine Chinese provinces with no missionaries at all. Getting money to support more workers had always been a problem. Hudson wrote articles about the need in China, challenging Christians to pray. Outside China he spoke wherever he could get an invitation to talk about China. Then one by one, Hudson received applications from eighteen young people who answered the call to come work with the China Inland Mission.

Hudson was not satisfied with temporary missionaries. He wanted to establish permanent mission stations in each of the provinces.

"God will provide the workers and the money," he had always said.

Hudson traveled several times back and forth to England, each time further

expanding the work. He eventually married again and his wife took up work among the Chinese women. In the meantime, Hudson began to make visits to America and Europe, always calling for more missionaries. Soon there were a thousand volunteers, but Hudson was spending less time in China than he wanted.

At 73, Hudson finally returned to China with his son and daughter-in-law, doing the very work he so loved. Together, they sailed the inland waterways telling people about Jesus. There was barely a city in the interior of China that had not been reached by missionaries whom Hudson had inspired and challenged. Hudson had seen his dream come true.

Main Events in Hudson Taylor's Life

1832 (May 21) Hudson Taylor is born in Barnsley, Yorkshire, England.
1849 (June) Makes personal commitment to Jesus Christ.
1850 (May) Begins medical studies in Hull as assistant to Dr. Robert Hardey.
1853 (September) Sails for China, sponsored by the Chinese Evangelization Society.
1854 (March) Lands in Shanghai.
1850-1864 Taiping Rebellion in China.
1854-1855 Makes ten evangelistic journeys.
1855 (Oct.-Nov.) Makes his first home in "inland" China.
1856 (October) Settles temporarily in Ningbo where he meets Maria Dyer who will become his wife.
1857 (June) Resigns from the Chinese Evangelization Society.
1858 (January) Marries Maria Dyer.
1859 (September) Takes charge, with Maria, of Dr. Parker's hospital in Ningbo.
1860-1865 Becomes ill and returns to England with Maria and daughter Grace. Three sons are born to the family. Hudson is in a spiritual desert. He translates the New Testament into the Ningbo Chinese dialect and attempts to recruit new missionaries for China.
1865 (June) Surrenders his dream to God. He founds the China Inland Mission (C.I.M.) and writes influential book,
China's Spiritual Needs and Claims.
1866 (May) The Taylor family sails to China with the first 16 volunteers for the C.I.M.
1866 (December) The C.I.M. settles in Hangzhou, China.
1867 (August) Oldest child, daughter Grace dies.
1868 Survives the riot at Hangzhou. House rebuilt and another son (their sixth child) is born.
1870 Sends four oldest surviving children back to England; one son (5-year-old Samuel) dies shortly before the trip.
1870 (July) Maria Taylor dies shortly after a newborn son dies.
1871 Returns to England and marries Jenny Faulding, a fellow missionary to China and family friend.
1872 (August) Forms the London Council of the C.I.M.
1872 (October) Returns to China with Jenny, the second Mrs. Taylor.
1874-1875 Is injured and returns to England; develops paralysis. Appeals for prayer for 18 pioneer missionaries for the nine unevangelized provinces.
1876-1878 Widespread evangelistic journeys throughout inland China.
1878 (autumn) Jenny Taylor leads woman missionaries far into the interior of China.
1888 (summer) Hudson's first visit to North America to appeal for volunteer workers to China.
1889 (November) Visits Sweden, Norway and Denmark.
1890 (August) Visits Australia.
1900 (May) Beginning of the Boxer Rebellion where foreigners were expelled.
1901 Retires from leadership of C.I.M. Eight hundred missionaries representing several denominations — nearly half of all evangelical missionaries in China— are with the C.I.M.
1904 (July) Jenny Taylor dies in Switzerland.
1905 (February) Hudson returns to China for the last time.
1905 (June 3) Hudson Taylor dies in China.

BOOK RESOURCES

Hudson Taylor's Spiritual Secret, by Dr. and Mrs. Howard Taylor (Discovery House Publishers, 1990).
J. Hudson Taylor: A Man in Christ, by Roger Steer (Harold Shaw Publishers, 1990).
God's Adventurer, by Phyllis Thompson (Overseas Missionary Fellowship, 1991).
Hudson Taylor, by J. Hudson Taylor (Bethany House Publishers, 1991).
Shanghaied to China, by Dave and Neta Jackson (Bethany House Publishers, 1993).
Hudson Taylor, by Susan Martins Miller (Barbour and Company, 1993).
The Church in China, by Carl Lawrence (Bethany House Publishers, 1985).

Mother Teresa

THE WOMAN WHO SERVED THE POOREST OF THE POOR

1910 — 1997

Great men and women are not in need of our praise.
We are the ones in need of getting to know them.

By Caroline Higgins

Illustrations by Giuseppe Rava

RATS, GARBAGE, AND A BOY WITH SAD EYES

Sister Teresa paused by the window of her simple bedroom on the second floor of the white marble building. At St. Mary's School and Convent in Calcutta, India she had a happy life teaching the children of wealthy British and Indian families. But this evening she looked longer than usual upon the alleyways below her in one of Calcutta's worst slums, the Entally district.

Teresa saw a scene which vividly contrasted with that of the elegantly landscaped gardens and pathways behind the high walls of St. Mary's. She saw narrow streets cluttered with every stall or business imaginable — textile factories, chemical manufacturers, and lean-to shacks set up to sell religious statues or cheap jewelry. And people were living in between the stalls, sleeping everywhere, in cardboard houses, doorways and on sidewalks, even on the concrete islands in the middle of the city streets. Teresa opened her window for some fresh air, but closed it again promptly; the smells of Calcutta's streets were sometimes unbearable to her. Rotting food and garbage lay heaped in the gutters, where rats scurried about. Smoke from small cooking fires mixed with exhaust from cars and buses. Cattle, considered holy by the Hindu religion, roamed through the streets freely. Their ribs stood out from under their hide. They, too, had a hard time finding food and shelter.

A beggar woman sat on the sidewalk. Her crippled feet were curled

under her filthy sari, the common dress worn by Bengali women.

"One rupee, sahib," she begged of the people walking by her.

Other women and men lay in their own vomit or waste beside her. Teresa knew they could not pay for hospital

care or doctors; many had been abandoned by families who did not even have enough food. Motorbikes and rickshaw drivers simply steered around the sick and dying.

Sister Teresa's heart was heavy with sadness. Ever since she had been a child, she had felt sorry for people who were struggling to find a meal every day, or who were lonely or hurting.

She asked herself, *How can I continue to live a comfortable life when there is so much suffering outside the convent walls? Perhaps I could avoid looking out the window.*

Teresa remembered the orphan child she had met on a winter trip into the city. A biting wind had blown against her sari as she hurried along the street. The sound of a hacking cough had caused her to look around. She had seen a small boy crouching in a doorway of a run-down warehouse, soulful and sad. And she had hesitated, then stopped.

"Are you sick?" she had asked.

The boy could not have been more than five years old. He nodded in reply to her question.

"Where are your parents?"

"Have none," he had replied, turning his head. A coughing fit had come from deep within his chest. Teresa guessed that he had pneumonia.

"I'll bring you some tea," Teresa had

said as she vanished into the crowd. She was back in a few minutes.

Temporary comfort was all she had been able to offer the boy. She could hardly bring people off the street into the quiet studious atmosphere of St. Mary's. *There are millions more just like that boy,* she thought. *What good can one person do in this sea of human misery?*

That night, when the moon was high in the sky, Teresa's eyes snapped open. In her dream she had seen the open wounds of dying people covered with maggots and she had heard the helpless cries of babies thrown onto garbage heaps as if they were nothing more than unwanted leftovers.

"I must do something," she determined the next morning.

CHILDHOOD GRIEF: A 10-YEAR-OLD LOSES HER FATHER

Teresa's childhood name was Agnes. She was 10 years old and living in Yugoslavia in the spring of 1920. Late one night, her sister Aga woke her up.

"Agnes! Agnes, come quickly," Aga said. "Father is ill, and the doctor is here."

Agnes shook her head, trying to focus on the meaning of her sister's words. She stumbled out of bed to join Aga, peering down the staircase into the room below.

"Nana, what's wrong with Papa?" Aga called down to her mother softly. Their brother Lazar appeared in a doorway. He was listening, too.

"Go back to bed, children, and say a prayer for Papa," their mother Drana responded. "We think it might be food poisoning."

Agnes thought soberly of Papa, usu-

ally so busy in his construction business and in political activities, but never too busy to listen to her silly jokes and laugh with her. Agnes remembered the many times Papa had joined the children's games outdoors on hot summer evenings or had taken her swimming in the river. Eventually that night she fell asleep. But in the morning she woke to the sounds of sobbing.

"Father's dead, Agnes, Father died during the night." Aga wailed.

HER MOTHER TEACHES COMPASSION

The days passed slowly after her father's death, and there was a dull ache in Agnes' heart. Now the family business in the Yugoslavian town of Skopje was gone. Agnes' mother, Drana, was forced to support the family on her own. Drana started a small business in her home doing embroidery and handicrafts. She sold the second house the family had always

rented out. Eventually her business grew, and many women came to buy Drana's brightly colored towels, smocks, and wall hangings.

Late one night there was a knock on the door. There stood a young woman, looking worried and in a hurry.

"Someone told me you do wonderful embroidery, but I've not come for that," she blurted out. "I'm very weak with a tumor, and my husband has left me. I was told I might find a place to stay here. I'm so sorry if I'm bothering you."

Drana's face softened with concern. She led the woman into the living room.

"Girls, put the kettle on and make up one of the beds, please," she told Aga and Agnes.

Agnes hesitated, knowing it was her bed that would go to their guest, while she would have to sleep with Aga. But she marched briskly into the kitchen where Aga was already setting the table for tea.

"Nana always says God calls us to serve Him and our neighbor," Agnes said to Aga. "Sometimes I don't like to hear it but I know she's right."

This was not the first time Drana had opened their home to the needy, but she always did it with little display. She often said, "Do good as if you were tossing a pebble into the sea." Agnes once helped her mother take a box of food to a poor family. She remembered many visits to a neighbor lady who was old and sick. Agnes noticed that helping people was a good way to get her mind off her own troubles and help her not feel so sad about her father's death.

Years later, Agnes said, "We were a very happy family. We lived for each other, and we made each other's lives very full and very happy. I have never forgotten my mother. . . ."

Teresa's Homeland

Teresa grew up in southeastern Europe, a part of the world that has been fought over for generations. When Teresa left home for India and until recently, it was known as Yugoslavia.

It is located on the Balkan peninsula just across the Adriatic Sea from Italy. This is a beautiful land with many mountains, lakes and sunny beaches. The Austrian composer Johann Strauss, Jr., was so inspired by the beauty of

Yugoslavia at the time of Teresa's birth in 1910.

the Danube River there that he wrote the famous "Blue Danube" waltz.

Sometimes earthquakes strike in the highland areas; in 1963 a major earthquake nearly leveled Skopje, Teresa's hometown and one of former Yugoslavia's largest cities.

This part of the world has been inhabited by many different kinds of people for hundreds of years. These groups moved into the area, bringing with them different languages and different ways of life.

The Croats called their region Croatia, and the Serbs established Serbia.

Other groups inhabiting the area include the Bosnians, Muslims, Macedonians, and Slovenes, as well as the Albanians and Turks. The country has three major religions, three official languages and two alphabets.

During Teresa's childhood all the different regions were united as one independent kingdom, eventually called Yugoslavia. After World War II it became a Communist state under the leadership of Josip Tito. In recent years, when other regions in that part of the world became independent of the USSR, Yugoslavia also broke its Communist ties. Since then, however, the Serbs and Croats have been fighting bitterly in a violent civil war over who should control the land.

For as long as Agnes could remember, Nana had taken the children to the Church of the Sacred Heart every morning and ended the day with family prayers.

"Love God with all your heart," Nana always told Aga, Agnes, and Lazar.

Agnes loved all the Church activities — acting in the Christmas plays, singing in the choir, even singing solo sometimes or playing her accordion. She began to wonder what it would be like to make solemn vows and become a nun in the Church, totally devoted to God and His work.

SHE FINDS HER CALLING

One day Agnes skipped along the busy boulevard between church and her home. The late afternoon sun glinted and bounced off the leaves of the lacy maple trees lining the street. She felt light-hearted and excited as she hurried to share with Nana the missionary stories she had heard at the Society of Mary, a Church group for girls that met after school every week. There were always missionaries visiting from faraway places or talks about projects to help the needy at home. Last year the group had worked together, making quilts for poor families in the neighborhood.

Agnes burst through the open door and found her mother knitting in the living room.

"Nana, Society was so great today," she bubbled over with enthusiasm. "Brother Anthony from India shared about his work with the orphan children. He brought pictures and said the children love the missionaries! I just love to hear about all those places with mysterious sounding names."

"I'm glad you enjoy it so much," Drana said. "Here, would you hold my yarn while I wind it into a ball?"

Agnes continued, "I wonder how you find out what God wants you to do with your life. One time, Father Jambrekovich told me that when you give your life to God's service, He will fill your heart with a calling, sort of a knowing inside to do a certain kind of work."

"That's right, my love. Just keep seeking God," Drana said.

A TEENAGE GIRL LEAVES HOME

Agnes put thoughts of the future out of her mind for the next few years. But when she was almost eighteen, she spoke again with the missionaries from India. Her earlier fascination with India was still alive.

"Could I be a missionary?" Agnes asked the priest.

"Yes, and since you've been tutoring other students during your school days," Father Jambrekovich said, "you might be happy as a missionary teacher. You could apply to join the Loreto nuns, who teach the daughters of India's leaders."

Making the decision to become a nun in the Church, especially in a foreign country, was not easy. A nun gave her whole life over to God. Nuns promised never to seek after money for themselves, never to get married, and to always obey God. But Agnes had a peaceful feeling inside about becoming a nun and serving God in India. It was what she wanted to do. She also felt it was what God wanted her to do.

Agnes made plans to leave her home country of Yugoslavia and travel west across Europe to Ireland, the headquarters of the Loreto nuns. There, women came from all over the world to be trained as missionary teachers. In Ireland, she would learn English, the official language of India.

Agnes' brother, Lazar, had left home to join the military. When he heard her news, he wrote back, "Have you lost your senses, leaving home to go halfway around the world? How can you leave mother and Aga?"

"Lazar, you serve a king of two million subjects, but I serve the King of the whole world!" Agnes answered. "Which of us do you think is in the better place?"

In those days leaving to become a missionary meant that Agnes would probably never return to Skopje, and never see her family again. There would be no money to use for travel. It was a family sacrifice. But Drana spent a day in prayer, then asked Agnes only to "be sure of your decision and strive only for God."

IRELAND: A NEW LANGUAGE AND A NEW WAY OF LIFE

In Ireland Agnes became a postulant, someone learning about becoming a nun. The young women were given time to decide if they were sure this was what they truly wanted to do with their lives. Agnes had to wear a dark, heavy habit, or robe, made of linen. The food was different, the English language strange, and there was a whole new way of living. Postulants learned about "the silence," when no one was allowed to talk from bedtime until the morning. This was a way of preparing them for Mass and Communion the next day. Silence was also maintained in the dining room, and the Bible was read during all the meals.

Agnes spent six weeks in Ireland. Then she started the long journey by ship and train to India. There she would begin her work as a teacher.

INDIA: THE MISSION COUNTRY

The train chugged into Darjeeling spewing steam and smoke as if exhausted from its long uphill journey. Traveling through rugged river valleys and thick jungle growth, it finally reached this scenic spot in the shadow of the Himalayan mountains. Darjeeling was one of India's most beautiful resort cities, built at the foot of a rugged mountain.

Emerging from the train station, Agnes began the long climb up three flights of stairs built onto the side of the mountain. This was in the middle of the city. She reached the Loreto School perched at the top and looked down on the bustle of Darjeeling below. *What a fascinating city*, she thought, *so many different kinds of people — Indians, British, Tibetans, Mongolians. And the narrow streets are so crammed with colorful markets, bazaars, and food stalls.*

Agnes settled in happily at the convent in Darjeeling. Her English skills improved quickly and she also learned Bengali, the common language of India. She studied the Bible and taught history and geography to the girls at the Loreto School.

After three years there, Agnes made her first promises to God to remain poor, chaste, and obedient to Him.

"I'm so excited," she wrote to her mother, "today I get my ring and will choose my new name!"

The thin gold ring she placed on the third finger of her hand meant that she was now married — but not to any ordinary man. A nun promises that she will be married to Christ alone.

The privilege of being a nun meant that she could also choose a new name. "I'll choose Teresa, after St. Teresa of Lisieux, the little French nun who died so young but kept a wonderful diary," Teresa said. "She wrote about doing the smallest jobs as perfectly as you can because you love God. I want to be like that." So Agnes became Sister Teresa.

CALCUTTA: A NEW ADVENTURE

Soon afterwards, Sister Teresa was transferred to work in Calcutta, India, at St. Mary's School. She enjoyed the peaceful, serene life inside the walls of St. Mary's. Every day was the same. Every morning she got up early for prayers and Mass. She spent the day teaching the girls and, just as in her childhood home, she ended the day in prayer. Teresa was a popular teacher; the girls loved her, and she soon became the principal of St. Mary's.

But Teresa could still not forget the horror of the bustees, the slums which she saw right outside the gates of St. Mary's. She could not forget the view from her window. Sometimes she took several students with her and went into the streets, bringing medicine or bandages to the sick, lying in the gutters.

One spring day Mother Cenacle said something that surprised Teresa and the girls at St. Mary's. "Perhaps we could help some of the street children by bringing them into the convent to care for and teach them."

Soon, about twenty children had been brought inside the school, but the idea simply did not work. Over several months' time, the children ran away one by one. Teresa realized that life inside the convent was simply too different for these children. They just could not adjust.

TERESA'S SECOND CALLING FROM GOD

The years went by and Teresa remained at St. Mary's. In September 1946, it was time for her yearly spiritual retreat to the mountains near Darjeeling. There she could be alone for prayer and meditation. How she looked forward to it!

Teresa climbed the steps near the rear of the train and found a worn seat by a window. The train rolled slowly through the streets of Moti Jheel, the worst slum in Calcutta. It would eventually head out into the countryside on its way towards the mountains. Hissing and belching, the train stopped every few minutes at stations throughout the city, taking on more passengers.

Beggars, the hungry, and the homeless, were camped out on station platforms. With outstretched arms they asked the train's passengers for coins to be tossed their way. Trash lay everywhere. Traffic in the nearby streets swerved to avoid the potholes. Ragged, barefoot children wandered idly or sat playing games with stones from the gutter.

Teresa did not turn away from the scene outside the train window. Instead, the thought came back, I must do something.

"Lord, is that You speaking to me?" Teresa prayed.

Teresa thought of the Bible verse she had read so many times. *"I was hungry and you gave me no food; I was thirsty and you gave me no drink; I was a stranger and you took me not in, naked and you did not clothe me, sick and in prison and you did not visit me."*

She remembered that Jesus had said if you helped the least important kind of people, it was the same as helping Him.

Teresa believed she was hearing the "still, small voice" of God speaking to her. She called this her "call within a call" to follow the Lord, not only to India, but now also into the slums. God was calling her to leave the convent and serve Him by living as a poor person and caring for the poorest of the poor. During her retreat time she prayed again and again about this.

OBSTACLES IN HER WAY

Teresa's hopes were high as she climbed the spacious staircase to the office of the Archbishop of Calcutta, the Church official who could give her permission to leave the Sisters of Loreto.

"I cannot give permission for one lone woman to go live on the streets. Wait a year and pray about it," he said.

The year passed slowly. On her second visit to the archbishop, he asked her to write the Mother General of the Loreto Nuns and Pope Pius XII for permission.

Mother Gertrude, the Mother General, wrote back, "If God is calling you, I give you permission with all my heart."

Teresa wrote to Pope Pius XII, requesting "to live alone outside the cloister among the poor of Calcutta,

with God alone as protector and guide."

Not long afterwards, Teresa received the Pope's permission. But again, making a change was difficult.

"Leaving Loreto was much more difficult than leaving my family and country to enter religious life," Teresa said later. "Loreto, my spiritual training, my work, it meant everything to me."

But God was calling Teresa, and she followed Him.

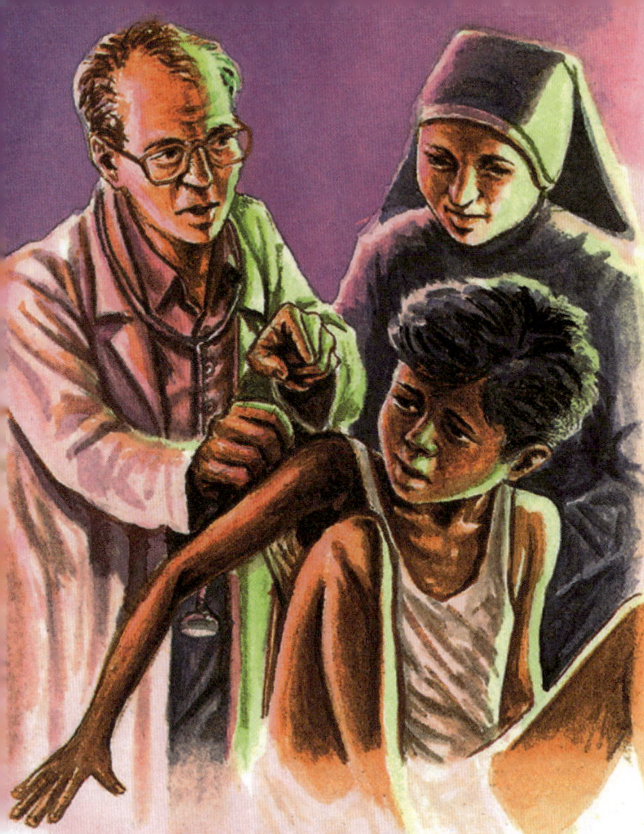

TERESA LIVES AS A POOR PERSON

Amidst tearful goodbyes, Teresa walked down the steps of St. Mary's and towards the train station. This train would not take her to the slums of Moti Jheel, but instead, to Patna, a city 240 miles away, where she would live and work with the Medical Mission Sisters for a time. Teresa knew she needed more medical training in order to help the sick people in the slums. She would spend the next four months learning how to give shots, administer medicine, first aid, and even how to deliver babies. She would learn to help patients suffering from the worst diseases — cholera, leprosy, smallpox.

One morning, Teresa stood talking with the sisters in the courtyard at the Medical Mission Hospital. On this particular day she was wearing something different. She had on a white cotton sari with three stripes of blue along the hem. It draped neatly across her tiny five-foot frame. This was the everyday dress worn by the women of India. She had pinned a small cross to her left shoulder and wore sandals on her feet.

"I'm not wearing my black veil and Loreto habit anymore," Teresa told the sisters. "I don't want to stand out too much. It's important for me and the sisters serving with me to dress just like the poor. We will eat only rice just as they do. We will preach Christ to them by the way we live."

But Mother Dengel of Patna objected to the food Teresa proposed to eat. "If you make your sisters eat only rice, you will commit a serious sin," she said. "How do you expect your sisters to work, if their bodies receive no sustenance? The very poor work very little, become sick and die young. But you must feed your sisters well. To resist disease, they must eat healthy food."

Teresa decided Mother Dengel was right. Her sisters would eat well.

India's Political History

People often wonder, why is English spoken in India? Why did the British have so much influence India?

Centuries ago, when Euro-ean explorers like Christopher ›lumbus and Vasco da Gama und new trade routes to the r East, the British East India ›mpany established trading posts at Indian ports. During the 1700s when the Mogul Empire in India was dissolving, the British East India Company took over the country, attaining political power in 1757. A century later, the British government itself gained control, and in 1877 Queen Victoria became not only queen of England but empress of India.

As the twentieth century began, there was much unhappiness among the Hindus and Muslims in India because of British rule. In 1919, after World War I ended, British troups fired on a crowd of Indian protestors, killing nearly 400 people and creating a climate of almost constant friction between the British and Indians.

When Sister Teresa first arrived

INTO THE STREETS: ONE CHILD AT A TIME

Moti Jheel looked the same on this day in December, 1948 as any other day. The flies buzzed furiously on the heaps of human waste lying in dark corners; there were no sewers in many parts of Calcutta. Women sat on the sidewalks in front of their makeshift shelters, rocking wailing babies. Their faces looked worn and tired and thin. Sick men held up their hands pleading, as Teresa walked by. Teresa had five **rupees** — less than one dollar — in her pocket as she left Patna. Early this day, her first living in Calcutta's worst slum, she had already given away four rupees to the poor.

A priest approached her and asked if she had a few rupees she could give him for a Church newspaper. Teresa hesitated but gave the priest the one remaining rupee in her pocket.

How will I pay my rent? *How will I buy my own food, let alone help the poor?* These thoughts tumbled about in Teresa's mind, but her faith held steady.

in Calcutta, the Indian independence movement was growing under the leadership of Mahatma Gandhi, an Indian lawyer who had been educated in London. In 1920 he became the leader of the Indian National Congress, India's most important political organization. Gandhi, a Hindu, believed strongly in living a simple life and in practicing tolerance for other people with different viewpoints. He believed in peacefully disobeying British laws if he felt they were unfair. Leading marches, sit-ins in the streets, and hunger strikes, he protested the British tax on salt and campaigned against a British law that would have made it illegal to organize opposition against the government. Many times Gandhi was jailed for his nonviolent disobedience; he felt it was honorable to be imprisoned for a worthy cause. Gandhi fasted many times to emphasize the importance of resolving issues peacefully. In time, more and more people joined Gandhi in supporting Indian independence.

During World War II the Japanese invaded neighboring Burm and many Burmese refugees crossed into India. Sometimes there were Japanese bombing raids. Once, the sisters at Loret had to evacuate their students t the countryside. In 1946 Muslim and Hindus clashed in bloody riots in Calcutta, killing 4,000 people. Sister Teresa went for food during the riot time and w stunned of the sight of so many dead bodies in the streets.

No, she thought, *if God is calling me, He will bless my work and never abandon me.*

But Teresa soon became exhausted. All day she had searched for a shelter for herself and a place where she could bring the abandoned. She walked until she could walk no more. She spent the day knocking on countless doors in the wealthier sections of Calcutta, asking for food to be donated to the poor. She asked for medical supplies and treated those in need as she met them. At some point she had stopped to hold a dying woman and comfort her. By the end of the day Teresa's arms and legs ached.

She wrote in her diary: "I couldn't feel sorry for myself because I thought how much the poor themselves must ache in body and soul, looking every day for a home and food and even good health."

Then, late that same day, the priest Teresa had seen earlier handed her an envelope containing fifty rupees. It was a gift from a man who had heard about Teresa's work and wanted to help. She had learned her first lesson about trusting God fully.

Even though the British had granted additional rights to the Indian people in many areas, Indians still wanted to rule themselves. In 1947 the British gave independence to India. But the violence between Muslims and Hindus continued, so Indian and British leaders agreed that India should be divided into two parts. India would become a Hindu country, and a new country, Pakistan, would be created for the Muslims. Each would be an independent nation. Gandhi was very grieved by this separation of the two peoples as he had fought so hard for unity. He was assasinated in 1948 by a man who did not agree with his views.

Jawaharlal Nehru, who had worked with Gandhi for an independent India, became prime minister of the new nation. Its form of government was a democratic republic. In the years since, the Indian standard of living has improved and industry expanded, but continuing rivalries among ethnic groups and border disputes still cause considerable strife. In the past ten years there have been two assasinations of Indian prime ministers. Indira Gandhi, who was Nehru's daughter and no relation to Mahatma Gandhi, was assasinated in 1984, and her son Rajiv Gandhi was assasinated in 1991. Today P.V. Narasimha RAO is prime minister and S. D. Sharma is India's president.

And yet the job before her seemed impossible. *Where do I begin?* she thought. *Where do I start? There are so many needs everywhere. Out of love for God, I desire to remain.* "Give me courage," she prayed.

The sight of so many wandering, ragged children tore at Teresa's heart. She would begin with the children. She cleared a spot in the street and began writing letters from the Bengali alphabet in the dirt with a stick. Some children gathered around her. Then she talked with them about what the letters meant. They were intrigued, as if it were some sort of secret code. A few days later there were thirty children coming to Teresa's school of the streets.

Teresa brought soap and water, and the children took turns getting washed. What a new experience this was for most of them! But it felt good and fresh. She gave out bars of soap for coming to school every day. Teresa brought them milk at noontime.

In the evenings Teresa cared for the sick and dying. Sometimes she felt overwhelmed by the screams of the sick, the smell of gangrene and vomit, and the long hours of back-breaking work. She remembered the peace and cleanliness of St. Mary's and was tempted to quit. But Teresa, called of God, was not a quitter.

When asked how she did manage to keep going, Teresa said, "One child at a time, one child at a time. If I can only help the closest one, that will be enough. And I feel it is the Lord I tend in the poor. It is His wounds I bathe, His sores I clean, His wounds I bandage."

Some of the sisters from St. Mary's came to the streets of Moti Jheel to see what Teresa was doing. They brought supplies she could use in her outdoor school. A priest helped her find a permanent place to live upstairs in a certain house. She was allowed to live there for free by the owner, Michael Gomes, an Indian teacher. He even provided her with food.

A REVOLUTION OF LOVE: TERESA'S HELPERS

One evening a knock at the door pulled Teresa away from her prayers. There stood Shubashini Das, one of Teresa's former students, a petite Bengali girl, smaller even than Teresa.

"Sister, I have come to join you," Shubashini said. "I know it will be a hard life but I am prepared for it."

"Come in, come in," Teresa replied, "Let's talk."

"You need to realize," Teresa said, "there will be only just enough to eat. . . he expensive saris will be replaced with the white cotton ones . . . we will not have fans in our rooms in the sweltering heat because the poor do not have fans . . . we will be caring for and loving society's outcasts. And all this must be entered into with a joyful heart."

"I'm ready, Sister," said Shubashini softly.

Soon more of Teresa's former students arrived. Shubashini became Sister Agnes. Sister Gertrude, Sister Margaret, Sister Bernard and others moved one by one into the upper story of Michael Gomes' house.

It was the beginning of the order of sisters Teresa had hoped for. She called them the Missionaries of Charity. The sisters now called her Mother Teresa. All nuns take the three vows of poverty, chastity, and obedience. But the Missionaries of Charity would have a fourth: to serve the poorest of the poor.

Teresa was excited. She wrote to her mother Drana, "It is beautiful to see our young people fully devoted, full of love for God's poor! What a wonderful gift of God. It is not the excitement of the work that is drawing them. It is something much deeper and more wonderful . . . it is a living miracle that impresses hundreds of people, even non-Christians, who come close to the sisters."

The sisters woke up every morning at 4:30 for prayers and Communion. "We must get the love and strength we need for the day from the Lord," Teresa said. "We are not social workers; we are in the business of doing something beautiful for God."

Then, after breakfast, the sisters washed one of their two white saris in a tin bucket, hung it out to dry, and mopped the floor by hand. Again Teresa insisted, "We will not have any modern conveniences that the poor do not have; we will do everything just as they do."

Eventually there were more than ten sisters living in Michael Gomes' upper

floor, all sleeping side by side. Teresa began praying for a larger place to live. Soon she heard of a Muslim man who wanted to give his house to the sisters.

"I received this house from God. Now I give it back to Him," he said.

The Missionaries of Charity moved into the first house of their own at 54a Lower Circular Road, Calcutta. The house was a quiet, peaceful haven where the sisters could become rested and refreshed before going back out to serve the suffering. Others like it would eventually be given to the sisters all over the world.

A PLACE TO LOVE THE DYING

The early morning sun sparkled and danced on the tin roof of the shanty. A garbage truck was parked in front of it. Teresa watched the dark-skinned men lift a dead body into the truck. This was something she had often seen, bodies being collected that had died on the street during the night.

She spoke to Sister Margaret, who stood next to her. "The biggest disease today is not leprosy or cancer or tuberculosis, but rather the feeling of being unwanted, uncared for, deserted by everybody."

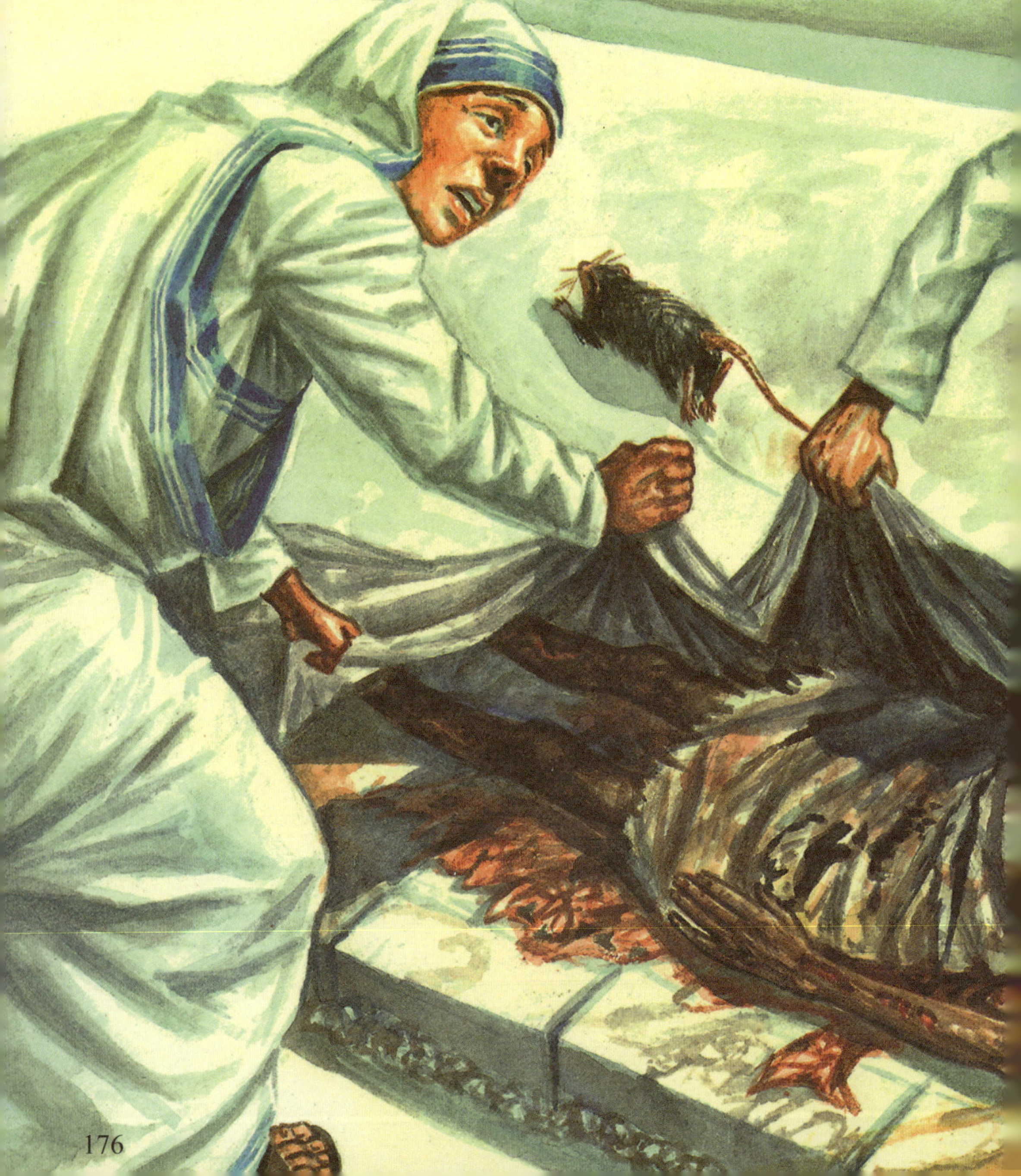

The two sisters walked on and turned the next corner. There something caught Teresa's eye. Near a trash bin she saw a heap of rags covering a body. *Another one to be picked up*, she thought. As she pulled the tattered cloth away from the body, Teresa gasped. Three rats scurried off it as she saw a woman's body, the feet eaten away by rats. Ants writhed on the open sores. The woman stirred slightly. She was not yet dead!

"She was dropped off to die here, no doubt," said Teresa. "People take better care of their dogs and cats, than they do their fellow human beings!"

Mother Teresa and Sister Margaret half dragged the woman to a nearby hospital. But the hospital refused to admit her. "She is too far gone for us to try and save her," was their reply. Teresa's strong will held firm.

"I will stay here until you admit her," she said with determination. The hospital gave in and admitted the dying woman.

People in India didn't help others very readily. Many were Hindus who believed that if a person was suffering, that was just his **karma**, or the hardship he had to endure because of what he had done in a past life. No one was supposed to help him.

The experience with the dying woman made Teresa more desperate than ever to find a place where she could bring such people. She wanted somewhere where they could die surrounded by love and kindness. She went to the city officials. They suggested the back rooms of Kalighat, a Hindu temple. There, three rooms, unused for months — and filthy — were promptly cleaned by the sisters.

A week later the first patients were moved into what Teresa called Nirmal Hriday, "the place of the pure heart." The sisters went out daily and brought in from the streets the dying of every race and every religion. Teresa washed and comforted the Hindu priest dying of cholera even though it meant she was in danger of catching the disease herself. Sister Frederick spoke words of love as she picked maggots off the wounds of a Muslim woman. The sisters respected each person's religious beliefs and did not try to change them.

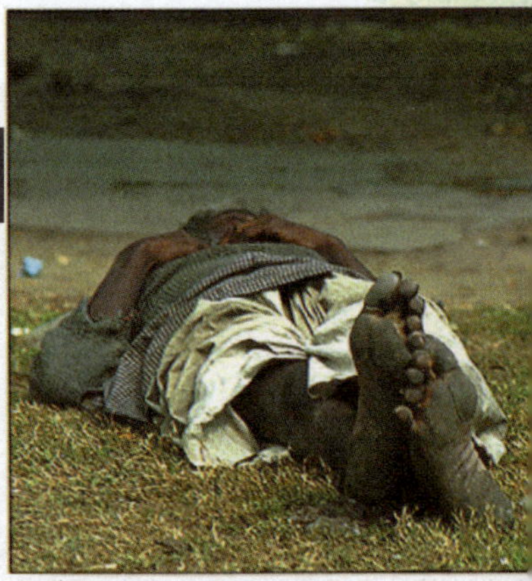

India's Caste System

"Untouchables! Those people are untouchables!" These words tell a story of India's social system, which had been in existence for thousands of years. It was finally outlawed in this century, just about the time Mother Teresa was working in India.

People in India used to be divided into groups, called the caste system.

If a person was born into one class, or caste, he couldn't change to another. He or she couldn't marry someone in a different caste. Sometimes it was even against the law for people to speak to someone from another caste.

The priests and scholars were on the highest rung of the caste system "ladder." They were called the Brahmans. Next came the rulers and soldiers, called Kshatriyas. The artists and merchants were the Vaisyas. Servants and laborers were called the Sudras. And at the lowest level were people who did not belong to any other groups so they were called

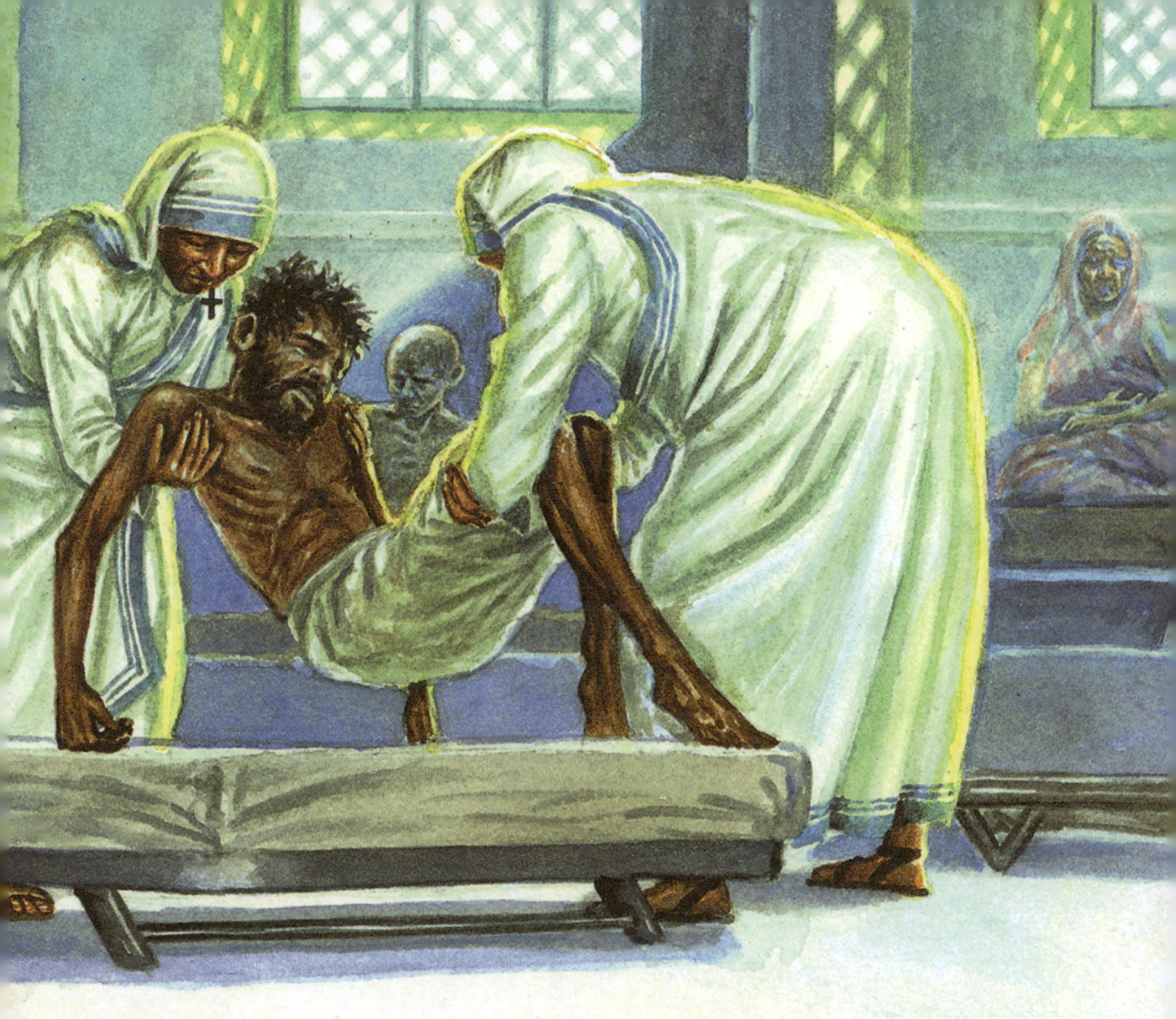

the pariahs, or untouchables.

The Hindu religion teaches said that people are reincarnated, that is they come back after death in another body. The only way a person could move to another caste was by living righteously and following the Hindu law in this life. Then there would be hope of being born into another caste in the next life.

Mother Teresa battled this ancient form of prejudice when she reached out to help the poorest of the poor, India's "untouchables." It was not a popular thing to do. Many in India thought the poor people were suffering because of their behavior in previous lives and that they deserved it.

Due to Mother Teresa's example, many families spoke out against this prevailing social philosophy. Some from highclass families came to Shishu Bhavan to adopt the orphans there.

A well-known Indian leader, Mahatma Ghandi, was also battling the caste system about the same time. He taught that people should accept all different kinds of people and their creeds and religions. He was assassinated in 1948 by a high-ranking Brahman who feared these ideas.

A few years later, in 1955, India's caste system was outlawed.

But many of the neighbors complained, "Why are they bringing these stinking people into our neighborhood? Are they trying to convert them to Christianity?"

Once, a group of men surrounded Mother Teresa and threatened to kill her. "You will just simply send me to Heaven sooner then," she had said. They turned and walked out the door.

Local Hindus were upset and accused Teresa of all sorts of crimes. They sent the chief of police to assess the situation. As he walked through the rooms, the man saw sister after sister washing away the filth, giving painkillers, and speaking words of comfort to the destitute people.

Stepping outside the building to address the angry Hindus, the police

chief said, "Unless you can get your own mothers and sisters to come here and care for these dying people, I will not make the Missionaries of Charity leave." The angry Hindus turned and walked away.

Once, an atheist came to the Home for the Dying. He watched a sister care for a man covered with maggots. He said to Mother Teresa, "I came here godless. I came here full of hatred. I am going full of God. I have seen God's love in action. Now I believe."

Suddenly public opinion started to change. People from the community stopped complaining and started volunteering to help. Medical companies donated supplies. Some people offered to pray regularly. One woman, Ann Blaikie, organized her friends to provide clothing. They became known as the Co-Workers of Mother Teresa. Today there are groups of Co-Workers all over the world.

GARBAGE-HEAP BABIES

One afternoon, Sister Marguerite and Sister Agnes were walking through Moti Jheel. Alert to the sights and sounds of the slum, they were searching for anyone who might need help. They fingered their rosary beads, praying as they went. The noisy din of the street was all around them — cattle bawling, the cries of vendors selling their wares, beggars calling out, the roar of cars and motorbikes. Then they heard the insistent, helpless cries of a newborn baby and followed the sound. A baby, not much larger than a man's hand, lay naked on a heap of cow dung near a pile of garbage. Sister Marguerite picked up the child, swaddled it in her sari, and the two nuns carried the baby four streets further, to Shishu Bhavan, a decaying gray building with a cross on the side.

This place was Mother Teresa's newest project. There were so many orphans. There were many children starving to death. There were many children who had simply been abandoned. Teresa had dreamed of a place for such children, and in 1955 Shishu Bhavan became a reality.

One night Mother Teresa heard a child crying at the gates of Shishu Bhavan. She found a small boy, not more than six years of age. Tears were running down his cheeks.

"I went to my father and my father didn't want me," he sobbed. "I went to my mother and my mother didn't want me. Do you want me?"

Yes, they did.

Dark-haired Rani, a mother at sixteen, sat in one corner of the big room and cradled another small boy in her arms. She could not support her son and had nowhere to turn but Shishu Bhavan. The boy's legs were grotesquely

deformed. Mother Teresa reached out and stroked the boy's head. "So beautiful," she whispered, smiling.

At Shishu Bhavan children of all ages were loved and fed, educated and made well. Sometimes the oldest child in a poor family from the streets was sent to public school by the sisters, so that he might help the others. Sometimes the sisters found husbands for the older girls. In Indian culture it is very important for a girl to find a husband and to have a dowry, gifts or money, to give him when they marry. Also, Teresa found parents to adopt children, even in faraway lands. People from India also came to adopt children from the Missionaries of Charity.

More and more people began to hear of Mother Teresa and her work. They sent money to her so she could support the children. Shishu Bhavan began to meet more needs. It became a clinic, a shelter for young unmarried, expectant mothers, and a soup kitchen.

"TOUCH A LEPER: TOUCH HIM WITH LOVE"

The ragged man looked grotesque. He sat in a dark doorway at the back of a warehouse. People who happened to look at him quickly turned their eyes away. He had no fingers, no toes, no ears; he did not even have a nose. There were just lumps of hardened flesh where these had been. He rarely came out into the daylight.

The man had a hideous disease that scared people more than any other — no one wanted to come near a person with leprosy. Leprosy is an ancient disease, dating back to biblical times. In those days a leper was required to ring a bell and call out, "Unclean, unclean" so that people would stay away. Leprosy spreads mainly where people are living closely together in unhealthy situations. Teresa knew there were many people with leprosy in Calcutta. She had seen them trying to hide themselves away, unable to work, abandoned by their families, digging through garbage for food.

"I must do something," she said again.

Mother Teresa went to the city officials. She knew that leprosy could now be treated and lepers could be healed if the disease was caught soon enough.

"Are there any hospitals in Calcutta that treat leprosy?" she asked. But the answer that came back to her was "No."

The place where Calcutta's many thousands of leprous people lived spread out along the railroad tracks. Teresa knew there were thousands of lepers in Calcutta, and maybe as many as fifty thousand in all of India. Inside one of the thrown-together shacks, one leper was bandaging another. They helped each other. There was no one else who was willing to do so. The woman dragged herself across the room; her foot was gone. She had lost all feeling in her deformed hands. There was no running water, no toilet facilities.

Teresa found a doctor, Dr. Senn, who, touched by the work of the Missionaries of Charity, left his own practice. He joined the sisters in their

efforts to help the lepers. He began training the nuns to care for them.

Mother Teresa said, "When we ask our young sisters who would like to go and work with the lepers, every hand is up. Every sister sees Christ in the lepers, even though they are disfigured."

The Missionaries of Charity decided they needed mobile vans equipped with medical supplies that could travel all over the city to treat the lepers in their own communities. To raise money for the vans, the sisters used the slogan, "Touch a Leper: Touch Him With Love." Money poured in from all over India.

But this wasn't enough for Mother Teresa. She wanted the lepers to have a beautiful place to live, and not be pushed away, living on borrowed property. She wanted them to be able to learn skills, grow gardens, support themselves without begging, and feel pride in themselves. She even wanted them to be able to die in a place surrounded by love and peace. Eventually, in 1957, Shantinagar, the Place of Peace, was built on donated land. It consisted of several small houses with trees and gardens.

At a Christmas party at Shantinagar, Mother Teresa told the lepers, "You are a gift from God. God has a special love for you."

An old man, deformed and misshapen, crawled up to Teresa. "I have always heard nobody loves me. It's wonderful to know that God loves me. Please say that again!"

MOTHER TO THE WHOLE WORLD

"Still working? Yes, I'm still working," Mother Teresa told a newspaper reporter who had come to interview her. Her weathered brown face was smiling as she bent over a sick woman, changing a bandage. "Yes, I've been in India for almost thirty years. The hot Indian sun is wrinkling my face, my back is stooped from bending towards the needy, but I never intend to retire."

The year was 1966. Politics or social work did not interest Mother Teresa — only seeing Jesus in one more needy person, one at a time.

Her name began to be spoken around the world. Young women came knocking, wanting to join the Missionaries of Charity. The sisters, new and old, continued to live just like the poor, squeezed together in their big house. They had to be physically, spiritually, and emotionally healthy in order to handle the long hours of hard, sorrowful work. Just as important, they had to be cheerful and full of joy. Teresa said, "A smile is the beginning of love."

Advice from Mother Teresa

Teach your family to be aware of the poor. Encourage them to go and do something for so many who are in need, for so many who are starving. Live simply. Give example through simplicity. The spirit of poverty is dependency on God. Trust him. Be with and love the poorest of the poor. You can and must expect suffering. It is a sign that Jesus is near when you are suffering. Jesus is very near, watching you.

Prayer is simply talking to God. He speaks to us: we listen. We speak to him: he listens. A two-way process: speaking and listening. Say this prayer often: "Jesus, in my heart, I believe in your tender love for me. I love you." The more you pray, the easier it becomes. The easier it becomes, the more you pray.

–from Mother Teresa, My Life for the Poor, Harper & Row, San Francisco 1985.

Even young men wanted to serve with Mother Teresa. So the Missionary Brothers of Charity was established. The brothers worked with the men and boys living on the streets and helped in places the sisters could not. Other people came to volunteer for short periods of time.

A British television producer, Malcolm Muggeridge heard about Mother Teresa and came to do a documentary about her in 1969. He called it **Something Beautiful for God.** In the film, Teresa did not ask for money for

her order or help for her sisters; she simply told people to love and understand their own neighbors and families.

Years passed. At Shishu Bhavan seven thousand people were being fed every day. People asked Mother Teresa to start Missionary houses in Rome and Bombay and New York and Caracas. The blue-striped saris of the sisters began to be seen all around the world.

To Mother Teresa nothing was impossible. "If God is doing it," she said, "He will bless it. We do nothing. He does everything. God has not called me to be successful. He called me to be faithful."

Sometimes Teresa needed to board a plane to travel to the Missionary houses in faroff places, but she had no money of her own. She asked one airline if she could pay her way by working as a stewardess! The prime minister of India, Indira Gandhi, heard about it and was amazed. She promptly arranged for Teresa to have a free pass on Air India flights anytime she wanted! Sometimes Teresa saved the food she received on the flights for the poor.

When the Pope visited India, he gave Mother Teresa the white Lincoln Continental limousine that had been given to him. Yet Mother Teresa had no use for such a luxury car. She promptly raffled it off for many rupees and used the money to help her lepers.

Awards and prizes of every description began to pour in for Mother Teresa's work. She received many honorary degrees, an award for International Understanding and the Peace Prize from Pope John XXIII. She was often invited to speak. Although she didn't enjoy it, she went anyway. It was an opportunity to tell people that we must all become carriers of God's love.

One day, one of the world's greatest honors came her way. Mother Teresa, almost seventy years old, was to be awarded the Nobel Peace Prize. She went to Oslo, Norway in 1979 to accept the award. On her way to speak before kings and presidents, she said, "I am unworthy."

Mother Teresa's message was simple: "You have an opportunity to love

others as God loves you — in the small things, with great love." She asked that the awards banquet be cancelled; the poor were the ones who needed the food.

Teresa decided not to accept any more awards; they took too much time away from her work with the poor. Even into her eighties, Teresa is visiting her houses, helping, speaking, praying. She calls herself a "little pencil in the hand of God." He does the thinking and the writing, she tells people, the pencil has only to be allowed to be used.

The Nobel Peace Prize

Alfred Nobel became one of the world's richest men in 1867 when he invented dynamite. His father was an inventor, and he was a chemist in Sweden. But over the years Nobel began to regret that he had created a substance which caused death and injury, and he feared it might be used for war. So he used some of his money to reward people for furthering the cause of peace in the world.

He set up the Nobel Prizes. They are awarded every year in six different areas to people who have done or created something for the good of all people everywhere. Awards are given in the fields of science, economics, medicine and literature.

Mother Teresa won the award for outstanding work in the interest of international peace. The awards consist of a medal and cash, usually over $150,000. A committee of five people, elected by the Norwegian parliament, chooses the winner of the peace prize. Winners receive their awards every year in Oslo, Norway. The prize is awarded on December 10th, the anniversary of the death of Alfred Nobel.

Main Events in Mother Teresa's Life

1910 Agnes Bojaxhiu is born on August 27th in Skopje, Macedonia.

1929 Agnes arrives in Darjeeling, India to work as a novice nun at the Loreto School and takes the name Teresa.

1931 Sister Teresa moves to Calcutta and begins teaching at St. Mary's School.

1937 Sister Teresa takes her final vows of service to the Church.

1946 On the train to Darjeeling, Sister Teresa receives "a call within a call" to serve the poorest of the poor.

1948 Sister Teresa leaves the convent and begins her work in the slums.

1950 Mother Teresa founds and heads the Missionaries of Charity.

1952 Mother Teresa opens Kalighat, a home for the dying in Calcutta.

1955 Mother Teresa opens Shishu Bhavan, the first children's home, in Calcutta.

1959 Mother Teresa opens the first leprosy clinic.

1965 Houses for Missionaries of Charity are opened outside India.

1979 Mother Teresa receives the Nobel Peace Prize in Oslo, Norway.

1981 Mother Teresa celebrates fifty years of service to God and people as a nun.

1983 Mother Teresa is admitted to the hospital for heart disease but recovers.

1983 The Missionaries of Charity help those injured by the poisonous gas leaked by a pesticide plant in Bhopal, India.

1994 The Missionaries of Charity have 3,439 sisters in 537 houses in 114 countries worldwide.

1994 Mother Teresa speaks in Washington, D.C. at the United States National Prayer Breakfast attended by President Clinton.

BOOK RESOURCES

Egan, Eileen, Such a Vision of the Street, Doubleday & Company, Inc., Garden City, New York, 1985.

Giff, Patricia Reilly, Mother Teresa: Sister to the Poor, Viking Kestrel, Penguin Books, USA, Inc., New York, New York, 1986.

Gray, Charlotte, Mother Teresa, Gareth Stevens Publishing, Milwaukee, Wisconsin, 1988.

Jacobs, William Jay, Mother Teresa, The Millbrook Press, Brookfield, Connecticut, 1991.

Johnson, Linda Carlson, Mother Teresa, The Rosen Publishing Group, Inc., New York, New York, 1991.

Mother Teresa, Contemplative in the Heart of the World, Servant Books, Ann Arbor, Michigan, 1985.

Mother Teresa, My Life for the Poor, Harper and Row Publishers, San Francisco, California, 1985.

Serrou, Robert, Teresa of Calcutta, McGraw-Hill Book Company, Maidenhead, England, 1980.

Watson, D. Jeanene, Teresa of Calcutta, Mott Media, Milford, Michigan, 1984.

William Carey

THE SHOEMAKER WHO PIONEERED MODERN MISSIONS

1761 — 1834

*Great men and women are not in need of our praise.
We are the ones in need of getting to know them.*

By Ben Alex

Illustrations by Giuseppe Rava

WILLIAM'S MUSEUM

"Look, Mary, this one is called Trollius laxus. It's a speci-member of the Ranunculaceae family." William turned excitedly to his little sister. Mary was more interested in the salamander she and William had caught that morning. It looked lonely. She wanted to put it back in the stream.

"Why do you want to keep these poor animals prisoner?" she asked. "I think they belong in nature where God created them,"

"I know," said William, "but I just want to study them for a while. Afterwards I'll let them go again."

"Promise?"

"Promise. Hand me my microscope, would you?"

Everything about nature interested William. He was always looking out for new things to add to his collection. Father said William's room looked more like a natural history museum. But he didn't mind his son's obsession with plants and animals. In fact, he was proud to show William's findings to his pupils at the little village school next door to the cottage.

"Let me show you Mr. Columbus' latest discovery," he used to say. So the children of the village nicknamed the schoolmaster's son Columbus. And if anyone, even an adult, wondered about some natural mystery, they were told to go ask William. "He'll explain it to you."

EXPLORING THE WORLD

William didn't mind his nickname. He was proud to be compared to the great Spanish explorer. Sometimes, when his Uncle Peter was visiting, he would walk with him through the Royal Whittlebury Forest to a big hill where they could see for quite some distance. Uncle Peter would tell stories about the Indians and settlers in Canada where he had lived, and William would gaze at the surrounding countryside. He dreamed of someday traveling to faraway countries, just like Columbus and Uncle Peter had done, exploring hidden lands and exotic people. But for now, the fields and forests of Northamptonshire would have to suffice. The only other way his imagination had access to the outside world was through the many books he borrowed. His favorite book was **Captain Cook's Voyages**, which contained fascinating illustrations of mysterious animals and far-off people with weird customs. Someday he himself might sail the South sea and maybe even go live in Tahiti.

Adventurous Captain Cook

James Cook (1728-1779) was an ambitious British explorer and cartographer, determined "not only to go farther than anyone had done before but as far as possible for man to go." He led three expeditions to the Pacific Ocean and sailed around the world twice. He discovered the Hawaiian Islands, claimed New Zealand and Australia for the British crown and helped develop hygienic reforms that made long voyages without scurvy possible. He proved that the existing maps of the Pacific were partly based on fantasy, and redrew them more accurately.

On his first voyage (1768), Cook led a scientific expedition to Tahiti to observe the planet Venus as it passed between the earth and the sun (June 1769). Afterwards he obeyed secret orders to find the alleged "Southern Continent."

(Geographers believed there was an unknown continent that kept the world in balance.) He never found it, but instead, discovered New Zealand and the eastern coast of Australia.

The second voyage (1772) was another attempt to find the hidden continent. Cook sailed farther south than anyone before him until finally, icebergs, winds and fog forced his ships back. Although he circled Antarctica, he never saw the mainland. Too much pack ice stood in his way.

During his third and final voyage (1776), as he was searching for the Northwest Passage (a sea route through North America that would make it easier to sail between Europe and Asia), Cook discovered the Hawaiian Islands on his way to the Bering Strait and the Arctic Ocean. Again ice pushed him back, and when he stopped at the Hawaiian Islands to repair a broken foremast, he was killed on February 14, 1779. It was Cook's writings about his expeditions that awakened the explorer and missionary in William Carey.

Captain Cook and his men witness a human sacrifice in Tahiti.

WILLIAM BECOMES A COBBLER

"You're a dreamer, William," said his mother as she wiped her hands on her apron. "It's time you learn a trade so you can support yourself. Someday you'll marry — and you may not be as lucky as your father or grandfather. They both started as poor weavers, but because they were clever, the Good Lord gave them the opportunity to better themselves and become village schoolteachers." Then she added with a smile, "You're smart too, son. I've no doubt you'll go far in life."

Little did she know just how far her son would go: all the way to the end of the world on a far more adventurous journey than Captain Cook ever had. As a missionary for Jesus Christ, Carey would open up a path to the East for thousands others who believed as he did, thereby changing the Christian Church's general attitude toward missions forever. He would reach more

people with the written Word of God than any other single Christian had ever done.

It all started in his father's classroom in the little insignificant village of Paulerspury in Northamptonshire, England. William's inquisitiveness and thirst for knowledge soon took him beyond what his father could teach him. When he was twelve years old he began to work as a gardener. He loved plants and flowers, but unfortunately he developed a painful rash on his face and hands that forced him to give upgardening. After a family meeting, his parents decided he should become a shoemaker — or a cobbler, as it was called in those days. They thought cobbling was a promising trade, because this was an age when people mostly walked in order to get from one place to another. William's father arranged an apprenticeship under a shoemaker in Piddington, nine miles away. William would be working seven years as an apprentice for a Mr. Nicholls.

A STRANGE LANGUAGE

Master Nicholls was a strict and irritable employer. He gave young William practically no time off. On Sundays Mr. Nicholls sent William out to deliver shoes to his customers.

"He shouldn't make you work on the Lord's day," said the other apprentice, John Warr. He was three years older than William. The boys shared the workbench during the day and a cold attic at night. Despite their age difference, they soon became friends, for William was intelligent and knew how to speak for himself.

One evening, when the boys were having a heated discussion about religion, John said, "William, I believe in God and Jesus, but I'm not good at arguing with you since you're so much smarter. Why don't you come with me to a prayer meeting at my church? I think you may become a believer too."

"I don't need to believe," replied William. "I need to know. And besides," he added, "prayer meetings are dull. I want to have some fun."

"The people in my church are not like the ordinary believers in the state church," continued John. "They know God in a very personal way and they're excited about it."

"Maybe later," said William casually, as he picked up a book from the stack which Master Nicholls had lent him that evening. His eyes widened when he noticed the strange letters on the page.

"Look John," he cried out, "have you ever seen such an odd language? I can't make head or tails of it."

John didn't know what the letters meant. The next day, when William asked Master Nicholls about it, he didn't know either. So William copied the letters from the book and showed them to an old weaver in his hometown. This man was supposed to know a great deal about words.

"No wonder you can't read this," exclaimed the weaver. "It's written in the Greek tongue, the original language of the New Testament." "How do I learn that language?" asked William eagerly.

"Well," smiled the weaver, "I think I can help you. When I was young I wanted to be a doctor. I went to a good school, but I threw away my chances, for I was more interested in having fun than studying. I regret that I didn't get a good education, for I ended up nothing but a poor weaver. But I still have my Greek grammar book — and I'll lend it to you if you like. Hopefully that'll help you."

In the months that followed, the Greek grammar became William's faithful companion at the workbench. The young boy would pore over the book and repeat the words and conjugations to himself as he went on mending shoes.

John kept quiet. He didn't want to disturb his friend. But in his heart, he prayed that God would open William's heart to the words he was reading.

MISSING MONEY

One day around Christmas, Master Nicholls sent William out to collect silver shillings from his suppliers. This was an old tradition among tradesmen in Northampshire. On his way back William bought a few things he needed with his own money. Too late, he realized he didn't have enough, so he borrowed some of the money he had just collected for Mr. Nicholls.

"Some of my money is missing," Mr. Nicholls said after William had returned. He was counting the shillings again.

"Sir," lied William, "this is the exact

amount I received. One of your suppliers must have given me less than required. I'm sorry I didn't notice."

Mr. Nicholls sent a man out to investigate the matter. In the meantime, William was praying in the attic, "God, please get me out of this trouble. If You'll help me not to be exposed as a thief, I promise I'll never do anything wrong again."

But God did not help him out of the lie. Master Nicholls found out and William had to confess the theft. He felt so bad about himself, that he eventually joined John at a prayer meeting at his church in nearby Shackleton.

The church was a non-conformist, or "dissenter" church — a church not affili-

ated with the Church of England, to which William and his parents belonged. The pastor was preaching on a passage from Hebrews 13: "Let us therefore go out unto Him without the camp, bearing His reproach."

William felt that the words were addressed directly at him. He realizedhe must break with his past sins and commit himself fully to God, even if it meant he would have to leave his parents' church and join this one. That night, William asked God's forgiveness and committed his life to Christ.

"WILL YOU MARRY ME?"

That same year, 1779, Mr. Nicholls died. William's apprenticeship was transferred to Thomas Old, a shoemaker who worshiped at the dissenters' church in Hackleton. William faithfully attended church as often as his job allowed him, for he loved God — and lately he had also become fond of a certain young girl in the congregation.

Dorothy Plackett was Master Old's sister-in-law, the daughter of the leading elder in the church. She was five years older than William — and uneducated. She could not even write her own name. But William thought she was the gentlest and most beautiful woman he had ever seen. One Sunday evening, as William and Dorothy were walking home across the fields, William stopped and said bluntly,

"Dorothy, will you marry me?"

Dorothy blushed. "But William," she stammered, "I'm a simple country girl, not a learned person like you. Are you sure you want to marry me?"

"Very," answered William. "I don't care how little you know. All you need to know is whether you love me enough to marry me."

"I love you dearly, William," Dorothy whispered.

"Then that's enough," beamed William. "I can't teach you to love, but I can teach you to read and write. You'll see!"

William and Dorothy were married on a beautiful June day in 1781. Their little cottage in Hackleton was neat and full of flowers from their garden. Soon the laughter and chatter of a little girl could also be heard around the house. But then little baby Ann became sick and died. Flowers from the same garden were placed on little Ann's coffin.

A few short months later, when Master Old died too, William and Dorothy took over his business, as well as the care of Master Old's family. William started an evening school for village children in Piddington in order to help pay all the expenses.

CAREY'S COLLEGE

William made a new friend, Thomas Scott, a noted Bible scholar and teacher of Latin, Hebrew and Greek. Mr. Scott traveled a great deal, but still managed to stop by often at William Carey's shoe shop. The young shoemaker often could also go where the famous preacher went and listen to his fiery sermons as long as it did not interfere with his work. Carey even began to travel and preach a little on his own. Every two weeks for three and a half years he walked twelve miles to Earls Barton, where he had been asked to preach in the dissenters.

This new calling involved a great deal of study. Carey always did things slowly and carefully, and he refused to preach without having thoroughly studied his topic. Many a late evening he sat bent over his books, especially his favorite, Help to Zion's Travelers. He also added Italian, Dutch and French to his language studies — and whenever he had an extra moment he plunged into Captain Cook's book and other books on natural science.

Thomas Scott called his modest workshop "Carey's college." On the wall behind his workbench Carey hung a homemade world map where he added facts about different peoples and countries as his studies progressed. He also made a globe out of leather scraps, often using this to fire the imaginations of his pupils. Sometimes he would point at some far-away country and cry, "These people are heathen! They have never heard the good news of Jesus!"

His other friends included Andrew **Fuller**, a Baptist preacher who encouraged Carey to keep up his language studies and also extend his preaching ministry to neighboring villages, and Dr. Ryland who baptized him in the Nen river on a cold October day in 1783.

As a Baptist, Carey was allowed to preach in several new congregations. This eventually led him to the pastor's pulpit in Moulton, and later in Olney,

and then in the big city of Leicester. In order to provide for his family he continued running his school and the shoeshop. But he sacrificed some independence when he hired himself out as a vendor for a shoe dealer in Kettering, named Thomas Gotch. Mr. Gotch was also a banker and deacon in Andrew Fuller's church. Every two weeks Carey tramped off to Gotch to deliver the shoes he had finished, returning with a new supply of leather. Carey enjoyed the long walks. It gave him time to think about spiritual matters. In his mind he envisioned the world map and the unreached peoples he had been introduced to through Captain Cook's book.

"Dear God," he prayed, "don't let these people die in darkness. Send someone to show them the light of the Gospel." It had not yet occurred to him that this "someone" might be himself.

GOTCH'S GRANT

One day, when Carey was delivering a load of shoes in Kettering, Mr. Gotch asked him, "Tell me Carey, how much do you earn each week as a shoemaker?"

"About nine or ten shillings, sir."

"How about making a deal with me, Mr. Carey. You give up shoemaking, concentrate on studying Latin, Greek and Hebrew. And I pay you ten shillings a week for your efforts. Mr. Fuller tells me this could turn out to be quite a profitable investment."

"Thank you, sir. I would consider working full time on my biblical studies as the highest honor on earth."

"Well then, it's a deal," concluded Gotch. He added with a twinkle in his eye, "Besides, then you won't have to spoil any more of my leather!"

A dream had come true for William Carey. He was now free to throw all his energy and skills into his calling. And it became increasingly clear to him that this calling involved a wider call to missions among the many indifferent Christians in the congregations he was serving.

A Call to World Missions

When William Carey began his preaching ministry, there were only a few hundred western Protestant missionaries in the world — and no missionaries originating from third-world countries. Today, two hundred years later, there are approximately 40,000 full-time American missionaries alone —and 48,000 missionaries from third-world countries.

In 1800, only one per cent of all Protestant Christians were living in Asia, Africa, and Latin America. Today, about 67 per cent of all Protestants in the world are living in countries once considered foreign mission fields. According to

'aul Pierson from the School of Vorld Missions at Fuller Theological Seminary in :alifornia, the modern mis-ion movement which William :arey helped launch has turned ne world upside down. Why? ierson says there are two main easons.

Old-World Religious Awak-ning During the first part of ne 18th century, a revival called ietism began in Germany and wept across Europe. It found s English counterpart in the vangelical awakening led by nen like George Whitefield nd John and Charles Wesley. America Jonathan Edwards d the movement. At the ame time, a deep concern for issions was born. In 1784 a esolution was passed in England to start monthly ecumenical meetings to pray for rivival in churches, and the spread of the Gospel. Five years later, when Carey wrote his mission manifesto the Enquiry, the moment was ripe for a global mission explosion. Following the establishment of the Baptist Mission Society in 1792, other British missionary agencies were formed: London Missionary Society (1795), Scottish and Glasgow Missionary Societies (1796), Church Missionary Society (1799), Religious Tract Society (1799), and the British and Foreign Bible Society (1804). Similar societies were formed elsewhere in Europe and in America. The Protestant church was finally responding to the Great Commission given by its founder, Jesus Christ.

New-World Commercial Interests Up until the 18th century, the third world had mainly been dominated by large Catholic countries such as Spain, Portugal and France. As a result, Catholic missions had been spreading for centuries. But as Protestant England gradually became the dominant maritime power of the world, the way was opened for new colonial enterprises and subsequent Protestant mission efforts.

Today, following the political independence of these former colonies, the spiritual influence remains. The third-world Church has grown to become the largest and most vital expression of the message of Jesus Christ today.

"SIT DOWN, YOUNG MAN!"

In 1786 William Carey finally had a chance to share his prayer burden at a ministers' meeting in Northampton. A topic for discussion was needed and Carey, still a young pastor, stood up and suggested that his colleagues consider whether the Great Commission, once given to the apostles by Jesus, was still a binding command. The pastors looked at each other, not sure what their response should be."

Sit down, young man!" snapped the chairman. "When God pleases to convert the heathen, He'll do it without your help or mine. Besides, there must be a Pentecostal gift of tongues if such an impossible task were to succeed."

When the discouraged Carey wen-thome that night, he sat down to write a pamphlet about the needs of the world,the subject he had not been allowed to discuss at the meeting. He poured all his knowledge and passion into the text which he called, **An Enquiry into the Obligations of**

Christians to use Means for the Conversion of the Heathens. The **Enquiry** lay on his desk for two years, until he met a man named Thomas Potts during a church business trip in Birmingham. Potts had been to America and witnessed the cruelty of the slave trade, and he had made friends among the Indians and blacks there.

"Come in and sit down, my friend," said Potts. "I hear you're interested in missions. I am, too. But how can we find able men willing to go?"

"I'm willing," answered Carey firmly. "If I can find sponsors who would agree to support me for one year, I'd gladly go."

"But where would you go? The needs are so great."

"I would go to the islands of the South sea, maybe Tahiti. But there's no mission society to send me."

"I fear the Christian public is not ready for such an impractical undertaking," sighed Potts.

"I know, sir," answered Carey. "That's why I have drafted a pamphlet with an appeal to world missions."

"Excellent! When will the book be published?"

"I don't know, sir. I have no money to print it."

"Then I will pay the expenses to have it printed," promised Potts.

A way was being paved for the message God had given to William Carey. God's hour for the modern missionary movement was approaching. But several obstacles still stood in the way.

A MANIFESTO FOR MODERN MISSIONS

The Enquiry was a literary masterpiece, pulsating with the vision of its author. It was a manifest for modern missions, a new way of seeing the world as one vast mission field. People were impressed with Carey's creativity and the knowledge of so many facts. And yet they still questioned the practicality of his ideas. As a result of the publication, thirty-one-year-old Carey was invited to address his colleagues at the next ministers' meeting in Nottingham.

The year was 1792. Carey spoke from his heart and slowly drove his message home like nails into soft wood. "Expect great things from God! Attempt great things for God!" he repeatedly hammered into the hearts of his listeners. The chapel seethed with quiet excitement, as if a spark from heaven had fallen among them. For a brief moment in their busy lives, the ministers witnessed all that God can do when fear and doubt and pride are banished. Fanned by the Holy Spirit, the spark of Carey's message set their hearts on fire.

When Carey sat down, there was total silence. Then a buzz started to rise from the excited crowd. "Quite a fiery preacher, this young cobbler from Leicester!" "God is no doubt speaking through him!" "What a glorious vision!" "Something must be done!"

By the next morning though, the excitement had died down. The church leaders discussed various business issues, but no one dared raise the matter of world missions. For the time being, it seemed it just wasn't quite practical.

Carey left the meeting heartbroken. But he refused to give up. He and his friend Andrew Fuller did manage to persuade the association to put world missions on the agenda for the next ministers' meeting though, to be held five months later. Then Carey went home and put together a plan. At the next meeting in Kettering, he presented this plan. Finally, then the spark caught fire in the hearts of the fourteen-member committee. They signed the document which became the birth certificate of

the first modern missionary movement in the world: **The Baptist Missionary Society,** established October 2nd, 1792.

The dream of a cobbler with a Bible and a simple world map had gone from the workbench to the drafting table of the Christian Church. From there it would be carried to the ends of the earth.

Birth Certificate of a Missions Movement

The resolution signed in Kettering on October 2nd, 1792, reads:"*Humbly desirous of making an effort for the propagation of the gospel amongst the heathen , according to the recommendations of Carey's 'Enquiry', we unanimously resolve to act in society together for this purpose; and as in the divided state of Christendom each denomination, by exerting itself separately, seems likeliest to accomplish the great end, we name this 'The Particular Baptist Society for the Propagation of the gospel amongst the Heathen'*"

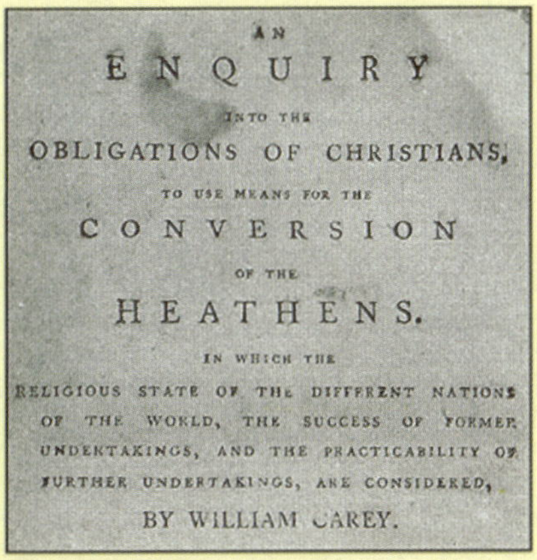

AN
ENQUIRY
INTO THE
OBLIGATIONS OF CHRISTIANS,
TO USE MEANS FOR THE
CONVERSION
OF THE
HEATHENS.
IN WHICH THE
RELIGIOUS STATE OF THE DIFFERENT NATIONS OF THE WORLD, THE SUCCESS OF FORMER UNDERTAKINGS, AND THE PRACTICABILITY OF FURTHER UNDERTAKINGS, ARE CONSIDERED,
BY WILLIAM CAREY.

Title page of Carey's Enquiry, the 87 page pamphlet which became the charter of the missions movement.

A GOLDMINE

The new mission society faced three immediate problems: How could the enormous task be financed? Who would they send? Where would they go? The answer to all three questions came from an unexpected source. Shortly after the Kettering meeting, Carey received a letter from a medical doctor, **John Thomas**.

Thomas, formerly an independent missionary to Bengal (India), had planned to be at the Kettering meeting but, unfortunately, had forgotten the date. Now he was eager to hear about the outcome, for he was planning to establish a fund in London and then return to preach the Gospel to the Bengalis. Would the Mission Society

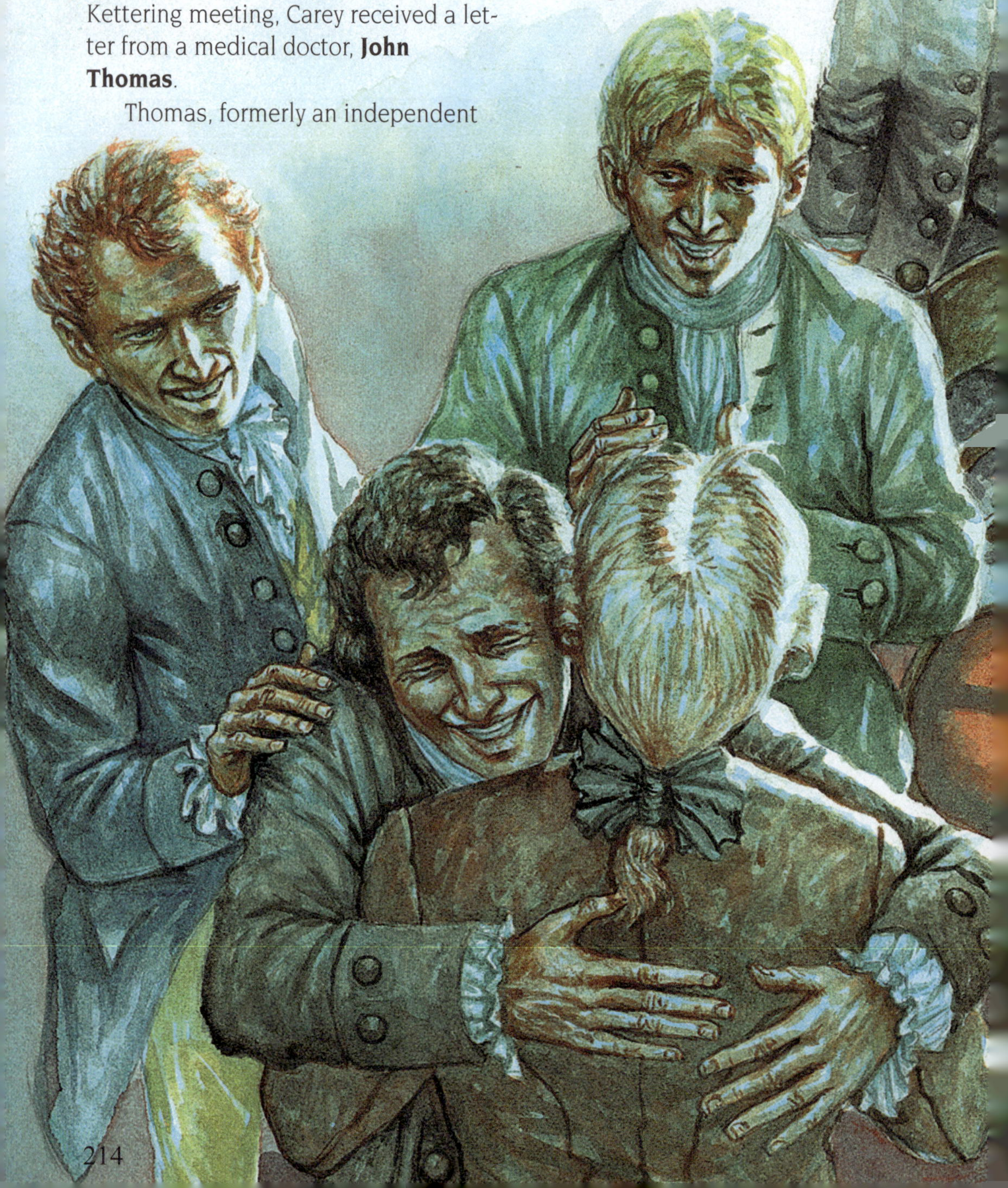

consider sending him? If so, they might want to combine their resources with his.

Carey recommended Thomas — and in so doing, set aside his own vision for the South sea and his desire to become the society's first missionary. The committee decided to study Thomas' credentials.

They didn't look good. First, the fact that he had forgotten the meeting date hinted at an unreliable character. Second, he seemed like the type of man who was an impulsive dreamer, a lot of enthusiasm but little practical sense. Third, the records showed he was often in debt. The good things about him: he was a physician, formerly employed by the British East India Company; he knew the Indian language and culture; and he was a believer and evangelist at heart. "I could do anything for Christ," he wrote the committee fervently. "I would suffer shipwreck and death to glorify Him but a little, but if He should tear me from the Indian people then I would be a bleeding, for my soul is set upon them."

The committee agreed to grant Thomas an interview, where he spoke eagerly about the needs and possibilities in India. Then he read a letter he had received from three Brahmans (educated Hindus). It stated, "Have compassion on us and send us preachers, and such as will forward translations of the Bible." These words won over the hearts of Carey, Fuller, Ryland and the other committee members.

Fuller, who was secretary, spoke for them all, "We realize Bengal is a goldmine though it's as deep as the center of the earth. Someone must go down and explore it, and we recommend that Mr. Thomas goes — and that Mr. Carey goes with him. The committee will hold the ropes at the top. . . ."

Before Fuller had finished his words, Thomas sprang to his feet and hugged Carey with tears of joy.

UNEXPECTED NEWS

Carey was less enthusiastic. Although his heart's desire was to do missionary work, he knew he also had a responsibility to his family. He and Dorothy had three boys under the age of nine, and she was five months pregnant. Dorothy refused to cross the sea to go to a distant land. She had never been further than thirty miles away from her hometown. Besides, Carey's father was furious and thought the whole idea was the folly of a mad-man. Nonetheless, after much consideration, Carey decided to leave anyway, even if it meant his family would remain in England.

Then, during a fundraising trip, he met a newspaper editor and printer, William Ward. "I would like you to join me in India someday," he said to Ward. "The Indian people need someone like you to print the Bible in their own language." Carey's words planted a seed in Ward's heart.

In the spring of 1793 William Carey, John Thomas and his family were ready to leave for India. A British cargo ship had agreed to take them to Calcutta.

But then came some unexpected news that threatened to ruin their plans. The British East India Company had decided not to issue any more permits to missionaries in India. They claimed that missionary work threatened the Indian way of life. This meant that Carey and his companions would have to go anyway, without a permit and, if they were discovered, that they would be sent back to England and have all their belongings confiscated. The missionaries decided to take their chances, and boarded the ship. But while they were waiting in Portsmouth for a convoy, the captain received an anonymous letter. It stated that he had a missionary on board and could have his license revoked as a result. The threat was so real, the captain ordered Carey and Thomas off his ship. Carey later learned that the letter had probably been written by one of Thomas' creditors.

The British East India Company

Established in 1600, the company was a private-trade enterprise, given charter (monopoly of trading rights) by the British government. It opened up India and the Far East to commerce by making trade agreements with the local rulers. At the beginning of the 18th century, when the Mogul Empire that ruled India began to dissolve, the company intervened and eventually took control of the country. A governor was installed as representative of the British government, and this eventually brought India under the British crown. In 1784 further limitations were placed on the company, and its monopoly on trade was terminated in 1813. But its administrative role in India did not cease until its dissolution in 1874.

Ships outside the Danish colony of Serampore

ON THEIR WAY

The disappointed missionaries returned to London. "The effort at present seems to be a failure," Carey wrote Fuller. But their misfortune was part of a bigger plan designed by God. For during the delay Dorothy changed her mind, and now she agreed to join her husband should the door to India ever open again. In the meantime, Thomas was busy trying to settle his personal affairs.

The season for a departure to India would not last long, though. One day, in a coffee shop in London, Thomas asked a waiter if he knew about any ships going to the Orient. The waiter scribbled down an address. This contact led Thomas to the information that a Danish ship bound for India was expected to arrive at Dover any day. The missionaries made their way as quickly as possible to Dover. There they were able to make the necessary arrangements and board the steamship **Kronprinsesse Marie**. This time, Dorothy and the children, including one-month-old Jabez, went with them.

On June 13th, 1793, the missionary party sailed away from the white cliffs of Dover. Their five-month voyage would take them past the southern tip of Africa into the Indian Ocean, then on to the Danish colony of Serampore, outside of Calcutta. The missionaries were clear of the anti-missionary restrictions posted by the British East India Company, and were welcomed by the Danish flag outside the consulate of Serampore.

FROM CITY TO JUNGLE

The missionary party arrived in Calcutta on November 11th, 1793. Despite the restrictions against missionaries in British territory, John Thomas began preaching in Bengali right away. His first sermon lasted almost three hours. A curious crowd gathered to hear the white man speaking in their language. Carey listened, trying to visualize the strange sounds and chop them into words. He watched the people around him and noticed the openness in their faces. Calcutta seemed to be an open door for the message they had come to deliver. He estimated the population in Calcutta alone to be at least 200,000. Beyond the city lived millions of people, as yet unreached by the Gospel. Three-fifths of the beautiful land was still uncultivated jungle. "I feel something of what Paul felt when he beheld Athens and 'his spirit was stirred within him,–" Carey wrote in his journal.

But there were many hardships which would still have to be overcome. As the months passed by, he realized that although these people were willing to listen, they were not so willing to receive the message and change their ways. The Hindu religion was deeply rooted in their hearts and culture. Anyone who might actually convert to Christianity would be considered an outcast — even by their own family.

The only Christian Carey had met who actually came from India was **Ram Basu**, a learned Brahman who had been

converted through Thomas' previous missionary work. Even though while Thomas was in England, Basu had returned to worshiping Hindu idols, now he had recommitted his life to Christ. He became a great help to Carey, not least as interpreter. This was especially true when Thomas had to leave and resume his medical practice due to pressure from his creditors.

Carey soon realized that Thomas had been too optimistic about their expected living expenses in India. The same amount of money that should have lasted them an entire year, had been used up in less than three months.

Carey's wife and Felix, their eldest son, became very sick with dysentery, so Carey had to move his family to less expensive lodgings. They moved to Debhatta in the **Sunderbans**, an area feared for its boas, cobras and tigers. But Carey had no choice. Inch by inch he cleared the jungle with his spade, planting a vegetable garden and building a small bamboo but for his family. After a while, he began to feel happy again. Then he was offered a job at **Mudnabatty** three hundred miles up the crocodile-infested Maharunda river. Carey accepted. The family was uprooted again.

VALLEY OF DEATH

Thomas had arranged for Carey to get a job as manager of an indigo plantation. The blue indigo dye was a popular article in the markets of Calcutta and abroad. The owner of the plantation was George Udney, an old friend of Thomas. He was eager for Carey to start work as soon as possible.

"I can't think of anyone more fit for the job than you, Mr. Carey," he said. "Especially with your knowledge of plants and agriculture, you're perfect for the job. And," he added, "I promise there will be time for plenty of your language studies and Bible translation."

The Carey family settled into a spacious two-story house. In time they turned it into a home with plenty of flowers and vegetables all around it. Yet the unhealthy climate took its toll on the family: Five-year-old Peter became sick and died; Dorothy became mentally ill; and Carey himself fought sickness, as well as depression. To add to Carey's distress, Ram Basu left him. Now, with both Thomas and Udney out of reach, he felt homesick and lonely. Not a single letter had arrived from England for nearly two years. When mail finally did arrive, the mission society at home had only criticism for his work.

"This is, indeed, the Valley of the Shadow of Death to me," he wrote in his journal on February 3rd, 1795. "O, what would I give for a sympathetic friend to whom I might open my heart."

Dorothy's Illness

Dorothy married and hesitantly followed her husband to India. Carey's biographers have not always been entirely fair to her. One wrote, "Never had minister, missionary, or scholar a less sympathetic mate." The truth may be that Dorothy wasn't mentally equipped for the hardships she faced in India. In 1795, after having lost family and friends in England, three children and several homes in India, and weakened by tropical diseases, she lost touch with reality and slipped into insanity. For the last twelve years of her life she was confined to a locked room.

Dorothy's illness is today referred to as psychosis or a delusional disorder. As the years went by and no treatment was given, her unhappiness turned to bitter resentment. She became increas-

ingly obsessed with the idea that her workaholic husband was unfaithful to her. Carey and Thomas wondered if she were demon-possessed. At one occasion Thomas wrote, "She has uttered the most blasphemous and bitter imprecations against him, when Mrs. Thomas and myself were present, seizing him by the hair of his head, and one time at the breakfast table she held up a knife and said, 'Curse you. I could cut your throat.' She has even made some attempts on his life."

In 1807, at the age of 51, Dorothy passed away. Her obituary reads, "Mrs. Carey, after having been ill about a fortnight, died."

Left: Dorothy suffered from the mental illness today referred to as delusional disorder. The only known "treatment" at that time was confining the patient. Below: An insane woman is released by physician Philippe Pinel, one of the first to believe that insanity resulted from other causes than demon possession.

WORKERS FOR THE HARVEST

In the midst of this dark and lonely period in Carey's life, some good news finally greeted him: A party from England had arrived in Calcutta — seven adults and four children. These were missionaries that Fuller and the Mission Society at home had sent him in answer to his many letters. In one he had written, "I earnestly entreat the Society to set their faces this way and send out more missionaries. We ought to have seven or eight families together. Our families should be considered nurseries for the Mission and among us should be persons capable of teaching school. . . ."

Carey's vision was to start a mission community where missionaries would live and work together. Using his savings, he had recently bought land at

Kidderpore for an indigo plantation which would house the mission and a school for the natives. The missionaries arriving in Calcutta would make this dream come true. God had sent workers for the harvest!

No sooner had Carey started to make accommodations for the newcomers, when he heard that the East India Company was refusing to allow them into India. Great was his disappointment when he learned the reason for the refusal. The new people had insisted on calling themselves missionaries on their entry documents. Carey, knowing about the government's attitude toward missionaries, had instructed them to say they were indigo factory staff instead. Now the new missionaries were stuck in the small Danish colony of Serampore, about twenty miles outside of Calcutta.

DEATH OF A DREAM

On the first day of December 1799, one of the new missionaries managed to visit Carey at his house in Mudnabatty. Carey was busy making arrangements for the move to his new plantation in Kidderpore.

"Mr. Carey, do you remember me?" said the missionary as he shook Carey's hand. "I'm **William Ward**, the printer from Derby. Seven years ago you told me to come to India and print the Bible for you."

Carey was thrilled. Here was the man who could run the printing press Mr. Udney had recently bought him as a gift. The only problem was, Ward and his fellow misssionaries were still being denied residence permits. But Ward offered a solution.

"We're all settled in Serampore — and we want you to come and join us!"

"Join you?" answered Carey puzzled.

"You were supposed to join me!"

"I know," continued Ward, "but Serampore is the only safe place for us. Besides, Colonel Bie, the Danish

governor at Serampore, has invited us as his 'honored friends' to start a mission and a school there. He has even offered to issue passports under his seal so we can legally travel into British territory!"

Carey didn't like Ward's idea. But the next morning, after a night of prayer and consideration, he began to wonder if this wasn't God's way of relocating him in a field that had yet to produce a single new convert, despite six years of preaching and hard labor. He decided to abandon his own plans — including the indigo plantation at Kidderpore —and join his new missionary partners.

On January 1, 1800, Carey and his family packed the printing press and all their belongings. Ten days later they arrived at Serampore, where they were made welcome by the new missionaries and Governor Bie.

THE DREAM FINALLY COMES TRUE

Serampore proved to be the perfect place for Carey to realize his vision. The Danish settlement was a busy port with ships and people from many nations. British Calcutta was too far away to pose any threat to the missionaries, yet close enough to be reached within two hours, if necessary. Carey immediately bought a large building on the riverbank which could accommodate the missionary families and a printing shop for Ward. There was room for other activities, too. One of the missionary couples, the **Marshmans**, opened a boarding school for children of wealthy European and Indian families. Both the printing business and the school became important sources of income for the self-supporting missionary settlement.

Joshua Marshman, William Ward and Carey became a trio whose commitment to each other and zeal for the Gospel laid the foundation for twenty-three fruitful years in Serampore. The families ate and worked together from six o'clock in the morning until late evening. Carey worked long hours on trans-

lations and language studies, especially Sanskrit, considered the mother tongue of India's many dialects. He insisted on equality for all adult members by rotating the chores and responsibilities. No one was considered any better than another. Only One was called Lord and Master: Jesus Christ, whom they all served with the talents He had given them.

Their first year in Serampore was mostly a happy one. By May, the New Testament was ready to be printed in the Bengali language — after seven years of hard labor. In November, a native worker named Sakira came to the mission to be baptized after being converted through Thomas' fiery preaching. Carey regained hope that God would eventually win the Indian nation to Himself. It was therefore a great disappointment to him when Sakira did not show up on the Sunday when he was supposed to be baptized. Some said Sakira was afraid of the persecution. Others said he had been killed by Hindus because of his decision to become a Christian.

But then one day, Thomas brought home **Krishna Pal**, a carpenter who had heard the Gospel through earlier missionaries. Pal said he was now ready to commit his life to Jesus — despite the persecution he faced. He publicly renounced the Hindu idols and then joined the missionaries for a meal. This was a sign of his determination to sacrifice everything for his new faith. Sharing a meal with Christians automatically meant a Hindu was breaking caste. This violated an important rule in Hinduism. A riot broke out around the missionary settlement.

"If Krishna Pal is baptized, we'll kill him," shouted the angry mob. But Governor Bie's soldiers dispersed them and stood guard outside the mission. On December 28th, 1800, Krishna Pal was baptized outside the mission in the Hooghly river, a branch of the holy Ganges river. Krishna Pal's baptism was the first native baptism in India.

A Long Workday

In a letter from 1806, William Carey describes a typical workday at the mission in Serampore: "I rose this day at a quarter to six, read a chapter in the Hebrew Bible, and spent the time till seven in private addresses to God and then attended family prayer with the servants in Bengali. While tea was pouring out, I read a little in Persian with a Moonshi [native assistant] who was waiting, when I left my bed room. Read also before breakfast a portion of the Scriptures in Hindustani.

"The moment breakfast was over I sat down to the translation of the Ramayuna [classical Indian text] from Sanskrit, with a Pundit (native teacher], continued this translation till ten o'clock, at which time I went to College [Fort William] and attended duties there till between one and two o'clock. When I returned home I examined a proof sheet of the Bengali translation of Jeremiah, which took till dinner time.

"After dinner translated with the assistance of the chief Pundit of the College, greatest part of the 8th chapter of Matthew, into Sanskrit — this employed me until six o'clock, after six sat down with a Tilingua Pundit to learn that language. Mr. Thomas called in the evening; I began to collect a few previous thoughts into the form of a sermon, at seven o'clock, and preached in English at half past seven. The congregation was gone by nine o'clock. I then sat down to write to you, after this I conclude the evening by reading a chapter in the Greek testament, and commending myself to God. I have never more time in a day than this, though the exercises vary."

FROM COBBLER TO PROFESSOR

The following spring Carey received a very special reward for his many years of linguistic study. The British governor of India asked Carey to become professor of Bengali at the prestigious Fort William College in Calcutta. This college had recently been established for employees of the East India Company who wanted to continue their education. Carey's nomination was not only a

gesture of appreciation for his translation work, but also of indirect recognition for his missionary work. "I am almost sunk under the prospect," he wrote Dr. Ryland in England, "having never known college discipline." Yet he accepted the offer "though with fear and trembling," and for the rest of his life he divided his time between the college and the mission. Tuesdays through Fridays he taught language classes in Calcutta; Fridays through Mondays he worked with Ward and Marshman in Serampore.

During these busy years Carey grew to become a linguistic genius, one of the greatest scholars of his century. With nothing more than a primary-school education he had taught himself everything he knew about science and languages — tutored only by Bengali teachers. When he started his lectures at Fort William, there was not even one book of Bengali prose or grammar. So the first textbook he introduced to his students was the Bengali New Testament he himself had translated. This he eventually revised in eight different editions. Then he compiled a grammar book. By the end of his first term he was also appointed as teacher of Sanskrit, the classic ancient language of India. Yet the humble professor still remained a student, always adding new languages and dialects to his repertoire. Within a few years he had produced grammars and dictionaries in the Bengali, Punjabi, Telugu, Marathi, Karanese and Sanskrit languages. Nothing was published by the government without his approval. And all this time, he still continued his translation work. By 1825 Carey and his staff had translated the New Testament into thirty-four languages, and the Old Testament into eight. In the seven years following that there would be another ten new translations. When Marshman, Ward and Carey were commended on this superhuman task, Carey answered, "Few people know what may be done till they try, and persevere in what they have undertaken."

THE HORRORS OF HINDUISM

Shortly after Carey was appointed professor at Fort William, the British governor asked him to investigate some of the brutal religious ceremonies that had been taking place among Hindus for centuries.

"Since you've gained great knowledge of the sacred Hindu writings," said Governor Wellesley to him, "I want you to study the principles upon which these practices are based — practices like the sacrifice of infants to the Ganges river, and suttee, the burning of widows on the funeral pyres of their husbands."

This was a task close to Carey's heart. During the annual festival at Saugor he had often witnessed how mothers would throw their babies into the holy river and sacrifice them to the Hindu gods (many were actually eaten

The Burning of Widows

In 1799, when Carey first witnessed suttee, he wrote: "The woman was standing by the pile, which was made of large billets of wood on the top of which lay the dead body of her husband. I asked them if this was the woman's choice, or if she were brought to it by any improper influence? They answered tha it was perfectly voluntary. I talked till reasoning was of nc use, and then began to exclai with all my might against wha they were doing, telling them that it was a shocking murder They told me it was a great ac of holiness, and added in a ve surly manner, that if I did not like to see it I might go furthe off, and desired me to go. I to them that I would not go, tha was determined to stay and s the murder, and that I should certainly bear witness of it at the tribunal of God.

"She lay down by the corp and put one arm under its ne

by crocodiles). He had also seen mothers suspend their babies in baskets from trees, so they would be eaten by white ants. Carey's son William had once seen how a boatman had saved a drowning child. He pulled him up on his boat, but when the man gave the child back to his mother, she took the child, broke his neck and threw him back into the river! By the time Carey had finished his report, infanticide practices like these had been banned by the British government.

Carey's research on widow-burning showed that it resulted in the deaths of about ten thousand widows every year. Many of the widows were young girls who had been married away to older men for a generous dowry. The Hindus believed that a wife would win "eternal happiness" only if she were burned together with her dead husband. Carey considered this a serious crime, but the government was reluctant to interfere. Not until December 1829 was suttee abolished by the government. Sunday morning, December 6th, Carey was asked by the government to translate into Bengali the declaration banning the practice. He immediately gave up his Sunday sermon and rushed into his study to translate it, believing that further delay would cause the deaths of even more innocent women.

and the other over it, when a quantity of dry cocoa leaves and other substances were heaped over them and then melted butter poured on the top. Two bamboos were then put over them and held fast down, and the fire put to the pile, which immediately blazed very fiercely.

"No sooner was the fire kindled than all the people set up a great shout. It was impossible to have heard the woman had she groaned, or even cried aloud, on account of the mad noise of the people, and it was impossible for her to stir or struggle on account of the bamboos which were held down on her like the levers of a press.

"We could not bear to see more, but left them, exclaiming loudly against the murder, and full of horror at what we had seen."

The Killing Practices of Hindduism

Because of his belief in God's goodness and com-passion for the oppressed, Carey also spoke out against many other evil practices within the Hindu religion, practices such as self-torture and assisted suicide.

Self-torture by Flesh Hooks

Shortly after arriving in India, Carey wrote deeply distressed, "I have already seen several, who have swung by the flesh hooks."

The cruel ceremony of "hook-swinging" was done by men who had hooks pierced through the flesh on their backs and tied to a bamboo pole. A group of men would hold the pole and run in circles while the poor man, suspended in the air, scattered herbs to the Hindu god Shiva.

Killing of Lepers

After witnessing the death of a leper in 1812, Carey wrote, "A pit about ten cubits in depth was dug, and a fire placed at the bot-tom of it. The poor man rolled himself and struggled for that pur-pose. His mother and sister, however, thrust him in again; and thus a young man, who to all appearances might have survived several years, was cruelly burned to death.

"I find that the practice is not uncommon in these parts. Taught that a violent end purifies the body and ensures transmigration into a healthy new existence, while natural death by disease results in four successive births and a fifth as a leper again, the leper like the even more wretched widow, has always courted suicide."

Exposure of the Sick

It was not uncommon that sick and dying people were dragged down to the Ganges river to die a slow and cruel death. William Ward wrote, "When a person is at the point of death, his relatives carry him on his bed, or on a litter, to the Ganges. A person, in his last agonies, is dragged from his bed and friends, and brought, despite the coldest or hottest weather, from whatever distance, to the riverside, where he lies, if a poor man, in the open air, day and night, till he expires."

The Curse of Karma

Karma (which means "to act, do, bring about") is a basic idea in several Eastern religions, especially Hinduism and Buddhism. The idea is that a person's present circumstances are the result of past actions, and that present actions will produce future circumstances.

According to these religions, life is seen as a cycle of cause and effect — a wheel of life and death — to which man is bound through his desires and actions. Bad actions build bad karma; good actions build good karma. And unless a person can reap the full karma in his present life (which is practically impossible since every moment adds new karma), he will have to continue life through rebirth (reincarnation). In this way man either regenerates to a higher status or degenerates to lower forms. A competitive, violent, egotistical person, for example, will sink down to still lower, animal-like lives, while a good, compassionate person will ascend to still better and happier lives. The pur-pose of life is to free oneself from the vicious cycle of death and rebirth through the practice of yoga which empties one of actions and karma, or through intervention and salvation by a god beyond the karmic realm.

Practices such as infanticide, self-torture, and suicide were popular, superstitious ways of trying to reduce one's bad karma by sacrificing something of great value. Carey realized such practices were not taught in the holy Hindu scriptures, so he was able to fight them on Hindu grounds. In addition, the doctrine of karma gave him a perfect opportunity to tell the Hindus about Jesus who came to deliver us from "bad karma." Through our faith in His sacrifice on the cross, God has intervened to save us from sin and death.

Left: The Hindu god Shiva standing on a serpent and surrounded by the fire wheel of life and death. Above: A holy Hindu detaching himself from karma by religious acts.
Below: Carey preaches the Good News that Jesus came to deliver us from "bad karma."

FIRE IN THE FOUNDRY

On a hot evening in March, 1812, Ward had dismissed his staff and was locking up the printing office. In the composing room he stopped and looked over the punches and cases of typeface representing many Asian languages. The Serampore Press was fast becoming the chief foundry for eastern-language typefaces in Asia.

Suddenly he smelled smoke coming from the next room where paper was stored. They had just received a shipment of 12,000 reams from England. As he opened the door, smoke poured out. He immediately shut the door and ran outside.

"Fire! Fire!" he yelled. Two servants came running. A few minutes later, Marshman and the other missionaries from the house were there, too. Carey was away at the college in Calcutta at the time.

Ward climbed up on top of the building and hacked a hole into the roof where the fire was raging. A human chain was formed and buckets, pots — anything that could carry water — was frantically passed between the nearby river and the roof. Ward poured water onto the bales of paper. Others ran inside and began to rescue the presses, manuscripts, proofs, frames of typeface,

ledgers and other valuable papers.

Four hours later the fire was finally under control. Everyone was greatly relieved that only the paper had been lost. It stood still smouldering in the room behind the composing room.

Then it happened. Someone made the terrible mistake of opening a window. The draft caused the fire to blaze up again. Within minutes the whole building was enflamed. Missionaries, workers and neighbors could do nothing but stand by and watch the fire do its work.

Carey cried when he saw the damage that had been done. Years of translation work were wasted —valuable parts of the Old and New Testaments in several languages — and the entire Sanskrit dictionary manuscript which he had just finished were all gone. Typefaces and fonts for Tamil, Chinese, Hebrew, Greek, Persian, Arabic, Nagari and Telugu were gone. Fortunately, the irreplaceable punches and matrices were later found undamaged in the debris.

Carey wrote home to England: "Our printing office was totally destroyed by fire. This is a heavy blow, as it will stop our printing the Scriptures for a long time. I wish to be still and know that the Lord He is God, and to bow to His will in everything. He will no doubt bring good out of this evil, but at present the providence is exceedingly dark."

Carey overestimated the time it would take to get the presses running again. But he was right about God's goodness. When news about the catastrophe arrived in England, money and items which had been lost in the fire were donated to the Mission Society's office by a variety of churches and private sources. Two months later, Andrew Fuller could proudly announce that the goal of $50,000 had been raised. "This fire," he wrote to Dr. Carey, "has given your undertaking a celebrity which nothing else could."

Within three months the presses were running faster than ever before. By the end of the year all the lost typefaces had been recast. And Carey and his helpers found that their re-translations were a tremendous improvement over the translations that had been lost in the fire.

THE CROWN OF CAREY'S DREAMS

The following years many new missionaries arrived, and the native staff grew, as well. Mission stations, schools and churches sprang up all over India. Carey could see the advantages of reaching India through education, rather than by preaching alone. The educational movement he started impressed the new British governor, Lord Moira, who visited the mission at Serampore with the newly appointed first bishop of Calcutta. Their visit was such an encouragement to Carey that he decided to press on with a vision that had stayed with him since the days of "Carey's College" in his shoeshop home in England. In 1818 he proposed a "college for the instruction of Asiatic, Christian and other youth in Eastern literature and European science." His intention was to offer advanced education both in Buddhist and Hindu belief systems, as well as in the Christian faith so that a new generation would thoroughly know the dogmas of the Christian faith and the religions around them.

To Carey's disappointment, the Mission Society in England did not share his enthusiasm. Being so far away, it was hard for them to understand his ultra-modern outlook on missions and Christian education. But once again the Danish governor came to his rescue by offering a piece of land close to the mission. Three years later the **Serampore College** became a dream come true. The beautiful brick building was one of the finest European buildings in Asia. The King of Denmark sent Carey and Marshman a gold medal in honor of their work, and the British king granted the college a royal charter in order to confer on its students "degrees of rank and honour." The Serampore College became the first college in Asia to offer degrees to its students.

FINAL DAYS

Carey was now sixty years old. He was busier than ever with his classes at two colleges, teaching several languages, classic Indian literature, botany, zoology and other sciences. At the same time, he was in charge of the growing mission work and of supervising twenty-two Bible translations, including translations in Chinese and Afghanistani. Yet he still had time to tend his garden at the mission and care for his family.

After Dorothy's death, Carey married an educated Danish woman, Charlotte Rhumohr. He loved her dearly, and she became a great help to the master translator, since she spoke several languages fluently. But after only thirteen years together, Charlotte died.

Carey's third wife, Grace Hughes, was seventeen years younger than him. She was a good companion and nurse for him during the last eleven years of his life. But it was Charlotte who had captured his heart, and before he died, Carey requested to be buried at her side.

Three of Carey's strong-willed sons, Felix, Jabez and William, became missionaries — Felix to Burma, labez to the Moluccas Islands, and William at a remote outpost in India. Eventually, Felix gave up his missionary work (he lost his whole family in a boating accident) to become an ambassador of the king of Burma to the British Governor General in Calcutta. His father commented, "Felix is shriveled from a missionary into an ambassador." But after some time, Felix came back', and helped Ward in the printing shop until they both died from cholera in 1823.

Carey spent his last days in a homemade wheelchair surveying his sanctuary — the garden he had developed into a botanical museum. When he finally was confined to his study, he insisted that the gardeners still consult him there. Many important people and celebrities visited him to praise his work, but Carey often answered, "You have been talking much about Dr. Carey. When I am gone, say nothing about Carey. Speak instead of Carey's Savior."

On the morning of lune 9th, 1834, at the age of 72, and with the last proof sheet of the eighth edition of the Bengali New Testament in his hand, professor Carey was found dead on his couch. Outside the governor's house at Serampore the Danish flag was flown at half-mast. lohn Foster, the famous essayist, wrote the words that summed up a forty-year ministry in India:

"Dr. Carey is unquestionably the very foremost name of our times in the whole Christian world. What an entrance it has been,into that other world!"

Main Events in Carey's Life

Year	Date	Event
1761	17 Aug.	Born in Paulerspury, England.
1775		Apprentice with Mr. Nicholls. Discussions with John Warr.
1776	Dec.	The stolen shilling. Religious awakening.
1779		Joins the dissenters. Apprentice with Old.
1781		Marriage to Dorothy Plackett.
1782		Begins preaching ministry.
1783	Oct.	Baptized by Dr. Ryland. First daughter dies. Seriously ill.
1785		Son Felix is born. Pastor at Moulton.
1787		Ordained minister.
1788		Son William is born.
1789		Baptist pastor at Harvey Lane. Son Peter is born. Writes the *Enquiry*.
1791		Daughter Lucy is born.
1792	May.	The *Enquiry* is published.
	31 May	"Expect great things, attempt great things" sermon in Nottingham.
	2 Oct.	The Baptist Missionary Society is established.
1793		Son Jabez is born.
	13 June.	Leaves England with family and Thomas.
	11 Nov.	Arrives in Calcutta.
1794	Feb.	Moves to Sunderbans.
	June	Indigo planting in Mudnabatti. Malaria.
1795	Feb.	Dorothy becomes mentally ill.
1796		Son Jonathan is born.
1797		First draft of Bengali New Testament.
1799	July	Buys plantation at Kidderpore.
	Oct.	Missionary party arrives in Serampore.
1800	Jan.	Moves to Serampore.
	Dec.	Felix and Krishna Pal are baptized.
1801	Feb.	First Bengali New Testament printed.
	Apr.	Professor at Fort William College.
1807	Dec.	Dorothy dies.
1808	May	Marriage to Charlotte.
1812		Fire at Serampore.
1815		Fuller dies. Tension between BMS and the Serampore mission.
1818		Serampore College is founded.
1821		Charlotte dies.
1822		Marriage to Grace. Felix dies.
1823		William Ward dies.
1829		Abolition of suttee.
1833		Abolition of slavery.
1834	9 June	Carey dies at Serampore.

BOOK RESOURCES

William Carey: Cobbler to Missionary, by Basil Miller (Zondervan, 1980, Bethany 1994))
William Carey, by Kellsye Finnie (OM, BMS, 1993)
People Whose Faith Got Them into Trouble, by John W. Cowart (InterVarsity, 1990)
Martin Luther: The Man and His Work, by Mary Drewery (Zondervan, 1979)
Dorothy Carey: The Tragic and Untold Story of Mrs. William Carey, by James R. Beck (Baker, 1993)
Christian History, Issue 36, 1994: William Carey

By Ben Alex

Illustrations by Giuseppe Rava

Florence Nightingale

THE LADY WITH THE LAMP IN BATTLE

1820 —1910

Great men and women are not in need of our praise. We are the ones in need of getting to know them.

A DISCONTENTED DAUGHTER

"Flo! Are you daydreaming again? Hurry up! It's time to dress for dinner! The guests will arrive in less than an hour!"

Florence turned from the window and caught a glimpse of her sister Parthe already disappearing down the hall. A tired smile passed over her pale face.

"Yes, I'm coming," she sighed and tucked her book under the pillow. As soon as she was dressed she hurried downstairs to help her mother and Parthe with the last-minute preparations before the guests began to pour in.

Florence had many aunts, uncles, cousins and friends who seemed to enjoy every opportunity for a family party. In a few days the Nightingale family would leave Lea Hurst, their summer

country home in Derbyshire, and move to their other country home, Embley Park, in Hampshire. And as was the custom in their wealthy family, relatives and friends had been invited to the good-bye party.

Florence's sister Parthe enjoyed these parties more than Florence. Parthe took after her mother, throwing herself wholeheartedly into the games and dances. Florence was of a quieter nature, although she, too, enjoyed good company and interesting conversation.

That night Florence's father, William Nightingale, watched his younger daughter from behind the smoke of his long Danish pipe. He could see her dancing, and she seemed to be enjoying herself. But William knew that his favorite daughter was deeply troubled to a point where her health actually suffered. Something was bothering her. And William did not know what to do about it.

A CALL IN THE NIGHT

After the party, as the mansion at Lea Hurst grew dark and quiet, candlelight shone through the window of Florence's bedroom on the second floor. The troubled young woman sat at the table by the window with her dearest companion, her journal. She dipped the pen into the ink and wrote, "O weary days! O evenings that seem never to end! For how many long years have I watched that drawingroom clock and thought it would never reach ten!"

She flicked through the book and read some past entries.

"July 16, 1835: Spent the day arranging flowers.

". . . September 17, 1836: Took a carriage ride with mother.

". . . October 14, 1836: Tried to paint a scene with watercolors. Horrible results!

". . . January 10, 1837: Parthe and I hosted a tea party. Dull."

All the entries seemed the same. Dull, dull, dull! Finally, she turned to a special entry on a dog-eared page. It read,

"**February 7, 1837: God spoke to me and called me to His service.**"

Florence had read those words so many times since, yet she shivered every time she read them. She recalled how one night, when she was only sixteen years old, she had woken up from her sleep and heard a voice. She knew it was God's voice. Since then she had felt that God wanted her to do something special for Him. The only problem was, she didn't know what.

Florence's Family

Florence, the beautiful city in Italy that inspired Florence Nightingale's name.

Florence and her sister Parthenope were born outside of England. Their parents, Fanny and William Nightingale, were having a three-year honeymoon in Italy. Parthenope was born in Naples in 1819 and named after the original Greek settlement there. Florence was born May 12th, 1820 in the city that inspired her name.

Their father was the son of a successful Sheffield banker, and had been born in Derbyshire in 1795. His original family name was Shore, but he had changed it to Nightingale, after the uncle whose lead mine and country estates he had inherited.

William could enjoy his good fortune without having to work. He liked to read and travel and introduce his family to the most fashionable

'lorence's
'ther,
'illiam
'dward
'ightingale.

places in Europe. In England they lived at Lea Hurst, the country home William had inherited.

Florence loved Lea Hurst. But her father decided the house was too small for company — there were only fifteen bedrooms — and besides, it was too remote and cold. So he bought another mansion, Embley Park, in Hampshire. The Nightingale family spent summers at Lea Hurst and winters at Embley Park. They also made several extended visits to London for shopping and entertainment.

The Nightingale sisters grew up surrounded by many cousins, uncles and aunts — and with lots of fun and dinners and parties. Their future was secure. All that was expected of them was to learn to become good wives and mothers and to carry on the proper family traditions.

Lea Hurst where the Nightingales lived during the summer.

SEEKING A FUTURE

This had happened many years earlier. Now Florence was almost thirty years old — and still, she didn't know what to do with her life. Oh yes, Mama and Papa knew! They wanted her to learn the latest dances, to look beautiful, and to manage the household successfully so she could someday marry a suitable gentleman and become an entertaining hostess. In fact, for some time now they had long had a certain gentleman in mind for her. And now she had disappointed their high hopes for a nearly perfect match.

Florence had first met Richard Monckton Milnes at a dinner party seven years earlier. Richard was wealthy, intelligent, funny, and had a good-hearted nature. He was always surrounded by numerous devoted friends. He was especially known for the breakfast parties he threw for his many friends at his rooms in Pall Mall — friends who included celebrities and artists.

Richard also had a serious side, though. He was a widely travelled linguist and a politician — and not a bad poet either. As a member of Parliament he was especially interested in reforming the schools. Besides, he was deeply in love with Florence. Her father was hopeful that marriage would cure his daughter's melancholy.

Florence herself was not opposed to

the idea. She adored Richard, and Richard was a frequent guest at the Nightingale residences in London, Lea Hurst and Embley Park. Yet she kept him waiting, and then finally, she turned down his marriage proposal after seven years of courtship. Somehow she felt that marriage would hinder her in following God's call. In those days, a married woman was expected to support her husband's work without pursuing a career of her own. And Florence was not willing to give up the idea that God had called her to do something special — whatever that may be.

"I would never feel fulfilled if I spent my life just supporting him and arranging domestic things," she wrote in her journal. "To be forced to continue my present life without hope of another would be intolerable to me. To give up the chance to form for myself a true and rich life would seem to me like suicide."

HAPPY CHILDHOOD DAYS

One winter evening in 1850, when she had finally dismissed the thought of marriage, Florence sat down in her bedroom and knew the time had come to make a decision. Her life up until then had seemed like a puzzle of scattered pieces. Why couldn't she be happy and careless like her sister Parthe? Why couldn't she be satisfied with the life that satisfied so many people? What was wrong with her? It hurt her to see that she worried and disappointed her parents. Where was the missing piece? Her thoughts flew back to her childhood.

She remembered the happy days when she and her mother went to visit the workers and tenants on their estate at Lea Hurst. How good she had felt when she delivered a ham or fresh vegetables to a family in need! How excited she had been when she was able to comfort a poor child with a bowl of warm soup! How fine it had been when she could nurse a sick animal back to health!

Once, when she was only six years old, she and the vicar had been riding through the countryside when they met a group of farmers talking together. Roger, the shepherd, had looked especially upset.

"What's wrong, Roger?" she asked. "Why are the sheep scattered? Where's your dog Cap?"

"Missy," answered Roger, "the boys threw stones at him and broke his leg, I'm afraid. I'll have to hang him and put him out of his pain."

"Oh no!" said Florence. "Where is he?"

Roger led them to a nearby shed. The collie was lying on the floor. Florence and the vicar examined the leg while Roger went out to find a rope.

"I don't think his leg is broken," said

the vicar relieved. "Florence, I think he can be nursed back to health!"

The two companions cleaned the collie's wounds and put hot compresses on its leg. When the shepherd returned with the rope, Florence announced triumphantly, "Throw away your rope, Roger! Cap will get well!"

Many, many years later, the vicar reminded her of the incident. He wrote, "I wonder whether you remember how, twenty-two years ago, you and I averted the intended hanging of poor old shepherd Smither's dog Cap? I can recollect the pleasure which the saving of the life of a poor dog then gave to your young mind. I was delighted to witness it. It was to me . . . a sign of what you were about to become. . . ."

Rosa, rosae, ro

MASTERING THE BASICS

Florence's heart jumped with joy when she thought about helping suffering people and animals. She remembered how she had even taken great pleasure in picking up Parthe's broken dolls and "caring" for them. She bandaged their "injuries" and "nursed" them by sewing them up and handing them back to her astonished sister.

When she was twelve, her father had begun to divert her childish mind from "useless" to more "useful" things. He decided to take over Parthe and Flo's education. Their mother Fanny had taught them good manners. Now he wanted to teach them about scholarly matters. He wanted his girls to be better educated than most upper-class girls of the day. Since he was a Cambridge graduate himself, he was determined to take them as far as possible. "Not because I want them to pursue a career, of course," he assured their skeptical mother, "but strictly because I intend to make them into as cultured wives and mothers as possible. A husband prefers suitable company, you know."

He arranged a lavishly equipped schoolroom and library where he then taught the two sisters French, German, Italian, Greek and Latin, as well as mathematics, history and philosophy. The library was stocked with classics he wanted his girls to read. Flo excelled and soon mastered the basics, whereas Parthe fell further and further behind. She was more interested in drawing and helping her mother with embroidery and flower arrangements. The two sisters grew farther and farther apart.

"You're pushing them too hard,"

complained Fanny to her husband. "Studying too much is not good. Not that it has done any harm to Parthe, I believe, but Flo is so unlike her sister."

"No harm comes from learning, my dear Fanny," smiled William.

"Well, it hasn't done Flo any good. She would be happier without it."

"Ah, she'll settle down allright," said William. "Give her some time to find herself."

GOD'S WORK

Later, William would wonder if his wife had been right about Flo. Maybe all the learning had gone to her head and put silly dreams into her mind afterall. Lately she had begun to study hospital reports! Florence had acquired hospital and asylum statistics from a Protestant sisterhood in Germany and now she had come up with the idea of starting something similar in England. Meanwhile though, the book her father had recently ordered her to read, "**Daughters at Home**," with religious

advice for discontented daughters, was gathering dust on the shelf.

But no matter how much Florence had wanted to please her parents, she found no rest in following their plan for her life. Now, by the age of thirty, she was more restless than ever — but in the midst of her distress a vision began to unfold. She wanted to relieve the suffering of the poor and sick. She wanted to become a nurse!

"Have you gone mad? This is absolutely out of the question!" thundered her father. "Nursing is not for respectable girls! How can you even think such an ungodly thought, you ungrateful girl?"

"But Father," objected Florence, "I want to become a good and respectable nurse! I have been thinking about going to an infirmary in Salisbury in order to learn the profession."

"I'd rather see you working in the kitchen! But a nurse? Never!"

That was that. Florence leaned back in her chair, arms crossed, and Parthe bent nervously over her drawing while their father continued reading aloud to his daughters from **The London Times**.

Flo did not listen. She was tired of **hearing** about what was going on in the world. Instead, she wanted to be part of it and make a difference. She was becoming more and more convinced that her parents' religion was superficial. She could not accept that serving God meant going to parties and chatting and endless evenings in theaters and concert halls. Dinner parties could not be done to the glory of God when there was so much misery among the poor! To serve God must mean to be a servant and do His work in the world — not to cultivate a spiritual state of mind for its own sake. To be a true Christian must mean more than handing out little food baskets and otherwise, shutting out the suffering of the world. To be a real Christian must mean to give yourself to God first and then follow His calling. Hadn't the Lord Jesus Himself been an example of this?

If God had called her to be different — why had He then seemed to slam every door in her face? The only reason she could think of was that God had found her unworthy of serving Him.

"I shall never do anything," she sighed. "I'm worse than dust and nothing."

That night, as Florence went to bed, she prayed, "Dear God, I'm a sinner and I must have grieved Your Holy Spirit. Is there any hope for me? Please forgive me of my vain and sinful life. I pray that You'll find a way I can be useful to others and to You." Little did she know that, in her lowest moment, God was preparing her for her highest achievements.

Nursing Before F

There was a good reason why Florence's parents reacted so strongly against her desire to become a nurse. In those days, only poor people stayed in hospitals. The huge wards were overcrowded, filthy, blood-splattered and infested with disease anc infection. There was no privacy. The "hospital smell" was not the smell of sanitation but of odors so strong that anyone who entered woul get nauseous from the stench. This was before Lister's use of antiseptics and Pasteur's discovery of how germs spread. The surgeons were often wearing coats caked with blood and usin dirty knives on their patients, who received no pain-killing drugs. The best way to survive the horrors of a hospital was by drinking gin or brandy.

The nurses then were mostly untrained, tough women often with bad reputations — unable to be trusted to carry out the simplest medical duty. They were often alcoholics, with

e Nightingale

Nursing was not for respectable women, as these 19th century cartoons show.

children they had to care for on their own. Sometimes these women would sleep with the doctors or the patients since they were not given a place of their own to rest, except for wooden cages outside the doors of the wards. Florence once wrote her father that a head nurse had told her that "in the course of her large experience she had never known a nurse who was not drunken and that there was immoral conduct practised in the very wards of which she gave me some awful examples."

The idea of professional nursing originated in the Roman Catholic church where there were special orders of nuns who took upon them the task of caring for the sick. These nurses inspired Florence Nightingale by their commitment, thorough training and disciplined way of life.

A VISIT TO ROME

"Good Lord! Flo, what's the matter with you? You look so pale and thin!"

Mrs. Bracebridge stepped back to take a better look at her young friend.

"Florence has been suffering from migraines and bronchitis lately," her mother apologized.

"I think she needs a change of climate," Mrs. Bracebridge said. "Flo, why don't you come with me and my husband to Rome? That will do you good."

Florence's parents liked the idea. A visit to the Eternal City might help her forget her silly ideas. They gave their permission for the trip.

The plan seemed to work. During the months in Rome, Florence was temporarily distracted from her obsession with hospital work. Together with the Bracebridges she visited ancient monuments, churches, museums and art galleries. She loved every minute of it, and was especially fascinated by the ceiling paintings in the Sistine Chapel. She spent a whole day staring at them while Mrs. Bracebridge wrote letters in the pew. It was like looking straight into heaven and seeing the angels, prophets and God Himself.

"Of all my days in Rome," she wrote afterwards, "this one has been the happiest and most glorious."

While in Rome, something even more important happened to Florence. She was introduced to a fellow Englishman, Sidney Herbert, the former British secretary of war. Herbert was the person God had chosen to open the door of opportunity for Florence. From the beginning, Herbert wholeheartedly supported her vision of hospital reform and gave her the names and addresses of people who thought along the same lines back in England.

"They're all very respected people. They'll help you," he smiled. Then he added, "Your parents can hardly object to them!"

IONAS

LEAVING THE NEST

When Florence returned to her family in England again she felt stronger than ever. Her new friends had helped her gather reports on institutions and hospitals from all over Europe. She soon knew more about health care than anyone else. Because she knew her parents disliked her interest in medical matters, she would get up before dawn to study hundreds of pages of reports on statistics about the outbreak of diseases, nutrition or drainage problems. Then when her family woke up, she joined them for breakfast and assumed her domestic and social duties. Then, whenever she had a

chance she would go off to care for sick relatives or visit the poor in nearby villages.

"Alas, we're ducks," wailed her mother, "but we've hatched a wild swan!"

She was wrong. It was not a swan Fanny and William had hatched. It was an eagle. And the eagle was about to soar.

A Visit to Kaiserwerth

When Florence was 31 years old she had the chance to visit the Institution of Deaconesses at Kaiserswerth near Dusseldorf, Germany — while her mother and Parthe had mud cures at a famous resort in Carlsbad. The Kaiserswerth institution was inspired by the work of Roman Catholic nuns, but run by Protestants. It had a hospital, two schools, an orphanage and an asylum for the mentally ill. The women serving there were mostly single or widowed women who wanted to serve out of their Christian faith.

At Kaiserswerth Florence received her first professional training. She had to get up at 5 a.m. and work till noon before she had a ten-minute lunch break when she ate broth and vegetables. She had another short break with tea and bread at 3 p.m., and finally the workday would end with one more bowl of broth at 7 p.m. The evenings were spent studying the Bible. Florence took all the training there was to be had at Kaiserswerth since there was nothing similar in England.

"I am as happy as the day is long," she wrote home. "Now I know what it is to live and to love life!"

But the joy was short-lived. After three months she had to go back to London to join her family. Her mother hardly spoke to her — and Parthe did not know what to think of her sister.

NURSE AT LAST!

In the summer of 1853, when Florence was thirty-three years old, she finally had a chance to break loose from her family and test her wings. The Institution for the Care of Sick Gentlewomen in Distressed Circumstances in London was setting up a hospital on Harley Street. A superintendent was needed and Sidney Herbert's wife suggested Florence Nightingale. Her family fought the proposal in every way they could.

"Florence, what will people say?" wailed her mother while almost fainting.

"But Mother," protested Florence, "this is a sanatorium for sick governesses. And it's managed by a committee of fine ladies."

"But Flo, you have absolutely no practical experience in running a sanatorium!" interrupted Parthe.

"Please Parthe," sighed her father, "you shouldn't interfere in your sister's affairs."

The atmosphere was poisoned with hysteria and threats. Yet Florence did not budge. She packed her bags and carried them down to the carriage waiting outside. Her father came outside to say goodbye.

"May God be with you, Flo," he said and added, "I'll make sure you receive an allowance of £500 ($1000) a year!"

Florence was on her way.

APPRENTICESHIP IN HARLEY STREET

Florence Nightingale surveyed the empty house at number 1 Harley Street. No beds, no furniture, no kitchenware, no curtains, no linen, no nurses! In ten days the patients would move in and there was still so much to do.

"By the way," said the chairman of the ladies' committee sponsoring the hospital, "we see fit that only members of the Church of England be admitted."

"We shall see," answered Florence quietly but firmly. "I think this place will be proper for any woman who is sick and poor — regardless of her faith!"

The ladies thought this new superintendent had some very strange ideas. "Only good women make good nurses," she insisted. In her opinion, the comfort of the patients and the well-being of the nurses were important for success, as were healthy nutrition, order and cleanliness. During her fourteen months as

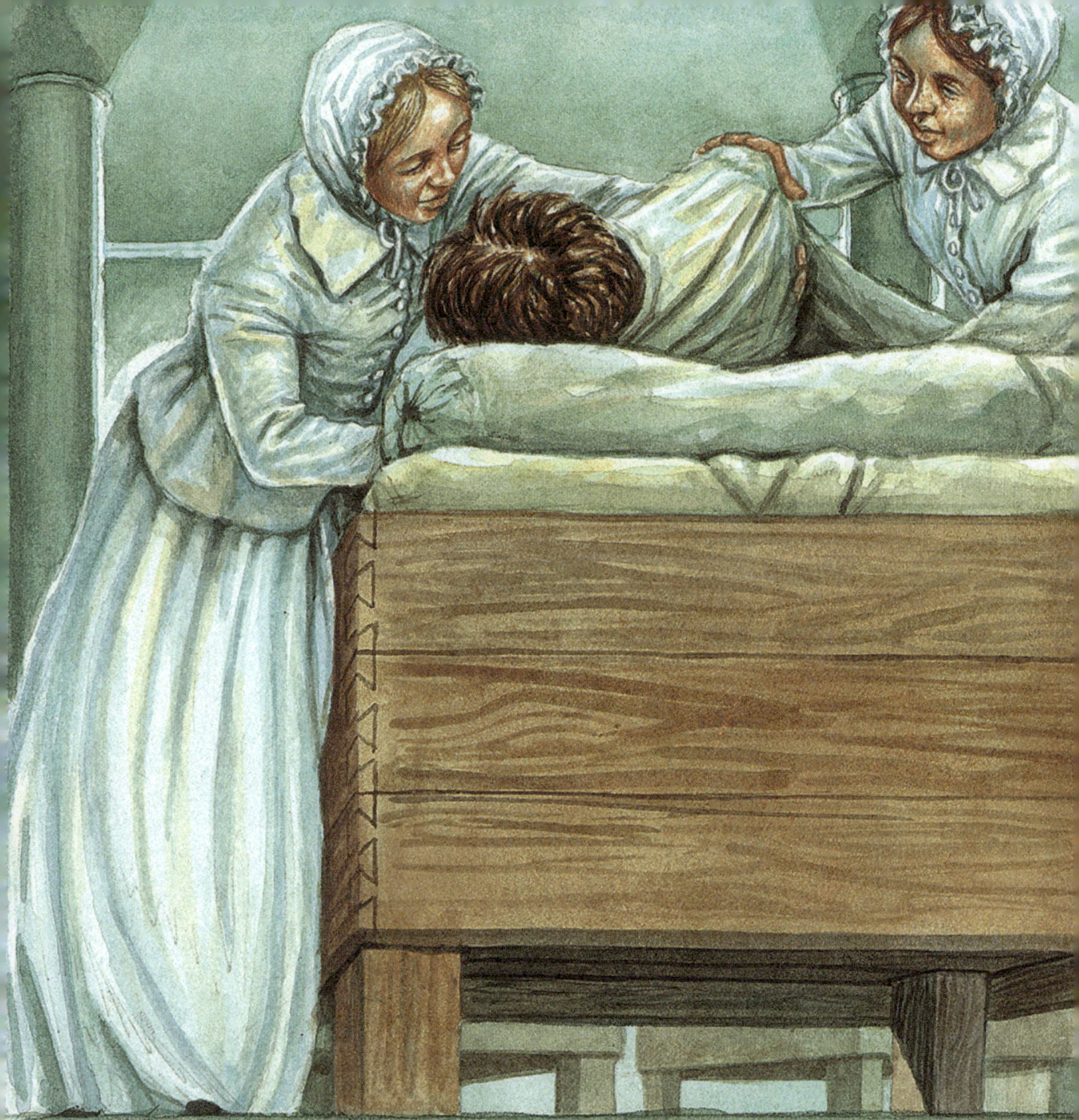

superintendent, Miss Nightingale modernized the profession of nursing. She invented bells for the patients to call their nurse — "a valve which flies open when the bell rings, and remains open in order that the nurse may see who has rung." She installed a food elevator to haul the patients' meals up to the wards from the kitchen. She bought food and supplies at bulk rate, organized jam making in the kitchen to save money, set up a laundry room and carefully selected her staff.

"I am now in the heyday of my power," she wrote to her father.

The ladies' committee was astounded. Instead of the ministering angel they had expected they were dealing with a human dynamo who was revolutionizing the concept of hospital work. Their superintendent had even managed to manipulate the men's committee from behind the scenes in order to have her way. Florence Nightingale always won.

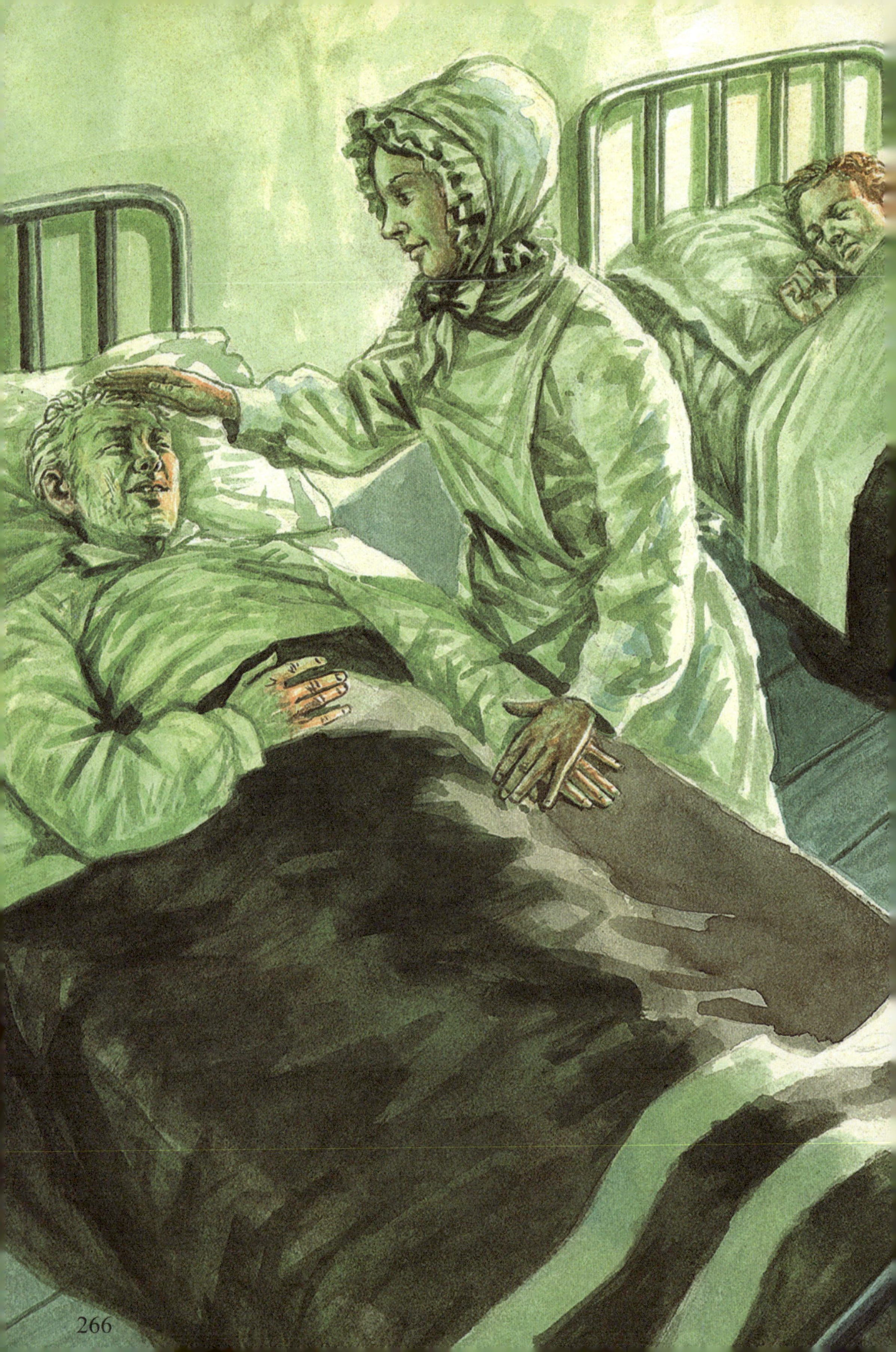

DRESS REHEARSAL IN LONDON

Her patients almost worshiped her. "Thank you, thank you, dearest Miss Nightingale," said one. Another wrote, "My kind Miss Nightingale, I send you a few lines of love." A third added, "Were you to give up, all would soon fade away and the whole thing would cease to be." One evening, as she was making the rounds to tuck her patients in, one patient jumped out of bed and stood at the fireplace, waiting for Miss Nightingale so she could rub her feet!

In the summer of 1854 a cholera epidemic broke out in London. Cholera is an infectious, usually fatal disease. Many people died and Miss Nightingale was rushed to the forefront of the battle — the new Kings College Hospital — to train nurses and care for the sick.

It was dangerous work. But it proved to be a final dress rehearsal for the nursing she would do on the front lines of the Crimean War, which would turn Miss Nightingale into a famous health-care reformer and national heroine.

APPEAL FROM THE BATTLEFIELD

It all began the following fall when war broke out between England and Russia. British soldiers were shipped to the island of Crimea in the Black Sea in an attempt to besiege Sevastopol and defeat their enemy. A British war correspondent, William Howard Russell, sent alarming eyewitness accounts, together with an appeal for help, back to The London Times — the first war coverage by a journalist ever.

"The wounded have just been left on the field," wrote Russell, "some for two nights, all of them for at least one. From the battlefield they have been bundled on board a ship for transport across the Black Sea to Scutari without medical attention. . . . The neglected gunshot wounds bred maggots, which crawled in every direction, infecting the food of the unhappy beings on board. The putrid animal matter caused such a stench that the officers and crew were nearly overcome, and the captain is now ill from the effects of the five days of misery. . . . The men must attend to each other or receive no relief at all. . . .

Are there no devoted women among us, able and willing to go forth and minister to the sick and suffering soldiers of the East?"

England was apalled. Their young men were dying like flies abroad — some from battle wounds, but more than sixty per cent were dying from curable diseases and a simple lack of medical attention. There was a desperate need for immediate relief work. Sidney Herbert, now British secretary at war, sent a hasty letter to his friend Miss Nightingale.

"There is only one person in England I know of who is capable of organizing the hospital work in Scutari," he wrote. "This person is you. Would you please go and oversee the entire situation?"

Within 48 hours after Russell's appeal in the Times, Miss Nightingale was ready to go. With her went a housekeeper, the Bracebridges and the best thirty-eight women she could find — some were regular hospital nurses, others were Catholic nuns and there were also Anglican nuns — all going to care for the wounded soldiers at Scutari.

Miss Nightingale's War Nurses

"Forty British females are more difficult to manage than 4,000 men!" said Florence Nightingale about her Scutari nurses.

They certainly were a hastily chosen and somewhat ill-fitting team — some were coarse, untrained women, others Roman Catholic nuns and Protestant sisters. The religious nurses would often argue over doctrine and sometimes accuse each other of preaching their own beliefs among the soldiers. The nonreligious nurses often lacked self-discipline and proper conduct. In fact, ten of them were sent home shortly after they arrived because of inappropriate moral behavior.

The uniform was a gray tweed jacket, cap and skirt, woolen cloak, brown scarf embroidered in red with the words "Scutari Hospital" — an unattractive outfit that would help "protect" the nurses from male admirers among the patients and hospital staff.

A month after their arrival, Florence Nightingale was notified that another team of 47 nurses was on its way. The Lady-in-Chief was furious. This was more than she could handle. Besides, there were no accommodations for them.

"I have toiled my way," she wrote her boss Sidney Herbert, "into the confidence of the medical men. I have introduced something like a system into the disorderly oprerations of these women. But to have women scampering about the wards of a military hospital all day long, which they would do if an increased number relax the discipline and increase their leisure, would be as improper as absurd."

The Lady-in-Chief received the new nurses coldly and shuffeled the old and new packs, sending thirty of them to Crimea and keeping fifty in Scutari.

Eventually she sent for more nurses, and before the war was over the nursing staff at Scutari had grown to 125.

One of Russell's dispatches for The London Times.

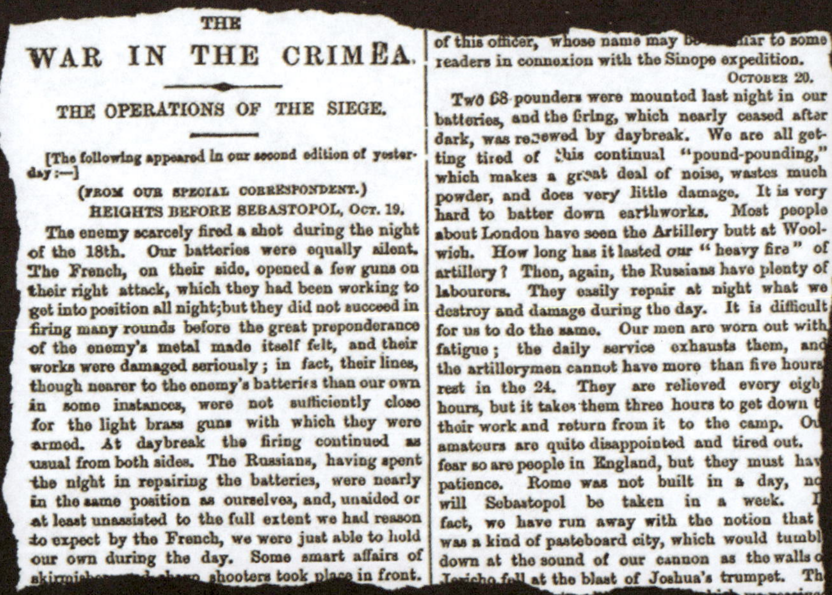

THE

WAR IN THE CRIMEA.

THE OPERATIONS OF THE SIEGE.

[The following appeared in our second edition of yesterday:—]

(FROM OUR SPECIAL CORRESPONDENT.)

HEIGHTS BEFORE SEBASTOPOL, OCT. 19.

The enemy scarcely fired a shot during the night of the 18th. Our batteries were equally silent. The French, on their side, opened a few guns on their right attack, which they had been working to get into position all night;but they did not succeed in firing many rounds before the great preponderance of the enemy's metal made itself felt, and their works were damaged seriously; in fact, their lines, though nearer to the enemy's batteries than our own in some instances, were not sufficiently close for the light brass guns with which they were armed. At daybreak the firing continued as usual from both sides. The Russians, having spent the night in repairing the batteries, were nearly in the same position as ourselves, and, unaided or at least unassisted to the full extent we had reason to expect by the French, we were just able to hold our own during the day. Some smart affairs of skirmish[illegible] shooters took place in front.

of this officer, whose name may be [illegible]iar to some readers in connexion with the Sinope expedition.

OCTOBER 20.

Two 68-pounders were mounted last night in our batteries, and the firing, which nearly ceased after dark, was renewed by daybreak. We are all getting tired of this continual "pound-pounding," which makes a great deal of noise, wastes much powder, and does very little damage. It is very hard to batter down earthworks. Most people about London have seen the Artillery butt at Woolwich. How long has it lasted *our* "heavy fire" of artillery? Then, again, the Russians have plenty of labourers. They easily repair at night what we destroy and damage during the day. It is difficult for us to do the same. Our men are worn out with fatigue; the daily service exhausts them, and the artillerymen cannot have more than five hours rest in the 24. They are relieved every eigh[t] hours, but it takes them three hours to get down t[o] their work and return from it to the camp. Ou[r] amateurs are quite disappointed and tired out. [I] fear so are people in England, but they must hav[e] patience. Rome was not built in a day, no[r] will Sebastopol be taken in a week. I[n] fact, we have run away with the notion that [it] was a kind of pasteboard city, which would tumbl[e] down at the sound of our cannon as the walls o[f] Jericho fell at the blast of Joshua's trumpet. Th[e]

The Crimean War

In 1853 Russia attacked the Turkish Empire in order to gain access to the Mediterranean from the Black Sea. In March the following year England and France sided with Turkey and declared war on Russia. Six months later the allies landed 50,000 troops on the Crimean peninsula and surrounded the strong Russian naval base at Sevastopol. The Russians lost several bloody battles, but not without inflicting heavy casualties on the allies who had already abandoned much of their equipment, including medical supplies. To make matters worse, deadly diseases such as typhus and cholera broke out, leaving the allies in chaos — despite their success on the battlefield. Unlike the French who had brought trained nuns and nurses with them, the British army proved totally incapable of coping with their sick and wounded. All they had was an ambulance corps of old pensioners. Florence Nightingale and her nurses were desperately needed!

The war dragged on until February 1856 when Austria finally joined the allied forces. Russia then capitulated and signed a treaty forcing it to abandon its naval bases on the Black Sea.

Top: War correspondent William Howard Russell. Middle: British and Russian soldiers fight the battle of Balaklava, October 25th, 1854. Bottom: The Crimean winter captured by the new medium of photography. Russell reporting in his tent while Florence Nightingale awaits wounded soldiers.

CHAOS AT SCUTARI

Miss Nightingale was optimistic — despite her ill-equipped and diverse band of nurses. Sidney Herbert had assured her that plenty of supplies had been sent on ahead — tons of lint, 15,000 pairs of sheets, medicine, wine, arrowroot, food and everything else needed to run an effective army hospital. There were also plenty of doctors — one to every ninety-five men — the highest proportion on a British battlefield ever.

Two weeks later, Miss Nightingale's rescue team landed on the shores just down the coast from the Turkish village of Scutari. Rain was pouring down and black clouds hung over an enormous, ugly building on top of the hill. This was the army barracks where the wounded had been brought. It looked more like a prison than a hospital.

Once again, Miss Nightingale came up against an impossible situation: The supplies promised her were nowhere to be found! Evidently, they had bypassed Scutari and either been confiscated by Turkish customs agents, or just disappeared somewhere in Crimea! There were no sheets! Hardly any blankets! No heat! No soap, no clean water, no towels, and no clothing! No furniture or tables — not even an operation table! No food except for chunks of meat full of gristle and fat! No kitchenware! Only one kitchen with thirteen copperpots to serve 2,500 patients! The place was overcrowded and filthy, infested with lice, maggots and disease. There were rats everywhere. The walls steamed with damp. From the sewers underneath the building rose a stinking odor which the cold wind blew up through the pipes into the wards.

And in addition to all this, the medical staff already there hardly welcomed the nurses with open arms. The medical officer in charge and the military commandant gave the nurses nothing more than a professional handshake. There was an obvious prejudice against women interfering with men's affairs. And here were two reasons for the men to be upset. Both war, and wounded soldiers belonged strictly to the men's world. Female amateur nurses were not wanted — especially when it meant that neglect and inefficiency would be exposed! The doctors forbade the nurses to enter the wards where the wounded lay, unless they were specifically asked to. So Miss Nightingale obeyed and ordered her helpers to clean and organize as much of the building as they could. Little by little she won over the doctors purely through her quiet and determined way of doing things.

One evening, as she was discussing a certain matter with a doctor, the doctor snarled, "But that's impossible! This cannot be done!"

"But Doctor," came the quiet reply, "it must be done!"

Then unforeseen events lowered the doctors' resistance even further. When a new battle was fought at Balaclava, a flood of wounded men were brought to the hospital at Scutari. Now the doctors had no choice. They needed all the help they could get.

THE LADY WITH THE LAMP

Miss Nightingale's nurses were finally permitted to do the work they had come for. They worked round the clock among the sick and wounded — the Lady-in-

Chief often twenty hours a day! Wherever suffering was at its worst and the need for help was greatest — there was Miss Nightingale! Night after night she walked with her lantern down the four miles of corridors and wards to check on the sick. She often sat down by a bedside to write a letter for a soldier unable to write himself — or to hold the hand of a dying man.

"I've seen her spend hours with men dying of cholera, or fever," said one patient. "Her slight form could be seen bending over them, administering to their ease in every way in her power, and seldom quitting their sides until death had released them."

Her mere presence and personal attention brought healing and hope. Not even the roughest soldier dared to swear in her presence.

"What a comfort it was even to see her pass by," remembered one man. "She would speak to one and nod and smile to many more. But she could not do it to all, you know, we lay there by the hundreds; but we could kiss her shadow as it fell, and lay our heads on the pillow again, content."

ORDER OUT OF CHAOS

And so, after six months of hard labor, the Lady-in-Chief could step back and evaluate all that had been accomplished: The mortality rate among soldiers had fallen drastically — from fourty-two per cent to two; the patients were properly clothed; the mattresses were covered with clean linen; the kitchens were organized; the hunks of meat had been replaced with well-prepared and appetizing meals; a laundry was running efficiently; a storehouse had been established with plenty of supplies; the sanitary system had been improved; and a new ward had been built.

But the Lady-in-Chief was still not satisfied. "I have been clothing the British army," she wrote Sidney Herbert. Now the time had come to care for her patients' spiritual needs.

A readingroom was furnished, and recreational activities started. There

were even classes to educate the soldiers and their families. The officers were amazed to see how the Lady-in-Chief treated their men.

"She's spoiling the brutes!" grinned one officer.

She was not spoiling them. She was treating them with love and dignity and helping them become better human beings.

It almost cost her life, though. During a visit to the battlefields at Balaclava, Miss Nightingale fell ill with "Crimean fever." She was carried in a stretcher to a nearby hospital, where the doctors did not think she would live much longer. When the news reached the hospital at Scutari, the men turned their faces to the walls and cried.

But the stubborn Lady-in-Chief was determined to recover. And recover she did — only to work more eagerly than ever before. In the summer of 1856, when the war finally ended, she left her last "children" in Scutari, and sailed back to England.

A NATIONAL HERO

A heroine's welcome awaited her. England wanted to celebrate their brave nurse. Military bands, triumphal arches, speeches and banquets were planned. Instead though, she managed to slip undetected into her homeland — disguised as a "Miss Smith."

She caught a train for Derbyshire and walked to Lea Hurst, her childhood home, where she took her family by surprise.

"Flo! My daughter!" beamed her mother. "The whole of England is welcoming you!"

"Welcome home," added her father. "We're proud of you, Florence!"

The next morning the bells at the village church announced her homecoming. England was ringing with her name. But Florence was not impressed by all the fuss. Her heart was still with the many soldiers who had died of neglect back in the hospital barracks at Scutari and Crimea.

That night she wrote in her journal, "I am standing before the altar of murdered men. As long as I live I will fight their cause."

VISITING THE QUEEN

And fight she did — determined that only thorough reform of the army medical service would prevent a repetition of the Crimean War fiasco. The following year she drew up an alarming report for the Royal Commission on the Health of the British Army — a committee she herself had helped appoint, with Sidney Herbert as chairman. The 1,000 page report was full of statistics and observations from army hospitals she had visited. The document was accompanied with this personal note from her days at Scutari: "No one can feel for the Army as I do. These people who talk to us have all fed their children on the fat of the land and dressed them in velvet and silk while we have been away. I have had to see my 'children' dressed in dirty blankets and old pairs of regimental trousers, and to see them fed on raw, salted meat. Nine thousand of my 'children' are lying from causes which might have been prevented in their forgotten graves. But I can never forget. . . ."

In those days it was still unthinkable for a woman to enter politics. So Florence Nightingale had to do her reform work from behind the scenes by bullying reluctant politicians to take up her cause. In the fall of 1856 she was invited to see Queen Victoria and Prince Albert and went fully armed with facts and plans, to plead her case at the highest level. The queen gave her a brooch with the inscription, "Blessed are the merciful."

After the audience the prince said, "She put before us all the defects of our present military hospital system, and the reforms that are needed. We are much pleased with her. She is extremely modest."

Queen Victoria remarked, "I wish we had her at the War Office!"

HEALTH REFORMS

Over the next few years many reforms followed — due to Florence Nightingale's persistence. In 1859 the War Office established a medical college in Kent. In 1861 a military hospital was opened in London. And the following year a permanent army sanitary commission was set up to make sure that the new practices were kept up to standard. In 1857, when the Indian army rebelled against British rule, another commission was appointed to ensure the soldiers' welfare in India.

Florence Nightingale was involved in all of this. But most of all, she was interested in reforming the nursing education itself, so in 1860 the Nightingale School for Nurses was opened in London.

Reforms in India

Florence Nightingale never set foot on Indian soil — and yet she came to be known as the "Governess of India" because of the important reform work she did for this former British colony.

The British first came to India as peaceful traders. But when the Mughal empire collapsed, the British took control, claiming the need to prevent crime and civil war. By the middle of the nineteenth century, law and order had been reestablished and a new Indian army under British command was in place.

Even though life for the Indians was hard under British rule, the British started many important projects to improve living conditions in India: construction of roads and railroads, canals to drain swamps and irrigate dry land, schools and hospitals. Yet many Indians preferred their traditional way of life. This led to a brief national uprising in 1857 which was put down by the British.

Florence Nightingale was deeply concerned for the welfare of the army and the general population in India. Two years after she returned from Scutari she began to work towards establishing a Sanitary Commission for India, headed by her friend Sidney Herbert. A questionnaire she drafted was sent out to every military station in the colony. When the results came in, she analyzed them

herself, then wrote a 2,000-page report, entitled **Observations by Miss Nightingale**. This comprehensive report discussed overcrowding in barracks, hygiene, water, diet, exercise, disease, drainage, hospitals and, of course, mortality statistics.

"The picture is terrible," admitted the commission, "but it's all true!"

Over the next twenty-five years, Florence Nightingale's reform ideas for the army developed into a program of reform for the entire public health administration of India — inspired by her next book, **How People May Live and not Die in India**. Every step of health progress taken in India during the latter part of the nineteenth century — military as well as civil — was more due to Florence Nightingale than any other man or woman.

The Nightingale Nursing School

When Florence Nightingale returned from Scutari many people wanted to support her work for the sick and poor. A fund was set up and money poured in from people who supported her idea of starting a training school for nurses.

During this planning stage Florence Nightingale wrote **Notes on Nursing: What it is and what it is not**. The book offered a great deal of practical advice and became extremely popular. More than any of her other books, this one helped outline a professional training program.

The Nightingale Training School opened at St. Thomas' Hospital on June 24th 1860, when fifteen applicants were chosen for the one-year course. Thirteen of them qualified to become certified nurses. The trainees were instructed by physicians and surgeons in not only bed-making, dressing of wounds and other simple skills, but also in the very scientific basis of their work.

The school became a great success. "I trust that our school may lead the way towards supplying a want long felt in England," said Florence Nightingale. New schools sprang up all over the country — even in other countries. All of the modern nursing profession is a result of Florence Nightingale's ideas.

This photo of a ward in St. Thomas' Hospital in London shows Florence Nightingale's lasting influence on the profession of nursing.

THE FINAL YEARS

Florence Nightingale never fully recovered from her exhausting years in Scutari. Even though she lived another fifty years, she was often sick and bedridden. As her sight failed, she withdrew from public life, cared for her parents till they died, and wrote many letters. These she often concluded with, "Should there be anything in which I can be of the least use, here I am."

Three years before her death, King Edward VII presented her with the Order of Merit, the highest honor a British civilian could obtain. Florence Nightingale was the first woman ever to receive the award, but it hardly meant anything to her.

"Too kind, too kind," she murmured.

At 90, she died peacefully in her sleep — lonely and almost forgotten by the general public. She had not wanted

a hero's burial in Westminster Abbey, only that her body would be used for dissection in a training hospital, but this wish was ignored. Instead she was buried next to her mother and father near Embley Park. The words on the memorial stone read, "F.N. Born 1820. Died 1910."

A couragous woman with extraordinary gifts and powers had passed through the world and left it a better place for us all. Thanks to her brave determination and stubborn love, thousands of people had been nurtured back to health — and nursing had been revolutionized and changed forever into an honorable profession.

Main Events in Florence's Life

1820	12 May	Born in Florence, Italy.
1837		Tours the European continent. Called to serve God. Victoria becomes queen.
1839		Presented at the queen's court.
1842	10 May	Introduced to Richard Monckton Milnes at a party.
1844		First hospital visits.
1845		Parents object to training at Salisbury Infirmary.
1847	Dec.	Visits Catholic hospitals in Rome, Italy.
1849		Decides not to marry Richard but pursue God's calling instead.
1850	August	Brief visit to Kaiserwerth.
1851	July	Training at Kaiserwerth.
1853	August	Superintendent of the Institution for the Care of Sick Gentlewomen in London.
1854	March	The Crimean War breaks out.
	October	Appointed to lead nursing mission to Scutari. Arrives in Scutari.
	November	Visits Balaklava.
1855	June	Seriously ill with Crimean fever. The Nightingale Fund set up in England to assist her work.
1856	March	The Crimean War ends.
	August	Returns to England. Meets Queen Victoria and Prince Albert.
1857		Rebellion in India. Royal Commission set up to investigate the army medical service.
1859		Notes on Hospitals (about hospital design) and Notes on Nursing (about guidelines and conduct) published.
1860	9 July	The Nightingale Training School opens in London.
1861	October	Helps the United States organize hospitals during the Civil War. Sidney Herbert dies.
1865		Moves into her Mayfair home in London, given to her by her father.
1868		Helps establish East London Nursing Society.
1871		Appointed head of the Nightingale Training School.
1874		Death of her father.
1880		Death of her mother.
1890		Death of Parthe.
1901		Loses eyesight. Queen Victoria dies.
1907	Dec.	Awarded Order of Merit.
1910	13 August	Florence Nightingale dies peacefully in her sleep.

BOOK RESOURCES

Florence Nightingale: God's Servant at the Battlefield, by David R. Collins (Mott Media, 1985). **Florence Nightingale: The Lady of the Lamp**, by Basil Miller (Bethany). **Florence Nightingale**, by Dorothy Turner (The Bookwright Press, 1986). **Florence Nightingale**, by Richard Tames (Franklin Watts, 1989). **Florence Nightingale**, by Irene Cooper Willis (Coward-McCann, 1931). **Florence Nightingale**, by Elspeth Huxley (G.P.Putnam's Sons, 1975) **Eminent Victorians**, by Lytton Strachey (Weidenfeld & Nicolson, 1989).

Francis of Assisi

THE MAN WHO GAVE UP EVERYTHING TO FOLLOW JESUS

1182 —1226

Great men and women are not in need of our praise.
We are the ones in need of getting to know them.

By Ben Alex

Illustrations by Musio Cosimo

ROWDY BOYS

It could have been a beautiful spring day in 1196 A.D. The sun glistened on the steeples and towers of the city on top of Mount Subasio. Larks fluttered in the air, making the whole landscape look like a fairy tale. The bell in the tower of San Giorgio church rang out the time. Siesta had begun.

A band of unruly boys ran out of the school annex and down the narrow, cobblestoned streets toward the city gate. On their way they pushed each other and shouted at the people they passed. An old woman with a basket of apples hurried out of their way. Some of the boys snatched an skipped through the gate.

The boys stopped on the slope outside the city. Below them they could see some lepers sitting and begging along the roadside.

"Look at those misfits," mocked one boy.

"Yes, they stink," yelled another as he hurled an apple at them. The lepers gathered their alm bowls and limped off. But one of the boys, a handsome fourteen-year-old with curly black hair and a strong face, took his apple and instead of throwing it, gently rolled it down the steep path to the lepers. Then he turned around and ran to catch up with his friends.

Francis — The Best or the Worst?

Pietro di Bernardone, Francis' father, was away on a business trip when Francis was born. His mother Pica was still confined to her bed when a beggar knocked on the door and made his way to mother and child. According to the legend, the beggar took the newborn in his arms and prophesied that two boys had been born in Assisi that day -the best and the worst among men.

Moved by the beggar's words, Pica decided to have the baby baptized right away. She called him Giovanni, which is Italian for John. She named him after John the Baptist because she remembered that Jesus had called John "the greatest among men." And she believed that a name is a blessing which leaves a mark on a person's entire life.

Her husband Pietro came back from his business trip to France, excited about its customs and people. But when he heard that Pica had named the boy Giovanni, he grew angry and renamed him Francesco, the little Frenchman. Pica could do nothing about it. She prayed for her favorite child, now named Giovanni Francesco di Bernardone, that he would become the best among men, and not the worst.

For a while it looked as though he might turn out to become the worst. According to Thomas of Celano, Francis' first biographer, "Until he was nearly 25, he squandered his time terribly. Indeed, he outshone all his friends in trivialities, suggested various evils, and was eager for foolishness of every kind."

A BEGGAR IN THE SHOP

Pietro di Bernardone was busy showing some new fabric to a customer when fourteen-year-old Francis stepped into the shop.

"Ah, there you are, my son," he beamed. "Come help me unroll this bolt of magnificent French silk. It's time you learned the trade of a merchant."

Francis took care of the customer and saw her out. As he opened the door, a beggar wrapped in a bundle of rags stuck his bowl rudely through the doorway.

"Good lord, give an alm for God's sake!" asked the beggar.

"Go away," rebuked Francis, "I have nothing to give you." Then he turned to the customer, smiled and said, "Good day, signora!"

But as soon as he was alone, Francis regretted his harsh words. Here he was, surrounded by the costliest fabrics of the world, the son of a wealthy merchant and owner of some of the finest vineyards and orchards around Assisi. Yet Francis hadn't been able to spare one alm for a poor beggar.

"If this beggar had come to borrow money for a noble friend, wouldn't I gladly have given it to him?" he asked himself. "How then can I turn him away when he comes in the name of Almighty God?"

Without another thought, Francis took the money which the customer had just paid him, ran out the door and pressed the coins into the beggar's palm.

Perugia — Assisi's Rival?

Francis was fifteen at the time in history when many Italian cities revolted in order to win independence from the Holy Roman Empire. In Assisi, the people stormed the garrison, broke down the fortress and formed a communal government which immediately began to rebuild the walls around the city with stones from the demolished fortress. Francis may have learned his building skills here. This was a talent which he later used in the restoration of demolished churches around Assisi.

After Assisi had gained its independence, the next step was to eliminate the feudal aristocracy which had for so long oppressed the citizens by means of heavy tolls and taxes. Many lords were imprisoned and executed, others managed to seek refuge in Perugia, to the west of Assisi. From there the lords stirred up hatred against their hometown until Perugia finally declared war on Assisi in 1201. The feud between the two cities lasted for over ten years.

It was most likely during the battle of Ponte San Giovanni outside of Perugia, in November 1202, that Francis was taken hostage.

PRISONER OF WAR

In 1202, the knights of Assisi were getting ready for war. On the plains below the city they mustered an army of brave young men who hoped to win honor and fame in battle. Among them was twenty-year-old Francis, the son of Pietro.

Pietro and Pica watched from the hill as the army rode off. They were proud of their son. He looked so handsome, dressed in armor and sitting on his black horse. They prayed he would come back safely, having earned the title of knight.

The battle against Perugia, Assisi's neighboring rival city, waged through all of November. Francis fought bravely but was finally taken prisoner in Perugia. For twelve months he was held hostage while his father tried desperately to negotiate a ransom. In prison he became friends with many of his fellow prisoners, some of whom were nobles and knights. They admired Francis' optimism and courage.

"How can you laugh at your chains?" they asked. "Don't you realize we may never get out alive?"

"I know I will get out," smiled Francis. "A great future awaits me. Someday I'll be famous thoughout the world."

Francis's Background

Francis grew up in an age of violence and war. The map of Europe looked very different then from what it does today. The Holy Roman Empire stretched from Germany in the north down across central Europe to the southern part of Italy. France was only half the size it is today, and most of Spain was occupied by the Muslim Turks. Central Italy, where Francis grew up, had alternately been in the hands of the emperor and the pope, and there were many wars and feuds among cities, states and noble families.

People were basically divided into two groups — majores (nobles, knights, lords) and minores (common people). The minores were again divided into villeins (independant laborers, merchants and craftsmen) and serfs (forced laborers, or slaves, under the lords).

Since the first Crusade (almost a hundred years before Francis' birth) and the discovery of the Byzantine Empire, new trade routes had opened up to the east. The markets of Europe were flooded with new raw materials and products. Many merchants and artisans reaped immense fortunes that eventually qualified them to cross their class lines from minores to majores.

Francis' father, Pietro di Bernardone, was a cloth merchant who prospered from the new materials and fabrics that came to Europe. In 1182, when Francis was born, his business was booming, for this was an age when people showed their wealth by the fancy costumes they wore.

From his shop in Assisi, Pietro traveled far to make business deals. Some day, he believed, his son Francis would follow in his footsteps and become the greatest merchant in Italy.

A VIVID DREAM

Francis did eventually get out of prison. But by the time he was released, Francis had grown sick and weak. He was forced to stay in bed for many months. When he finally began to recover and took his first walk in the countryside, the beauty of the vineyards and fields seemed less than what he remembered. He went home sad and depressed.

"What's the matter with me?" he wondered. "Why do I feel so restless and sad? How can I become happy again?"

One night, as he tossed and turned in bed, trying to sleep, he had a vivid

dream. In his dream he was led into a banqueting hall decorated with coats of arms and different types of knightly armor.

"Whose palace is this?" he aske in the dream.

"It is the palace of Francesco di Bernardone and his knights," answered a voice. "And in the innermost hall a princess is waiting for her bridegroom."

He woke up feeling hopeful and happy, sure that the dream was telling him he had a destiny and would meet with success, after all.

THE DEATH OF A DREAM

In 1204, Pope Innocent III was gathering an army against the German princes from the north. The pope managed to hire Gautier de Brienne, a famous and successful Norman captain, as his army general. Young men from allover Italy volunteered for the pope's army, hoping to win glory and knighthood. Francis, still tempted by his dream of the banqueting hall, decided to join.

One night outside Spoleto, a town southeast of Perugia, the voice from his dream spoke again. "Francis," it said, "where are you going?"

"I'm going to war to make my dream come true."

"Whom are you serving?" continued the voice. "God's servant, the pope."

"What is better: to serve the servant or the master?"

The Age of Chivalry

The parish school at San Giorgio was where Francis went to school. There he learned his catechism and a little rhetorics and grammar, but it was not much of an education. All his life Francis was, in his own words, an idiota, a man without any worldly knowledge. And he considered this an advantage for the pious life he was to lead later.

The ideals for youngsters in Francis' day were taught by troubadours (traveling singers and poets) rather than by schoolmasters. They taught about courtship, chivalry and bravery in the battlefield. Francis' favorite story was that of Saint George, the valiant knight who freed a princess and killed the dragon with his lance. Francis loved to daydream of himself as a knight returning triumphantly from battle to be welcomed by the lady of his dreams.

"The master, of course."

"Then why do you serve the servant?"

Francis was awestruck. Before he could reply, the voice said, "Francis, you're trying to make your dream fit your own ambitions. You must wait and listen to its deeper meaning. Go home now, and think about it."

Early next morning, the downcast youth rode back the way he had come. As he approached Assisi, a peasant in a field pointed and said, "Look, there's Don Pietro's son! He's running away from the war."

"Ha! He calls himself a knight," said another. "Some even say he was imprisoned in Perugia because he turned himself in."

Francis refused to listen. He kept his eyes fixed on the road. "I'll show them," he mumbled to himself. "Some day I'll be more than a knight. I'll be a prince of the King of kings."

SURPRISED BY LOVE

Pietro was furious. What was all this nonsense about a king and a palace? Hadn't he spent a fortune on his son's armor, horse and squire so he could become a real knight? And now Francis had the nerve to come running home to his mother with his tail between his legs. Rumors of his cowardly return had already spread through town.

Pica was worried too, but not angry like her husband. She was trying to find the secret source of her son's sorrow. Maybe he just needed to have some fun. Maybe he needed a wife. After all, he was now in his early twenties, and it was time to think of marriage. She thought maybe if they threw him a party he might cheer up.

Even though some of Francis' best friends were with the papal armies, a feast was prepared in honor of his homecoming. There was a great deal of wine and food. As the party got louder, a friend stuck a scepter into Francis' hand and shouted, "Here's to Francesco,the king and his palace!"

Everyone cheered. Then they ran out into the streets and sang some more drunken songs.

But Francis walked away, still clutching his scepter. He stared up at the stars in the sky and listened to the crickets in the trees. For a moment he felt a tremendous sense of belonging to the whole of the universe and creation. A feeling from beyond himself flooded his soul with peace and love. After a while, when his friends came back to get him, they could sense that something had happened to change him.

"What's wrong with you?" they asked. "You look like you're madly in love. Who's the girl?"

"You're right, I am in love," he replied, "and you have no idea of just how beautiful my Beloved is."

That was Francis' final feast. From that point on he was no longer interested in superficial amusement, chivalry and forms of worldly love. He was obsessed with the kind of love that comes only from God.

MEETING JESUS IN A CAVE

After some time Francis found a friend, someone he could tell everything to. The two men would often take long walks together beneath the black firs of Mount Subasio to a cave they had found. Francis would go into the dark cave while his friend waited outside. Inside the cave, far from the noise of the city, Francis lay facedown on the bare rock floor and prayed.

"God," he agonized, "what do You want? Please show me what to do. I'm listening." But there was no answer. All he could hear was the beating of his own heart.

So he began to listen to his heart. And the more time he spent in the cave, the more he realized his heart was like a dark, damp grotto filled with evil thoughts and monstrous temptations. Slowly he began to see his heart as God sees the human heart, and he trembled and wept over his past sins.

"What did God say?" asked his friend when he came out.

"Not much," answered Francis. "I told Him that if He goes on showing me my sinful heart, I shall break."

"And then?"

"Then He said, 'Break!' and right there I felt as if my heart really broke."

After many nights of praying inside the cave, Francis finally came out with a look of peace and joy on his face. His friend realized something had changed.

"What happened?" he asked.

"Jesus stood in front of me, and He touched me with His wounded hands. All I know is that grace and peace and love filled my heart. God has forgiven me all my sins."

That morning, as the sun came up, the two companions ran all the way back to Assisi, dancing and singing their praise for the mercy of God.

THE SPEAKING CRUCIFIX

As they approaced the city gate, they noticed a leper on the road. In the past, Francis had often panicked whenever he came across lepers, trying to find a way to avoid them. But this time he stopped, then he walked right up to the leper. He could smell the odor of rotting

flesh, and tears began to slide down his cheeks because he doubted himself. Then he almost jumped at the man, flung his arms around his neck and kissed him. The two men held each other for a moment, then Francis took the leper's head between his own, looked into his eyes and said, "Peace and good!"

"Peace and good!" the leper smiled back.

One of Francis' favorite places to pray was the San Damiano chapel outside of Assisi. The building was falling apart, inmiserable condition, guarded only by a priest who lived in a nearby hut. But Francis loved the quietness of the chapel, and he prayed for hours in front of an old crucifix which hung above the altar, as he thought about Jesus' sacrifice for his sins.

One day, as he was praying, the voice spoke to him again, this time from the crucifix.

"Francis," said the voice, "as you can see, My Church is in ruins. I want you to rebuild My Church!"

Naive as he was, Francis took the command from the cross literally. He hurried home, packed some bolts of his father's cloth onto his horse and rode off to the market in nearby Foligno. There he sold the goods as well as the horse and walked the ten miles back to San Damiano.

"Here's money to rebuild your church!" Francis handed a bag of gold coins to the priest living near the chapel. But he refused to accept the money without the permission of Francis' father. After all, the things that had been sold belonged to Pietro. Francis left the money behind and went home confused.

The next day he went door-to-door in Assisi, begging for stones to repair churches. Here was the son of one of the richest men in town, unkempt and dressed in filthy rags, begging for stones! Many people thought Pietro's son must surely have gone mad.

GOD'S FOOL

Pietro was furious when he found out Francis had sold off some of his best cloth. Now he thought, not only is Francis a madman, but also a thief! Pietro went looking for Francis so he could bring him before the magistrate. But Francis hid in a cave, and the San Damiano priest secretly brought him food. After a month in the cave Francis finally decided to face his father.

"Look," pointed the people of Assisi as Francis passed through the city gate, "there's Pietro's crazy son!"

"Pazzo! Pazzo! Madman!" they cried and threw rocks at him.

He caused such a commotion that Pietro sent some of his servants out to seize him and drag him into the house. Once inside, Pietro beat Francis. Then he chained him and locked Francis in a dungeon inthe hope that Francis would

come to his senses. But the trial only strengthened Francis' resolve. "I fear no chains, and no blows," he told his desperate father. "I can endure anything for Christ."

Pica felt compassion for her son. She admired his courage and even wondered if Francis was following his heart in ways she could not understand. One day, when Pietro was away on business, she unlocked Francis' chains and set him free. "Go, my son," she said, "and do what God has called you to do." Francis immediately headed back to San Damiano. When Pietro came back, the prisoner was gone. Then Francis' father wrote a complaint to the bishop, stating that his son was a thief, and the bishop ordered Francis to appear before his tribunal.

BEFORE THE BISHOP

This was the winter of 1206. Francis was twenty-four years old, and determined to stand up to his father and the lifestyle he represented. A crowd had gathered outside Bishop Guido's palace, eager to see what would happen to Pietro's son. The bishop cleared his throat and began, "Francesco di Bernardone, are these accusations against you true?"

"Yes, my lord," answered Francis.

"Then return your father's money. Otherwise you'll be punished as a thief."

"Gladly, my lord." Then Francis threw the money bag onto the ground. He stepped aside, undressed himself and stepped back into the square naked, holding his clothing in his hands. The crowd gasped. Francis looked at the bish-op and spoke firmly so everyone could hear, "Not only do I give back my father's money, I also return the clothes he gave me. From this day on, I no longer call Pietro di Bernardone my father. There is only One who is my Father—our Father who art in Heaven!"

No one said a word. Even the bishop was speechless. The strange, twisted expression on Pietro's face revealed the anguish in his heart. The bishop finally stood up, walked slowly over to Francis, opened his arms and covered Francis with his bishop's mantle. Francis bowed his head, then turned around and walked away through the dumbfounded crowd. Some burst into tears, others mumbled a prayer for the brave young man who had renounced his inheritance forever. The bishop's gardener ran up to him and handed him an old shirt. Francis took it, drew a cross on its back before he put it on and walked out of sight. Francis was free at last, a different kind of knight, having fought to serve his heavenly Father.

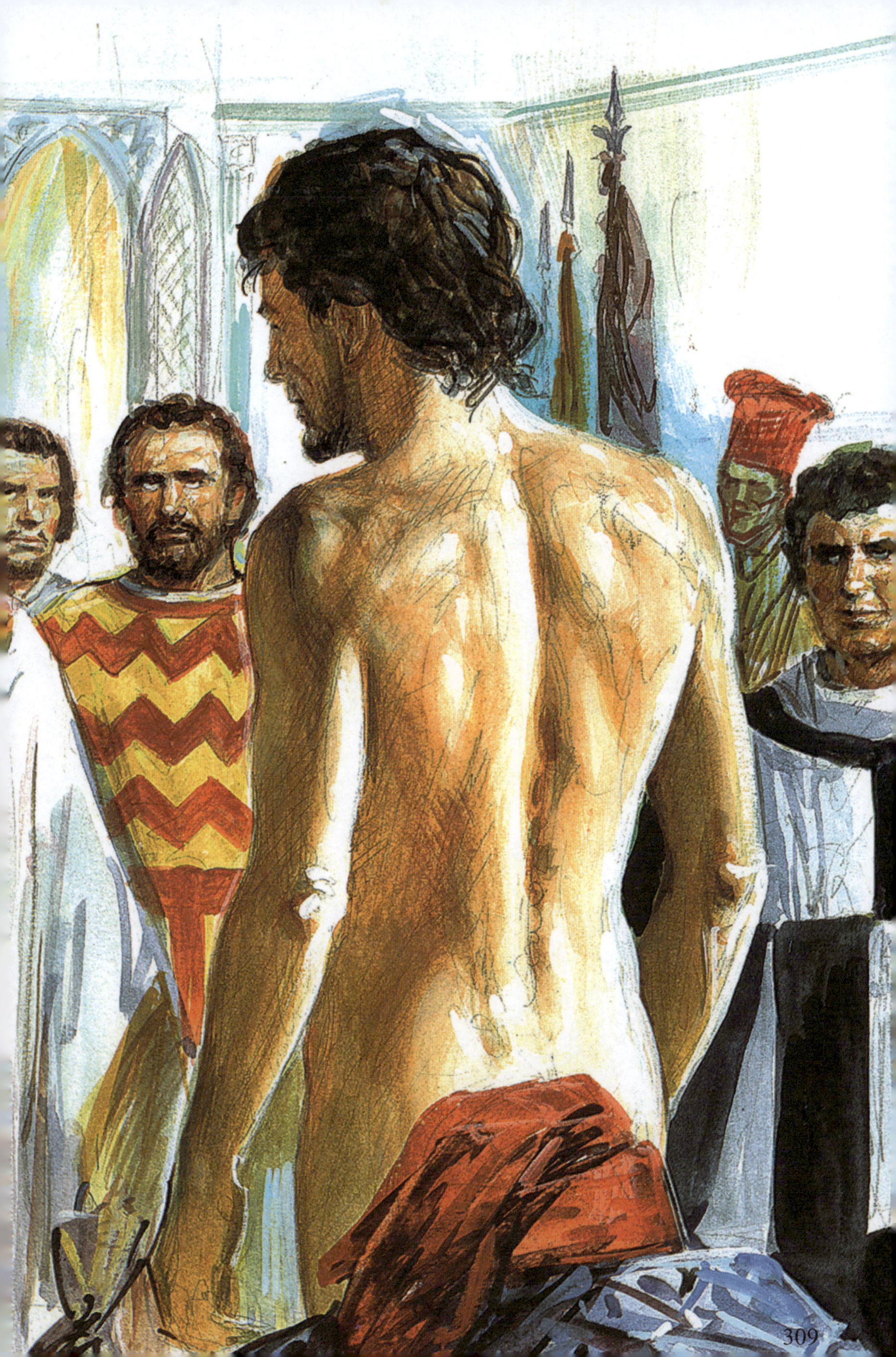

GOD'S HAPPY TROUBADOUR

Francis wanted to stop somewhere first before he returned to San Damiano. He was so filled with joy that he wanted to sing his heart out, and even though snow lay on the ground, he felt no cold. He sang and danced as he walked down the trail.

Suddenly he heard a noise in the thicket. A band of robbers stepped forward, blocking his way. They were surprised to see how poor Francis looked.

"Who are you? And why are you singing?" they demanded.

"I am the herald of a great King," smiled Francis.

The robbers beat Francis and left him bleeding in the snow. But Francis stood up, blessed his tormentors and walked all the way to Gubbio singing. There, the monks gave him a hermit's

outfit — a cloak, a belt, sandals and a staff. Francis spent his next days in a leper colony outside Gubbio, serving the lepers and taking care of their needs.

When he returned to San Damiano, the priest told him he would accept his offer of restoring the demolished church building.

Francis ran all the way to Assisi, eager to beg stones for the task. And this time people did not make fun of him. Some even helped haul the stones to the church.

One day, as Francis was rebuilding a wall, his brother Angelo came by with a friend.

"Look at poor Francis," teased Angelo. "Let's ask him if he wants to sell us his sweat."

But Francis just smiled and said, "I won't sell you my sweat. I serve a Lord who pays much better than you do."

TO LIVE LIKE JESUS

Over the next couple of years, Francis restored three ruined churches and cared for many lepers, washing their sores and attending to their needs. Everything he did, he did out of love for Jesus, filled with trust in the calling God had given him.

One of the churches he restored was the little chapel of Portiuncula. At a morning Mass there on February 24th, 1208, the priest read this text to Francis from the Gospel of Matthew: As you go, preach this message: "The kingdom of heaven is near"... Do not take along any gold or silver or copper in your belts; take no bag for the journey, or extra tunic, or sandals or a staff; for the worker is worth his keep. Whatever town or village you enter, search for some worthy person there and stay at his

house until you leave. As you enter the home, give it your greeting.

"Father, please explain this tome," begged Francis. The priest did so, and suddenly Francis realized what God wanted him to do: to live like Jesus and preach the Gospel. Suddenly he understood that God was not just calling him to rebuild churches, but to restore the Church of God, God's people. Immediately he threw away his hermit's staff, took off his shoes and his leather belt and replaced it with a simple rope. Then he went out to visit people and greet them with God's peace.

Restoring The Church

At Francis' time, the Roman Catholic Church was in decay. The clergy were busy managing worldly affairs, and had neglected their priestly duties and compromised their religious and moral beliefs. Many clergy were living openly sinful lives. Pope Innocent III had been forced to issue many papal bulls against the most scandalous excesses such as usury, venality, gluttony, luxurious living and other forms of moral misconduct,

Practiced even among the high-ranking servants of the Church.

Prophets, lay preachers and spiritual reformers within the Church had spoken out against these abuses. St. Elizabeth of Schonau said, "The world has become darkness! The Lord's vineyard has perished. The Head of the Church is sick and his members are dead!"

St. Hildegard of Bingen prophesied, "God's justice is about to strike. The empire and the papacy have fallen and shall go down together. But from their ruins, the Holy Spirit will cause a new people to rise."

Some prophets and preachers were branded as heretics by the Church because their ideas ran contrary to Church teaching. Yet many of these heretic reformers were moving through Europe, gathering support in city after city.

Francis knew about the Church excesses, yet he never was shaken in his loyalty to the Church and its representatives. Whenever he had a new idea, he first sought counsel and approval from the Church, honoring its authority. And because of his humble and charming appearance, he did not need to criticize the Church, attack its servants or invent any new teaching that might eventually be considered herecy. Instead, he simply presented to his listeners the teachings of Jesus in a new and fresh way through the example of his own life. This is what won him followers for his Gospel of penance and peace.

After Francis' death, Brother Elias built a magnificent basilica in Assisi to honor his beloved friend. Ironically, Elias did not realize how contrary this was to Francis' ideas.

BROTHER BERNARD

One night Francis was staying in the home of a wealthy merchant named Bernard of Quintavalle. Bernard wanted to hear what Francis had to say, and after a long night's talk they both went to bed. But as soon as Francis thought Bernard was asleep, he left his bed, knelt down and began to softly cry out to God. Bernard, pretending to be asleep, watched Francis and listened to his fervent prayers.

The next morning Bernard said, "Francis, I want to follow you in the footsteps of Jesus."

"But you're a rich man, Bernard," objected Francis.

"I still want to follow Jesus," said Bernard firmly.

"Then we'll have to find out what God wants of you," concluded Francis. They went to a church right away and opened the Bible three times. The first time they read: "If you want to be perfect, go, sell your possessions and give to the poor, and you will have treasure in heaven. Then come, follow Me."

The second time they read: "Take nothing for your journey, neither staff nor knapsack, shoes nor money."

The third time they read: "If anyone would come after Me, he must deny himself and take up his cross and follow Me."

"That will be our life and rule," said Francis to Bernard. "If anyone wants to join us, they must follow this rule." Then Bernard went home, sold all he had and gave away the silver and gold coins to the poor people in the streets.

"Come and take as much as you want," he called to them. "I need to be rid of this money." As he and Francis gave all of it away, they had so much fun doing it, they both laughed and sang until everything was gone.

FRANCIS' "KNIGHTS"

Soon a man named Pietro asked to join them; then another named Giles. Then came Barbaro, Morico, Philip, Sabbatino, Giovanni and others. Within a few months they were twelve. Francis began to recognize his old dream of a palace banqueting hall and the armor of knights.

He found comfort in Giles' cheerfulness and simple faith,especially when the group grew and there began to be complaints and arguments. He had first met Brother Giles in the woods around Portiuncula. Giles had come running up to him and thrown himself at Francis' feet.

"Please receive me as your disciple," begged Giles.

"Brother," smiled Francis as he raised him to his feet, "you have

received a great honor today. Think if an emperor had come and chosen you as his knight — then you would have felt proud. How much more honored you must feel that the King of kings has chosen you to His court. Welcome among our little band of poor Brothers!"

Then Francis, Bernard, Pietro and Giles had shared a meal together, rejoicing in their newfound,brotherly love. Afterwards, Francis and Giles had walked to Assisi to find a proper outfit for Giles. On their way they met a beggar woman.

"Why don't you give her your beautiful cloak, Brother Giles?" suggested Francis.

Giles gave her his cloak, and he did so joyfully. And when Francis dressed him in the coarse tunic they all wore, his joy only deepened.

THE POPE AND THE BEGGAR

As the group of Brothers grew, they met with growing suspicion from both civil and Church authorities. In the past, there had already been too many religious fanatics identifying with the poor who had stirred up trouble with their revolutionary ideas. In order to make clear what his group stood for, Francis decided to write down a more detailed rule of life for the Brotherhood. He also decided to go to Rome and appeal for the pope's blessing and protection. He would bring his Brothers with him. They arrived in Rome in the spring of 1209.

At first, Pope Innocent III did not give Francis a warm welcome. But Bishop Guido of Assisi who was in Rome at the time, and his friend, Cardinal Giovanni, both persuaded the pope to grant Francis and his humble Brothers another audience.

"What do you want from us?" the pope asked from his throne.

"Holy father," answered Francis, "we want you to approve our rule and consider us the lowest servants of the Catholic Church."

When the pope heard the details of Francis' rule, he objected. "It may be possible for you to live according to such a strict program of poverty. But those who come after you will hardly be able to follow your example."

"Do you mean to say, Holy father, that the Gospel of Jesus cannot be practiced?" asked Francis. "Isn't this the same as saying that Jesus was a liar?"

Francis' sincerity touched the pope. "My son, go pray to God for us so we can give you an answer," he said.

That night, Pope Innocent had a dream which radiated the power of a vision. In his dream he saw his Church leaning to one side, ready to topple over. Then a little poor beggar, which he recognized as Francis, walked up to the tumbling wall and pushed it back into place. Pope Innocent woke up convinced that God had spoken to him. At the final audience he approved Francis' rule, the Order of the Lesser Brothers of Jesus. He even stepped down from his throne to embrace Francis

"Go in peace, little Brother," he said with tears in his eyes, "and preach the Gospel as God reveals it to you. And if your order grows, come back to me, and I shall give you an even greater inheritance."

In the pope's embrace Francis felt the promise of something much greater than what he had once renounced when he left his earthly father Pietro. From that day on, Francis considered the pope his father on earth, and he always thought of Pope Innocent as a member of his order.

The Rule of the Lesser Brothers of Jesus

The rule Francis had presented to Pope Innocent III was based on a series of Gospel texts. The second rule (revised in 1223) states: Let those who wish to join us sell all their goods and strive to distribute them to the poor. If they should not be able to do this, their good will suffices. And the brothers . . . must take care not to be solicitous about their temporal affairs, that they may freely do with their affairs whatsoever the Lord may inspire them. . . . I indeed counsel, warn, and exhort my brothers in the Lord Jesus Christ that when they go through the world they be not litigious nor contend in words, nor judge others; but that they be gentle, peaceful, and modest, meek and humble, speaking honestly all that is fitting.... The brothers shall appropriate nothing to themselves, neither a house nor place nor anything. And as pilgrims and strangers in this world, serving the Lord in poverty and humility, let them go confidently in quest of alms, nor ought they to be ashamed, because the Lord made Himself poor for us in this world.

SISTER CLARE

Later that year, more members joined to the Brotherhood, so Francis began to look for more suitable quarters. Finally, an abbot gave him the little church called Portiuncula, which he himself had restored two years earlier. But Francis refused to own anything, so he arranged to rent the church instead.

One day in 1212, three years after Pope Innocent had approved the Order of the Lesser Brothers, a woman named Clare came to Portiuncula with her cousin. Clare was seventeen years old, a beautiful young woman of nobility. Even as a child she had loved the poor and gone out of her way to minister to their needs. Now she wanted to live like the poor Brothers.

On Palm Sunday, 1212, Clare and her cousin presented themselves as brides of Christ at the altar at Portiuncula and promised to follow the same rules as the Brothers. Francis then cut off their beautiful long hair and gave them coarse beggar habits and nuns' veils. Two weeks later, Clare's younger sister Agnes followed her example. The women moved into a nearby convent until, four months later, Bishop Guido gave them San Damiano as a place to

stay. It was here that the Order of Poor Sisters, or Poor Clares, was born. Clare's other sister Beatrice, her mother Ortolana and two more cousins also joined the Sisters.

Sister Clare and Brother Francis loved and respected each other deeply. Clare saw in Francis a spiritual father she could look up to, and Francis admired Clare for her purity and firm resolve in becoming a poor bride of Christ. Sometimes he wondered if Clare might be the princess of his old dream about the banqueting hall. Francis, who was now ordained as a deacon with permission to preach, would often walk over to San Damiano to instruct the Poor Clares. The contents of only one of these sermons has been passed down through the years. It is a sermon without words which Francis gave a few years before his death. Without saying a word Francis knelt on the floor at the altar where Jesus had spoken to him many years earlier. He lifted his hands toward heaven and silently prayed. Then he put ashes on his head and sprinkled some in a circle around him before he rose and walked back to Portiuncula. Francis had wanted to show the Sisters that it is a repentant heart that counts before God, not eloquent words.

A HAPPY MEAL

Francis was concerned that the Brothers and Sisters remain apart unless there was good reason to be together. So he decided that he too, should minimize his contact with the Sisters at San Damiano and leave their spiritual instruction to others.

One day the Brothers came to Francis and said, "Sister Clare has been asking for some time that you join her for a meal. Why don't you go? After all, she is your spiritual daughter and the abbess of the Poor Sisters."

"Do you think I should go?" asked Francis.

"Certainly," answered the Brothers.

"Well," continued Francis, "if it seems good to you, it seems good to me, too. We will prepare a meal for Sister Clare here."

When Clare arrived, Francis had made a meal and set the places on the ground, his favorite place to eat. The Brothers joined the two of them. They were just about to start eating when Francis began speaking softly about Jesus. He did so in such a moving way that they all forgot about the meal and started praising God instead. They lost all track of time and became quite lost in worship

Suddenly, there was a crowd from Assisi shouting at the door, "We saw flames in the forest. We thought there was a fire. What is happening?"

The men were shown into the room where Francis and his guests were still holding hands, praising God. Then they realized that the fire they had seen was the fire of divine love among the Brothers and Sisters. The crowd left, also praising God. Francis, Clare and the others hardly touched their food that evening. They were so full of the love of God.

Many stories are told about Sister Clare's devotion to God. The Legend, a collection of stories written by three of the Brothers shortly after Francis' death, tells about a miracle that happened in September, 1240.

Frederick II was the Holy Roman emperor and king of Sicily. His gruesome army invaded central Italy, "burning cities, cutting down trees, laying waste to vineyards,and torturing women and children." Even nuns were not safe from the raping and killing. When the soldiers arrived at San Damiano, they began to scale the walls and knock down the gate. But Sister Clare walked out, straight at them, praying, "Lord Jesus, do not permit these defenseless virgins to fall into the hands of heathen men. Protect them now, for I can do nothing for them. And protect the city of Assisi as well."

What happened next was like watch-

ing events in reverse. The soldiers stopped in their tracks as if hit by an invisible power. Then with horrified faces, they retreated back over the walls they had just scaled. God had saved the Sisters as well as the inhabitants of Assisi.

Another miracle occurred after Francis' death. Many cardinals, bishops and popes often came to San Damiano to ask Sister Clare's advice. The Fioretti (Little Flowers), another collection of stories written by the Brothers, tells how Pope Gregory IX sat down to eat with the Poor Sisters.

"Holy father," asked Clare,

"would you be so kind as to ask the Blessing?"

"You ask the Blessing," replied the pope.

Then Clare blessed the food and made the sign of the cross over the loaves. Suddenly there appeared a cross on each loaf. The pope knew he had witnessed a sign from God.

A SERMON FOR THE BIRDS

Years went by. Francis' eyes were getting weaker and his health was failing. Yet he refused to slow down and always remained alert and attentive to the world around him. He traveled to many places where people wanted to hear him. He had even been to Egypt to preach before the Muslim sultan. One of Francis' most famous sermons, however, is the sermon he preached to birds.

The Fioretti tells about a preaching tour when Francis and his two companions came across a field with a beautiful tree full of migrating birds. Francis stopped and watched the strange birds for a while. Then he said to Brother Masseo, "Wait here on the road. I will preach to our sisters, the birds."

The idea of preaching to animals may seem strange, but it wasn't to Francis. Since that night so many years earlier when he had looked up at the night sky and seen God's presence in all of creation, he had felt a special kinship to nature. To him, everything had some of God's love in it, and those who spoke in love were able to communicate with things around them. So Francis greeted everyone and everything he saw as his brother and sister in God.

Francis quietly walked into the field and over to the birds. As he began to speak, the birds gathered around him to listen.

"Sister birds," he said, "you owe God much praise, for He has created you and given you wings and songs of praise. He has given' you feathers to warm you and food to sustain you. He has given you fountains to drink from and mountains in which to take refuge. He has given you trees to nest in and air to fly in freely. He must love you very much, so never forget to sing His praises."

As Francis finished speaking, the birds began to open their beaks and spread their wings. Then he blessed them with the sign of the cross and dismissed them. And the birds flew off, singing praises to God.

BROTHER WOLF

By 1220, several thousand people had joined the Lesser Brothers and Poor Sisters. New convents wereestablished and many missionary teams sent out all over Italy and Europe, even into northern Africa. Even though Francis was not even fifty yet, his poor health restricted him to staying in the valley around Assisi.

According to the Fioretti, one day as Francis was preaching in Gubbio, a town northeast of Perugia, he heard about a ferocious wolf in the area. The wolf had even killed several men and women, and no one dared leave the city, they were so terrified it would attack them.

"I will go talk to the wolf," said Francis. The citizens of Gubbio climbed onto the tops of their houses and ramparts to watch how Francis would do such a thing.

When the wolf ran towards Francis, foaming at the mouth, Francis stopped, made the sign of the cross and said, "Wait a minute, brother wolf. In Christ's name I forbid you to harm me or anybody else." The wolf stopped, lowered its head and began to listen. Francis continued, "Brother wolf, not only are you killing animals, you have also killed men and women made in the image of God. You deserve a cruel death, and this is why these people are angry at you. But I want you to make peace with them and promise that you will no longer harm them."

The wolf lay down at Francis' feet to show he would obey. Francis continued, "Brother wolf, if you promise this, I can promise you that no one will hurt you and that you'll never go hungry again. The people of Gubbio will feed you every day until you die. Now give me your paw to show you'll agree to my terms." The wolf lifted his right paw and put it gently into Francis' hand. Then they both got up and walked into Gubbio side by side. In the town square Francis preached a wonderful sermon while the wolf lay at his feet. From that day on, the wolf harmed no one, and the people of Gubbio made sure he never starved again.

THE MANGER IN GRECCIO

Christmas was Francis favorite feast. He loved to celebrate how God came to earth as a baby — how He had put Himself into the hands of men and trusted in their welcome. The Christmas story always brought tears to Francis' eyes and joy to his heart.

In December, 1223, when Francis was visiting Pope Honorius III in Rome, he wondered how he and the Brothers could celebrate Christmas in a special way that year."

I would like to arrange a Christmas Mass and recreate the nativity scene, with a manger and real animals," he said to the pope. "Would that be all right with the Church?"

"Yes Francis, do as you wish," answered the pope. "You have our blessing."

So Francis asked a friend in Greccio to arrange a nativity scene in a grotto on the mountainside. His friend built a

A Prayer by Francis

Lord, make me an instrument of thy peace. Where there is hatred, let me sow love; where there is injury, pardon; where there is doubt, faith; where there is despair, hope; where there is sadness, joy; where there is darkness, light.

O Divine Master, grant that I may not so much seek to be consoled, as to console; not so much to be understood, as to understand; not so much to be loved, as to love. For it is in giving that we receive, it is in pardoning that we are pardoned, it is in dying that we are born again to eternal life.

manger and brought straw, an ox and a donkey and invited the people of Greccio to celebrate Christmas with Francis and his Brothers.

On Christmas Eve, shortly before midnight, people from all over the area lit torches and walked up the mountain trails toward the grotto. It looked like streams of light surging through the woods toward that spot where God had become one with men. As the people gathered around the grotto, the placed azzled with light. A priest came to say the Mass, using the manger for an altar, and Francis preached a joyous sermon about God's love. Afterwards, several people claimed to have seen the real Baby Jesus in Francis' arms. The child had smiled at Francis and stroked his beard.

When the ceremony was over, people went home singing and praising God through the woods. Since that memorable night at Greccio, the nativity scene has become a way of celebrating Christmas all over the world.

MUSIO

THE WOUNDS OF JESUS

Francis was now over forty, and knew he soon would die. He was already almost blind, and his long fasts and many cold nights spent on the bare ground had exhausted his weak body. After the joyous Christmas celebration at Greccio he spent the winter alone, preparing himself for what he called his sister Death.

On Easter Day, 1224, the Brothers at Portiuncula had put together a feast in honor of their spiritual father. The table was covered with a tablecloth and set with fine dishes and glasses. The Brothers were waiting anxiously for Francis.

Suddenly they heard a knock on the door. Outside in the darkness stood a beggar, wearing an old hat. "For the love of God," pleaded the beggar as he held out a bowl, "please give an alm to a sick pilgrim!" The Brothers handed him a piece of bread. Then they realized it was Francis.

"Brother," they exclaimed, "we have prepared a feast for you. Please come sit at the head of the table."

But Francis sat down on the ground in front of the fire. "Your table is too fancy for a poor beggar like me," he said. "I prefer to sit on the ground like a real Lesser Brother." Then he quietly ate the bread they had given him.

On September 14th, 1224, something remarkable happened to Francis. He had been spending some weeks in prayer on the mountain of La Verna. One morning at dawn he was pleading, "Lord, I ask You to grant me two wishes before I die: Let me experience the pain You experienced for me on the cross, and let me feel the love You felt when You died for me."

All of a sudden there was a dazzling light. The sky opened, and Francis saw the figure of Christ nailed to the cross. Light beams shot from the crucified Christ and pierced Francis' hands, feet and right side. Francis felt the pain tear through his body as blood streamed from his side. Then a love he had never experienced before overwhelmed him.

"From that moment," says St. Bonaventure, an Italian writer born a few years before Francis' death, "Francis was marked with the wounds of the Divine Redeemer. His hands and feet appeared as though pierced with nails, with round black heads on the palm of the hands and on the feet, and with bent points extruding from the back of the hands and the soles of the feet. In addition, there was a wound in the right side, as if made by a lance, from which blood frequently flowed, moistering his drawers and tunic."

Many others also testified to the stigmata of Francis, among them Pope Alexander IV who later claimed to have seen the wounds with his own eyes.

SISTER DEATH

Francis' health worsened, and in the summer of 1226 he was moved to Assisi. A doctor came to see him. When Francis asked him about his condition, the doctor assured him all would be well.

"Doctor," said Francis, "tell me the truth. Whether I live or die makes no difference to me."

"In that case," replied the doctor, "I think you will die at the end of September or the beginning of October."

"Welcome Sister Death!" exclaimed the invalid, raising his arms in the air. Then he turned to the Brothers around his bed. "Sing the 'Canticle of Brother Sun,— he asked. Then they all sang this song which Francis himself had written. Francis felt much better, and he persuaded the Brothers to carry him back to Portiuncula where he wanted to die. "My work is done," he said. "May Christ teach you to do yours."

A few days later, on October 3rd, 1226, Francis asked the Brothers to lay him on a coarse cloth on the ground, what he called his beloved Mother Earth. At twilight Francis felt the cold draft of death creep through the door. "Sister Death, I welcome you," he whispered, "for it is you who are going to introduce me to eternal life."

Then he asked the Brothers to sprinkle dust and ashes on his body and sing Psalm 141. Francis' lips moved the same as the Brothers' as they sang. When they had finished, though, there was silence. Francis was no longer with them.

Their spiritual father had died in the midst of a hymn.

A Poem by Francis

A year before his death, while Francis was staying with Clare and the Sisters at San Damiano, he wrote "The Canticle of Brother Sun," a technically complex work of music, and one of the first poems ever written in Italian. Francis wrote most of the stanzas after a night when he had experienced extreme physical pain and spiritual attacks from the devil. The canticle radiates a deep love for God and reverence for what Francis called his Brother Sun, Sister Moon, Brother Wind, Sister Water, Brother Fire and Sister Mother Earth. This is the closing stanza, which Francis added on his deathbed:

Praised be You, my Lord, through our Sister Bodily Death,
from whom no living man can escape.
Woe to those who die in mortal sin.
Blessed are those whom death will find in Your most holy will,
for the second death shall do them no harm.
Praise and bless my Lord and give Him thanks
and serve Him with great humility.

Main Events in Francis' Life

1820 Born in Assisi.
1190 Attends parish school at San Giorgio.
1194 Clare is born in Assisi.
1202 Captured in the battle between Assisi and Perugia.
1203 Ransomed from prison. Becomes sick.
1204 Joins Pope Innocent III's army. Returns to Assisi.
1205 Hears the crucifix speak at San Damiano.
1206 Comes before the Bishop of Assisi.
1209 Pope Innocent III approves of the Order of the Lesser Brothers of Jesus. The Brothers settle at Portiuncula.
1212 Clare founds the Poor Sisters. Settles at San Damiano.
1217 The Brothers number five thousand. Mission teams sent out.
1219 Sails to the Holy Land and Egypt.
1223 Christmas at Greccio.
1224 The stigmata at La Verna.
1226 Dies at Portiuncula, October 3. Buried at San Giorgio.
1228 Proclaimed a saint.
1230 Body transferred to the
1223 Basilica of Saint Francis in Assisi.
1253 Clare dies at San Giorgio, August 11. Buried the same place.
1818 Francis' body rediscovered after 600 years.
1928 Pope Pius XII proclaims Francis Patron of Italy.
1980 Pope John Paul II proclaims Francis Patron of Ecology.

BOOK RESOURCES

St. Francis of Assisi, by Omer Englebert (Servant Books, 1979).
Francis: The Journey and the Dream, by Murray Bodo (Saint Anthony Messenger Press, 1972).
The Little Flowers of St. Francis, translated from the Italian by Blaiklock and Keys
(Servant Books, 1985).
Christian History, Issue 42, 1995: Francis of Assisi.
St. Francis of Assisi, by John Moorman (SPCK, 1963).

Dietrich Bonhoeffer

THE PASTOR WHO FOLLOWED CHRIST TO THE CROSS

1906 —1945

Great men and women are not in need of our praise.
We are the ones in need of getting to know them.

By Ben Alex

Illustrations by Music Cosimo

THE GALLOWS OF FLOSSENBURG

It was early on Monday morning, April 9th, 1945. The sun had barely risen above the small town of Flossenburg, Germany. Outside town, behind the barbed wire of one of Hitler's most notorious concentration camps, walked several men in single file. S.S. Black Guards escorted the prisoners with machine guns.

The men mounted the gallows scaffold and an officer read their death sentence out loud to them. Then he ordered them to take off their striped prison clothing and step up to the nooses that closed tightly around their necks. One of them, 39 years old, gestured to the guard to wait. Then he knelt on the platform under the gallows and prayed. The guards watched him with a mixture of embarrassment and annoyance. But the man did not notice.

"Father," he prayed, "I thank You for the cross where Jesus suffered rejection and shame for me. Now it is my turn to walk to my cross and follow Him to the end. I pray for strength to do so. And I

pray for those around me – Maria, my family, my friends, my fellow prisoners, and even for my executioners whose sins I bear."

Then he stood and put his head through the rope. An officer gave the order to the hangman, his voice cracked the air like a whip. The hangman obeyed, and within seconds dead bodies were dangling in the air.

The camp doctor stepped up to confirm that the bodies were dead. Then he turned to a guard, pointed at the man who had prayed and said, "I'm deeply moved by the way this man prayed, so devout and so certain that God heard his prayers."

The man he was talking about was Dietrich Bonhoeffer, one of the greatest martyrs among the twelve million people killed by the Nazis during Adolf Hitler's brutal Third Reich.

FASCINATED BY DEATH

From an early age Dietrich thought a great deal about death. In their childhood home at what was then called Breslau, he and his twin sister Sabine had often sat in the window watching the funeral processions with black-draped horses and white caskets arrive at the cemetery across the street. Later, after the family moved to Berlin in 1912, they would often talk about what it must feel like to be dead.

One night, after their mother had prayed with them and turned out the lights, Sabine whispered to Dietrich, "It must feel very dark and lonely."

"I'd like to try it," said her brother. "I'd lay on my deathbed with all my mourning friends around me, and then I'd tell them that it's not hard to die when you believe in God. God gives eternal life."

"Dietrich," she went on, "what does 'eternal' mean?"

"It means forever."

"That sounds long and gruesome to me."

"Not if God is there. Death is a glorious thing. I'd like to die young."

Sabine sighed. Dietrich folded his hands behind his head and stared at the shadows on the ceiling. After a while they both drifted off to sleep.

Dietrich's Family

Dietrich was born on february 4th, 1906, only minutes before Sabine. Their parents, Karl and Paula Bonhoeffer, had eight children: Walter, Karl-Friedrich, Klaus, Ursula, Christine, Dietrich, Sabine and Susanne. Karl Bonhoeffer was a well-known neurologist and professor and psychiatry, and his family was cultured and wealthy. He nourished an attitude of discipline and independence in his children, while his wife Paula, a daughter of a chaplain in the court of Kaiser William II, raised them in the tradition of the Lutheran faith. The Bonhoeffers took an early stand against Nazism by supporting the Jews. Several of the children were later married to Jews or involved in the German resistance.

The Bonhoeffer family at their vacation home in 1991 Dietrich is the blonde boy third from right.

AN IMPORTANT DECISION

When World War I broke out in 1914, death suddenly became less desirable to eight-year-old Dietrich. Two of his older brothers were drafted and sent to the front. When one of them died, along with several cousins. his mother became withdrawn and quiet.

Then came the postwar years with poverty and economic depression. Dietrich's father was a university professor and leading authority on psychiatry and neurology. During the years when the German currency was devalued and became worthless, he was able to collect some of his fees in much more valuable, foreign currency. Another source of help was Dietrich's uncle who lived in the country. He provided the family with vegetables and other foods that most people in the city were unable to get. Dietrich and his brothers and sisters did not suffer much. The older brothers had almost finished their studies and could look forward to promising careers as lawyers and scientists. Dietrich was wondering what he would do.

A War that put Germany to Shame

New York American

WAR WITH GERMANY

BAKER ASKS AN ARMY OF 1,200,000

THREE BILLION AND A HALF IN WAR BUDGET

FOUR GERMAN SHIPS TOWED TO CITY PIER

CARRANZA'S TROOPS MASS UPON BORDER

HOUSE BACKS UP WILSON, 373 TO 50

GERMANS TWIST WILSON SPEECH

NAVY TO TOTAL 187,000 MEN

NO BREAK WITH AUSTRIA NOW

World War I (1914–1918) cost the lives of almost 10 million troops. The war broke out as a private feud between Austria–Hungary and Serbia. But soon France, Great Britain and Russia (the Allies) joined Serbia against Austria–Hungary and Germany (the Central European powers). Later on, more nations took sides until finally, in 1917, the U.S. joined the Allies. In the autumn of 1918, the Central European powers were forced to "surrender unconditionally."

The postwar Weimar Republic of Germany, which overthrew the monarchy, had no choice but to accept the harsh terms of the Versailles

The New York American front page on April 7, 1917, the day after America entered World War I.

One day in Greek class the teacher turned to Dietrich and asked, "Dietrich, what are you going to study at university?"

"Theology, Sir," said the boy, surprising even himself. He almost felt embarrassed at what he had said. But as soon as the words were out, he knew they were right.

"Then you'll be in for some surprises," replied the teacher.

Dietrich's father did not like the idea of his son becoming a theologian. He thought Dietrich was destined for greater things than an obscure existence in a country parish. At least he could see to it that his son became a professor of theology.

Dietrich's older brothers teased him about his decision. "Come on, little brother," they laughed, "the church is a boring, outdated institution full of hypocrites."

"In that case, I'll change it!" retorted Dietrich.

peace treaty of 1919. The treaty, which held Germany responsible for the war, was mainly intended to crush Germany and make any recovery from the war impossible. The German people felt humiliated and unjustly treated. Even Bonhoeffer said in America in 1930, "I will tell you frankly, that this is the wound that is still open and bleeds in Germany. When the war broke out the German people did not consider very much the question of guilt. We thought it would be our duty to fight for our country. I personally see many faults in our policy before the war, and I'm not going to defend my country on every point. But other countries had committed the same or greater faults than Germany."

The peace settlement created in Germany the conditions which eventually gave rise to Adolf Hitler's National Socialism (Nazism) and a second world war.

PASTOR AND THEOLOGIAN

University life came naturally to a boy who had grown up in an academic family. After a year at the University of Tubingen and an excursion to Rome and north Africa, Dietrich began to pursue serious theological studies in Berlin. Three years later, at the young age of nineteen, he received his doctoral degree with highest distinction. Dietrich's father and his professors were relieved. A career at the university seemed secured.

But even though Dietrich had a theologian's mind, he also had a pastor's heart. His enthusiastic first sermon at the Stahnsdorfer Church in Berlin, which he delivered at the age of nineteen, reflected both his mind and heart. "Christianity," he preached, "means decision, change, denial, yes even hostility to the past, to the men of old. Christ smashes the men of the past into total ruin. He smites and cuts through with His sword to the innermost nerve.

And that is where the wound hurts the most, where the apparently most noble feelings meet with a satisfied morality."

Dietrich's father was impressed, for although the controversial sermon was a bit above his head, he realized that Dietrich was attacking the very core of conventional Christianity. Later on he admitted, "When you decided to devote yourself to theology, I sometimes thought to myself that a quiet, uneventful minister's life, as I knew it . . . would really almost be a pity for someone like you. Now, seeing the Church in a crisis that I never thought possible, I see what you have chosen is very right."

BARCELONA AND BACK

The following year (1928) Dietrich Bonhoeffer was offered a job as curate to a German-speaking church in Barcelona, Spain. The congregation consisted mostly of diplomats and businessmen out of touch with the restless events in their homeland. Theseproblems of the Weimar Republic climaxed in the Great Depression of 1928. The conservative attitude of his congregation became too much for the young minister. After a year he decided to return to Germany and write a theological thesis which would qualify him as a university lecturer.

Dietrich Bonhoeffer found Germany in the grips of a severe crisis. The exchange market had just crashed; people were dying from hunger in the cities; members of both Communist and Nationalist political groups roamed the

streets of the homeless. One such group called themselves the National Socialists.

During this turbulent time Dietrich Bonhoeffer published two works that laid the foundation for his theology: The Communion of Saints (his doctoral thesis) and Act and Being. The books were an academic attempt to bring the Church down from its spiritual ivory tower into the streets of society.

In 1930, at the age of twenty-four, he became a lecturer in Systematic Theology at Berlin University. With a career as university lecturer secured, Bonhoeffer decided to accept a scholarship from the famous Union Theological Seminary in New York. He was granted a leave of absence from his own university for one year in order to study in America.

Bonhoeffer's Friends in America

Franklin Fisher

After the summer of 1931, when Bonhoeffer returned to Germany, the two friends never saw each other again. Unfortunately, Fisher hasn't left any written account of their friendship. Bonhoeffer often spoke about his black friend. One evening, years later, at the Finkenwalde seminary, Bonhoeffer was playing Negro spiritual records for his students. He said, "When I took leave of my black friend, he said to me, 'Make our sufferings known in Germany. Tell them what is happening to us, and show them what we are like.' I wanted to fulfill this obligation tonight."

Jean Lasserre

Lasserre was a French foreign student at the Union seminary. He especially helped Bonhoeffer in developing a global vision for world peace. Also, many of the ideas in "The Cost of Discipleship", Bonhoeffer's best-known book, must have been inspired by discussions with Lasserre.

The two friends stayed in contact during the war and met briefly at a peace conferences in Fano, Denmark.

THE "GREAT LIBERATION"

His year in America was not an academic success. Bonhoeffer thought the theology was shallow, compared with that of Germany, which had struggled so deeply with the issues of Martin Luther's reformation. The rewards were of another sort. Bonhoeffer later referred to his American experience as a "great liberation."

From America Bonhoeffer was able to view the present political situation in his homeland through foreign eyes. He realized the serious threat posed by Hitler's National Socialists (Nazis) who, at the September elections, had increased their power by almost one hundred seats in the parliament. The Nazis had suddenly gone from being a minor party to becoming a national movement. Bonhoeffer also realized that many of his friends in Germany sympathized with the Nazis' arrogant and hateful patriotism. "The Nazis are not like the Russian Communists," they wrote him. "They support the churches. All they want is to restore order and a feeling of dignity in Germany." Through his discussions with American friends, Bonhoeffer saw this was a lie.

One such friend was Franklin Fisher, a fellow student at the seminary. Fisher was a black man, and through him Bonhoeffer learned firsthand about the struggle of black Americans. When Fisher took him to a black congregation in Harlem, Bonhoeffer really saw for the first time the view "from below," from the perspective of the poor and oppressed. At a restaurant where Fisher was refused service because he was black, Bonhoeffer got up and walked out to demonstrate his opinion of racism. The whole party left the restaurant with him. As they walked by a Baptist church for white people, the angry German said about the black churches, "They'll remain long after this temple of Baal has been destroyed."

Unfortunately, all Bonhoeffer's letters to Lasserre were burned. During World War II Lasserre worked for the French Resistance, and it was too dangerous for him to keep them.

Paul Lehmann
Lehmann, a Presbyterian working on his doctorate at Union, was Bonhoeffer's closest American friend. Through their conversations, Bonhoeffer began to understand the American concern about Nazism in Germany. Lehmann was probably the one friend who best understood the paradoxes existing in Bonhoeffer's mind. Lehmann later said this about his friend, "One did not notice the solitude which prepared him for fellowship, the discipline which sustained his abandon, the quiet piety which nourished the acumen of his lively mind."

Reinhold Niebuhr
Niebuhr, a professor at Union, is still considered one of America's greatest theologians. His many books have influenced the Church immensely. Both Niebuhr and Bonhoeffer benefited from each other's theological differences. They kept in touch and met briefly in England, where Niebuhr arranged Bonhoeffer's escape to America in June 1939. After only a month in the States, however, Bonhoeffer's conscience and love for his people forced him to return to Germany.

YOUTH SECRETARY AND YOUTH WORKER

Once back in Germany, in the autumn of 1931, Bonhoeffer was invited to a conference held by the World Alliance for International Friendship through the Churches. Here he was elected youth secretary for Germany and Central Europe. The international delegates took a strong stand for world peace against war. War as a means of settling international disputes, they claimed, is against the Spirit of Christ and the Church. The conference broadened the young theologian's contacts and views.

In Berlin, Bonhoeffer was ordained as a Lutheran minister, and the university lecturer threw himself into parish work. He especially enjoyed teaching a confirmation class in the slums of northern Berlin. "This is real work," he wrote a friend. "At the beginning the young men behaved like mad things, so

that for the first time I had real problems with discipline . . . . Now there is absolute quiet, the young men see to that themselves, so I need no longer fear the fate of my predecessor whom they quite literally worried to death!"

The reason for his success was that he told the simple Bible stories with great emphasis and related them to the personal experiences of the young people. He eventually rented a room in the slums to be near them, and he told his landlady to always let the boys in – even if he wasn't there. His trust and genuine concern touched and impressed the boys.

The World Council of Churches

At the Edinburgh Conference of 1910 churches throughout the world came together for the first time to try and overcome their differences. Their goal was to discuss their common mission in the world. The organizations and efforts initiated then are generally referred to as the Ecumenical (universal) Movement. The World Alliance for International Friendship through the Churches, which appointed Bonhoeffer as a member of the Youth Commission, became the forerunner of the World Council of Churches, founded in 1948 in Amsterdam.

The World Alliance's lack of reaction to what was happening in Germany was a big disappointment to Bonhoeffer. In 1937 he eventually resigned as youth secretary in protest of the World Alliance's failure to support the German Jews.

Today the World Council has a membership of about 300 Christian churches with a total of 400 million Christians from 100 countries. The World Council's programs include world missions, education, church renewal, refugee aid, racial justice and the promotion of world peace. It has its headquarters in Geneva, Switzerland.

LOOKING FOR JESUS IN 1933

Bonhoeffer continued to lecture at the university. Most of his students liked their young teacher, for he wasn't stuffy and aloof like his colleagues. They noticed he had changed while being in America. He went right to the heart of the questions he raised and tried to answer them using modern applications. "Every sentence went home," wrote one student later. "Here was a concern for what troubled me, and indeed all of us young people, what we asked and wanted to know."

When Bonhoeffer was asked what had happened to him, he simply replied, "I've become a Christian."

During the next couple of years the tone in Bonhoeffer's lectures changed. "The Church has gone adrift," he told his students. "All too often it has sought the comfort of the privileged, instead of suffering with the oppressed. The Church has to confess anew its faith in Jesus with courage and reject all secular idolatries!

"Who is Jesus in the world of 1933?" he thundered. "Where is He to be found today? In a Church that bows to idolatry? No. You'll find him in the prisoners, the persecuted Jews and the homeless people in our streets."

When he started saying such things, students began to boycott his classes. They knew what he was aiming at. Adolf Hitler had just been appointed prime minister by President Paul von Hindenburg, and the Nazis were speaking openly against the Jews. Germany's youth was fast becoming attracted to Hitler's ideas.

Meeting Karl Barth

In 1931, on his way back from America, Bonhoeffer had the opportunity to meet the famous Swiss theologian Karl Barth in Bonn. Barth became the most significant theological figure in Bonhoeffer's life, except for Martin Luther. Barth's attack on liberal theology and his revival of the great themes of the Reformation not only changed Bonhoeffer's life, but the life of the entire Evangelical Church as well.

Barth read Bonhoeffer's doctoral thesis and called it a "theological miracle." The two became friends, although they did not always agree (Bonhoeffer considered Barth too vague, and Barth considered young Bonhoeffer too rigid). Together they battled against the "German Christian" idea of the Nazis. When Bonhoeffer later left Germany for England, Barth critisized him for leaving at the very moment his country needed him most. But in London Bonhoeffer rallied pressure against the German Nazi Church, and he returned much better equipped for the battle ahead. Later Bonhoeffer blamed Barth for failing to carry his revival of Christian doctrines into everyday life.

Karl Barth

HITLER BECOMES PRIME MINISTER

By 1933, the National Socialists had become a strong political movement with over two hundred seats in Parliament. President von Hindenburg was forced to appoint their leader, Adolf Hitler, as prime minister.

Hitler thought he knew what Germany longed for – discipline and self-respect in a Europe which still despised the Germans for being responsible for World War I. Hitler promised a destiny and a glorious future as soon as the country was purged of foreign elements and the true Germans (Aryans) came to power. The young people of Germany were ecstastic. Here was a man completely different from the fickle democrats of the Weimar Republic – a man who would restore their glorious past that had been lost in the war.

Bonhoeffer, made alert by his faith in God and his broader perspective

from having been abroad, thought differently. Two days after Hitler came to power, in February 1933, Bonhoeffer was scheduled to broadcast a message about leadership principles. He used the opportunity to speak out against Hitler publically. First, he gave a theological background for leadership, then he spoke of how easily youth can be seduced by "old fools," who are then made into "idols." The danger for the leader ("fuhrer" in German!), he said, lay in the temptation to "give in to the wishes of those he leads, who will always seek to turn him into an idol. Such a leader soon believes himself to be infallible, making himself and his office an idol, thus mocking God . . . ."

Bonhoeffer never finished his message. The broadcast was interrupted and the sounds of military marching bands took its place.

GERMAN CHRISTIANS SUPPORT THE FUHRER

The German Church was easy prey to Hitler's ideas. During the Weimar Republic it had been "homeless" in the sense that it had been left to itself, having lost the government support it was used to. By 1933 its leaders had realized that it belonged neither to the state, nor to the people. They were afraid that the Church would not survive as a free Church. Bonhoeffer had addressed this concern in his early books.

Now Hitler was welcoming the Church back to the state. He promised a strong Church for the people – a Church that was to become the moral conscience of a new and pure Germany.

Many Church leaders were fascinated by the idea. Hermann Gruner,

spokesman for the so-called "German Christians," went as far as saying, "The time is fulfilled for the German people in Hitler. It is because of Hitler that Christ . . . has become effective among us. Therefore, National Socialism is positive Christianity in action."

Bonhoeffer could not allow such a statement to go unchallenged. Again he protested. Prior to the church elections in July 1933, he had preached, "Church, remain a Church! Confess, confess, confess!" But the German Christians had Ludwig Muller, a member of the Nazi party, elected national bishop. Many churches began to display Nazi flags with swastikas at their services.

"Whoever reviles this symbol is reviling our Germany," said one pro-Nazi minister.

"In the pitch-black night of Church history," claimed another, "Hitler became . . . the wonderful transparency for our time, the window of our age, through which light fell on the history of Christianity. Through him we were able to see the Savior in the history of the Germans."

"Christ has come to us through Adolf Hitler," triumphed a third.

The Church leaders were too excited to read the writing on the wall. Had they read carefully this haunting passage from a school textbook in 1934, they might have listened to Bonhoeffer and other Church leaders' warnings later on:

"As Jesus set men free from sin and hell, so Hitler rescued the German people from destruction. Both Jesus and Hitler were persecuted; but, while Jesus was crucified, Hitler was exalted to Chancellor. While the disciples of Jesus betrayed their master and left him in distress, the sixteen friends of Hitler stood by him. The apostles completed the work of their Lord. We hope that Hitler will lead his work to completion. Jesus built for heaven, but Hitler built for the German soil."

THE "CONFESSING CHURCH"

During the scandalous Church elections in the summer of 1933, there emerged an underground movement of Christians opposed to the German Nazi Church. Martin Niemoller and Bonhoeffer became the leaders of this reform movement. In April 1934, while Bonhoeffer was in London, Niemoller gathered five thousand pastors and lay people in Ulm. This was the basis of the "Confessing Church." Bonhoeffer wanted a free Church that once and for all had broken its ties with the state. However, a more moderate majority voted to remain within the German Evangelical Church, even though it was dominated by German Nazi Church

"To walk out will only split the church in two," warned Niemoller.

"In that case," replied Bonhoeffer, "we'll walk them out."

"What do you mean?"

"I mean, they're not the true Church in Germany, right? The Confessing Church is the true Church, right? We'll simply excommunicate them from the German Evangelical Church – pastors, bishops, Muller and all!"

The following month the Confessing Church held its first national meeting at Wuppertal–Barmen, where they signed a new confession, the Barmen Declaration. Its purpose was to show that the ideas of the German Nazi Church were against the doctrines of the Christian faith. One paragraph in this long document reads, "We reject the false teaching that there are areas in our life in which we belong not to Jesus Christ but another lord [meaning Hitler], areas in which we do not need justification and sanctification through Him."

This clause did not disturb the Nazi Christians at all. Two months later, when President von Hindenburg died and Hitler became both prime minister and president, Reich Bishop Muller proposed that all pastors swear an oath of obedience to the Fuhrer.

During this time Bonhoeffer was living temporarily in England. He had longed to do parish work, and since he no longer was able to be a pastor in Germany (for that he had to be approved by the German Nazi Church), he decided to pastor two German-speaking churches in London. During his sixteen months there, he was able to expand his international contacts and gather support against the German Nazi Church. He did not want the outside world to accept the Nazi church as the true representative of Christianity in Germany. His friend, Bishop George Bell of Chichester, wrote a letter to ecumenical leaders in several western nations, urging them to take measures against the German Nazi Church.

Martin Niemoller

As Karl Barth was the theologian of the Confessing Church, so Niemoller was its strategist. In 1933 he founded the Pastors' Emergency League with a membership of 6,000 pastors. The league became the core of the Confessing Church.

On July 1, 1937, Niemoller was arrested by the Gestapo. Edwin Robertson, one of Bonhoeffer's biographers, tells the story: "It was the first day of the school holidays. Niemoller's two oldest boys had already left on their bicycles; Mrs. Niemoller had just returned from seeing off the girls on an early train for the Baltic; Niemoller himself, after a late night at a church conference, was not yet dressed, but playing with his youngest son, Martin. The Gestapo arrived at 8:30 a.m. and asked him to come for interrogation. He dressed and went, thinking he would return a little later. These interrogations had happened before. But this time he waited for hours. There was no interrogation. He was put in prison, without charge, for the next eight years."

At the end of the war Niemoller was released from the Dachau concentration camp and appointed president of the World Council of Churches. These words by him have become famous: "First, they came for the socialists, and I did not speak out because I was not a socialist. Then they came for the trade unionists, and I did not speak out because I was not a trade unionist. Then they came for the Jews, and I did not speak out because I was not a Jew. Then they came for me, and there was no one left to speak for me."

Niemoller did speak out, however. He has become a symbol of the Confessing Church – and a role model for persecuted Christians everywhere.

SPEAKING OF PEACE

The conflict between the German Nazi Church and the Confessing Church finally came to a head at the end of the summer of 1934, when the World Alliance of Churches held a conference in Fano, Denmark. Since the Alliance had not been notified that there were now two churches within the German Evangelical Church, they invited the official church (the German Nazi Church) to send a delegation. Bonhoeffer was invited as speaker. Through his influence the conference approved a resolution against the German Nazi Church. However, Bonhoeffer's lasting contribution to the conference was an unforgettable morning sermon on world peace that left the delegates breathless with excitement.

"Peace must be dared! It's the great

venture!" preached Bonhoeffer. "The churches of the world must speak out so that the world, though it gnash its teeth, will have to hear, so that the peoples will rejoice because the Church of Christ in the name of Christ has taken the weapons from the hands of their sons, forbidden war, and proclaimed the peace of Christ against the raging world.

"The hour is late. The world is choked with weapons, and dreadful is

the distrust which looks out of all men's eyes. The trumpets of war may blow tomorrow. For what are we waiting? Do we want to become involved in this guilt as never before? Who knows if we shall see each other again another year?"

Bonhoeffer had planned to visit the great Indian pacifist Mahatma Gandhi the following spring. He wanted to study Gandhi's ideas on nonviolence, and learn about quiet community life. But the hour was late. Nazism marched forward. There was no time for a three-month trip to India. Instead Bonhoeffer stayed in England to study Anglican communities. The idea of similar community-based seminaries for aspiring pastors of the Confessing Church began to take form in Bonhoeffer's mind.

"The Cost of Discipleship"

While Bonhoeffer was teaching at Finkenwalde, he wrote two important books, "Life Together" and "The Cost of Discipleship." The latter has become Bonhoeffer's most famous book. Here are some quotes:

"When Christ calls a man, he bids him come and die. It may be a death like that of the first disciples who had to leave home and work to follow him, or it may be a death like Luther's, who had to leave the monastery and go out into the world. But it is the same death every time – death in Jesus Christ, the death of the old man at his call."

"Cheap grace is the deadly enemy of our church. We are fighting today for costly grace . . . . Cheap grace is grace without discipleship, grace without the cross, grace without Jesus Christ. Costly grace. . .is costly because it calls us to follow, and it is grace because it calls us to follow Jesus Christ. It is costly because it costs a man his life, and it is grace because it gives a man the only true life. It is costly because it condemns sin, and grace because it justifies the sinner."

"We Lutherans have gathered like ravens round the carcass of cheap grace, and there we have drunk of the poison which has killed the life of following Christ. It is true, of course, that we have paid the doctrine of pure grace divine honors unparalleled in Christendom; in fact, we have exalted that doctrine to the position of God Himself."

"The Law of Christ, which it is our duty to fulfill, is the bearing of the cross. My brother's burden which I must bear is not only his outward lot . . . but quite literally his sin. And the only way to bear that sin is by forgiving it in the power of the cross of Christ in which I now share. Thus the call to follow Christ always means a call to share the work of forgiving men their sins. Forgiveness is the Christ-like suffering which it is the Christian's duty to bear."

TRAINING DISCIPLES

In the early summer of 1935, after Bonhoeffer had returned to Germany, the Confessing Church opened its first Church Training College at Finkenwalde in northern Germany. Bonhoeffer became its director. Most of his twenty-five students already had studied at universities. Now they were being prepared for active pastoral ministry.

Bonhoeffer was more interested in equipping these young men for the spir-

itual battles ahead, than giving them theoretical knowledge. From the beginning he inspired them to prayer, discipline, and brotherly love. Instead of studying the Bible, he taught them to listen to God's Word. Instead of giving them answers, he helped them raise important questions. Instead of defending their own rights, he showed them how to give up their rights for the sake of others. Sometimes Bonhoeffer would give his students a very difficult Bible text, then ask them to prepare a sermon. Afterward he showed them by example how the text could be preached. At other times he just relaxed and chatted, or walked with them on the beach.

Two years later, by 1937, the Gestapo began to put restrictions on the Confessing Church. Some of its pastors were arrested, among them Martin Niemoller. Several students from Finkenwalde were interrogated and persecuted. In September 1937 Hitler's police closed the seminary.

"WHERE'S YOUR BROTHER ABEL?"

Bonhoeffer had been extremely concerned about the persecution of the German Jews since 1933. Anti-Semitism was nothing new in Europe. The difference now was that Hitler had begun a massive propaganda campaign against this minority group consisting of about one per cent of the German population. Hitler accused the Jews of being greedy and anti-German. Many Christians condemned the Jews for having crucified Jesus. They felt somewhat justified in their hatred since their church father, Martin Luther, had also not always spoken well of them. But Bonhoeffer believed these people had misunderstood Luther. He felt that one of the major tasks of the Confessing Church was to speak up for the Jews. The primary purpose of the Barmen Declaration was to defend the Jewish people and oppose the "Aryan clause" of 1933, which the government had used to exclude Jews from ministry in the Church. As more time went by, Bonhoeffer became increasingly disappointed in the Confessing churches, mainly because he felt they were not sufficiently exposing the great injustice being done to the Jews.

In 1938 Jewish people were being openly harassed and denied privileges which other German citizens had. Bonhoeffer's twin sister Sabine and her Jewish husband were forced to escape into Switzerland. Thousands of Jews had no choice but to leave their houses and

The Night o

On "Crystal Night," November 10th, 1938, it became obvious to the world how evil Nazism was. On this night in Germany, young followers of Hitler burned and looted 195 synagogues and 8,000 Jewish shops. Then Nazis arrested twenty thousand Jews and deported them to concentration camps.

It had all begun two weeks earlier, when a young, frustrated Jewish refugee, wanting to revenge his suffering family in Poland, walked into the German embassy in Paris and shot a Nazi official. The episode supplied Hitler with an excuse for retaliating against the Jews. A "spontaneous" riot broke out in Germany (organized by the Nazi Security Service). The next day the New York Times carried the following: "NAZIS SMASH, LOOT AND BURN JEWISH SHOPS AND TEMPLES — A wave of destruction, looting and arson unparalleled in Germany since the Thirty Years' War, and in Europe generally since the Bolshevist revolution, swept over greater Germany today as Nazi cohorts took vengeance on Jewish shops, offices and synagogues for the murder . . . of . . .[a] third secretary of the German embassy in Paris. Beginning systematically in the early morning hours in al-

Broken Glass

most every town and city in the country, the wrecking, looting and burning continued all day. Huge but mostly silent crowds looked on and the police confined themselves to regulating traffic and making wholesale arrests of Jews 'for their own protection.'"

That night Bonhoeffer underlined Psalm 74:8 in his Bible ("They say to themselves: Let us plunder them! They burn all the houses of God in the land") and marked it "November 10th."

Two days later the Nazi government fined the Jews one billion Marks ($400 million) for the death of the embassy secretary. Not only that, but the government also forced the Jewish community in Germany to repair the damaged buildings out of their own funds.

The world was outraged. Yet no one intervened.

businesses with only a few marks in their pockets and some extra clothes on their backs. They were rounded up and deported. At the end of 1938, during the horrible public attack on the Jews now remembered as "Kristallnacht" (Crystal Night), a systematic extermination of this national minority began within the concentration camps of Dachau, Sachsenhausen and Buchenwald. During World War II, an estimated six million Jews were murdered by the Nazis.

DOUBLE AGENT IN THE ABWEHR

By 1938, Bonhoeffer had grown disappointed with the compromises of the Confessing Church in Germany as well as with the many empty words of the ecumenical movement abroad. Slogans or carefully worded resolutions just did not count anymore. Now was the time for political action. He distanced himself more and more from the Church until he felt he was "a Christian without a church." He resigned from his duties in the World Alliance and began searching for what his next move should be. The Gestapo had closed down the seminary, and he was not allowed to preach anymore. He knew the Gestapo was watching him. When would they come for him?

Should he escape? Unsure of what he should do, Bonhoeffer out of desperation accepted an invitation to lecture in America. He went there in June 1939, but after only a month, he decided he had to return to his homeland and fight a government he felt was inherently evil. "I have made a mistake in coming to America," he told his host, Reinhold Niebuhr. "I will have no right to participate in the reconstruction of Christian life in Germany after the war if I do not

share the trials of this time with my people."

In September 1939 Germany invaded Czechoslovakia and Poland. Britain and France declared war on Germany. Second World War had finally begun.

Hans von Dohnanyi, Bonhoeffer's brother-in-law who was married to his sister Christine and worked for the German secret intelligence agency (the Abwehr), managed to get him a job as civilian agent in the intelligence service. This kept him from being drafted into the German army, where he would have been required to swear allegiance to Hitler. Bonhoeffer just could not do that. And since von Dohnanyi and other top leaders in the Abwehr were secretly cooperating with the Resistance, it also opened up an opportunity to travel abroad and pass important information about the situation in Germany on to its enemies.

During the next two years Bonhoeffer managed to leak secret information to the Allies. He also tried to negotiate a potential peace plan between the German Resistance and Britain for after Hitler's fall. And he became involved in "Operation 7," a secret rescue plan for Jewish people.

THE CONSPIRACY

For several years some of the top officers in the Abwehr had been secretly planning to remove Hitler – not because they wanted the Nazi government's defeat, but because they believed Hitler was a madman. They were waiting for the right moment when public opinion would turn against the Fuhrer. They waited for several years, until Hitler invaded Czechoslovakia in 1939 against the advice of his generals, and it looked as if the moment had arrived. Hans von Dohnanyi, together with Admiral Canaris and General Oster, his superiors in the Abwehr, had made plans to arrest and prosecute Hitler. They had arranged for Karl Bonhoeffer, Dietrich's father, to declare him insane. But Hitler's popularity only rose. The opportunity went by. Hitler achieved an almost godlike status. He could make no wrong move. Every move he took seemed successful. He ordered his troops to take Stalingrad in Russia – also contrary to his generals' advice – and succeeded. Plots against him failed one after the other. One such plan,

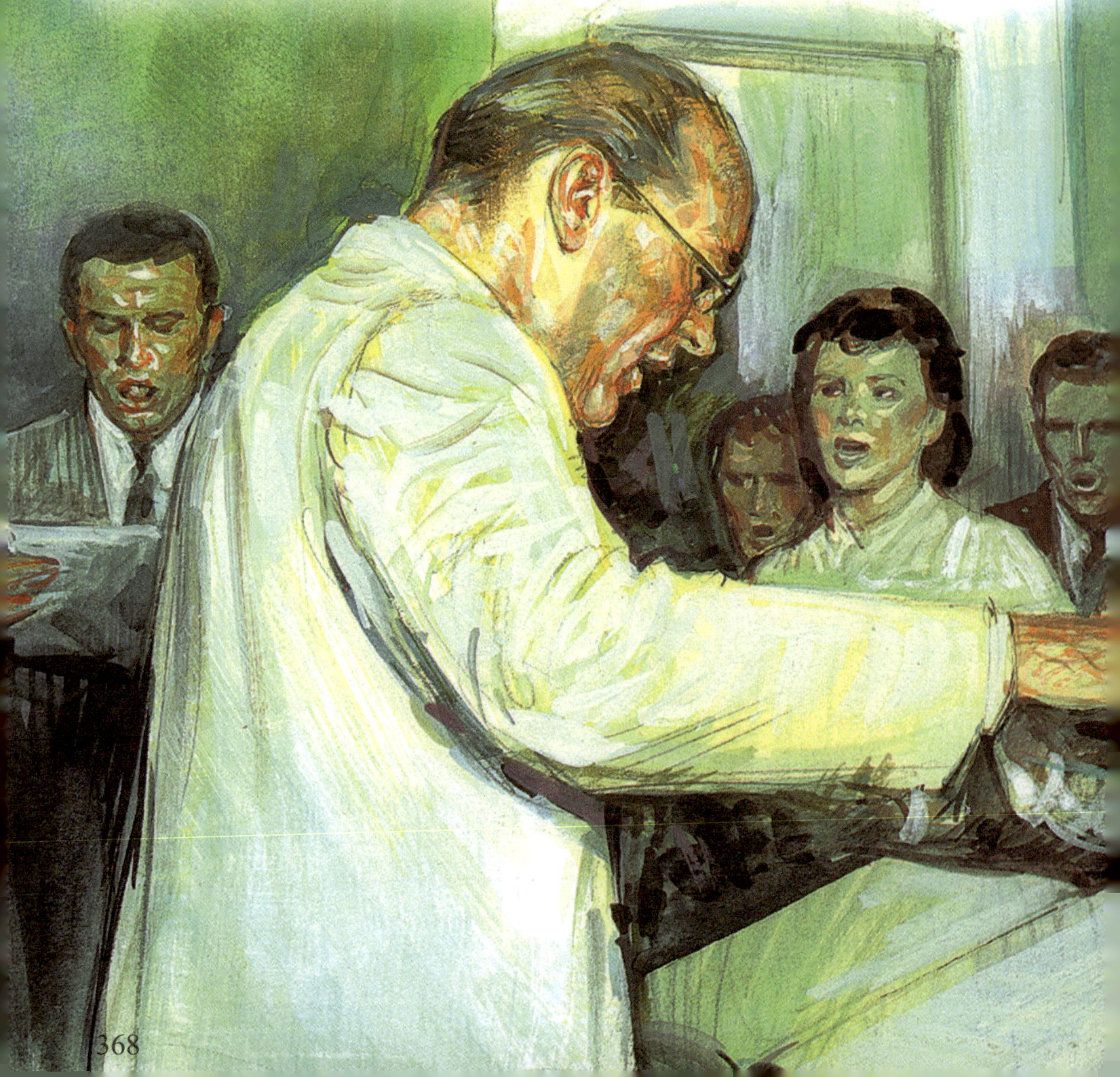

"Operation Flash," involved a bomb being secretly planted onboard Hitler's private airplane, because the bomb never went off. Many Germans seriously believed that higher powers protected the Fuhrer.

One afternoon in 1943, Hans von Dohnanyi was together with Dietrich and the rest of the family at their childhood home. They were getting ready for Karl Bonhoeffer's seventy-fifth birthday. Hans and Dietrich were waiting for an important phone call as they rehearsed "Lobet den Herrn" with the others. The phone call would inform them that Hitler had finally been assassinated and that they should come to the Abwehr office at once. Hans' car was waiting outside the door.

The hours went by, and there was still no phone call. Dietrich looked nervously at Hans while trying to concentrate on the music. Finally, when the rehearsal was over and the family dispersed, Dietrich and Hans knew that another attempt on Hitler's life had failed.

THE ARREST

After the assasination attempt in 1943, when the Gestapo searched the Abwehr office, they found evidence that the office had been involved in smuggling Jews across the border to Switzerland. This made them realize that the Abwehr officers were also involved in the Resistance. Bonhoeffer's brother-in-law Hans was suspected of being "the intellectual head of the movement to overthrow the Fuhrer."

A few days later, when Bonhoeffer telephoned Hans, a stranger answered the phone. Bonhoeffer realized immediately that the Gestapo must be ransacking Hans' house and that Hans and Christine had been arrested. When he hung up, Bonhoeffer went over to his other sister's house and asked her to prepare him a good meal. In the meantime he destroyed every document that could possibly incriminate him. He even managed to leave behind some false papers which would put the Gestapo on the wrong track. Later that afternoon, two men knocked on the door and took Bonhoeffer to the Tegel Military Prison in Berlin.

Letters and Papers from Prison

While Bonhoeffer was in prison, he wrote many letters to Eberhard Bethge, a former Finkenwalde student and his closest friend. In order to hide the letters from the Gestapo, Eberhard's wife Renate buried most of them in gas mask cases in the backyard of her parents' house. After the war Eberhard submitted the letters for publication. The book, entitled "Letters and Papers from Prison," became an instant success. More than any other work by Bonhoeffer, this book guides the reader to the heart of a great visionary and theological thinker. It has been translated into many languages.

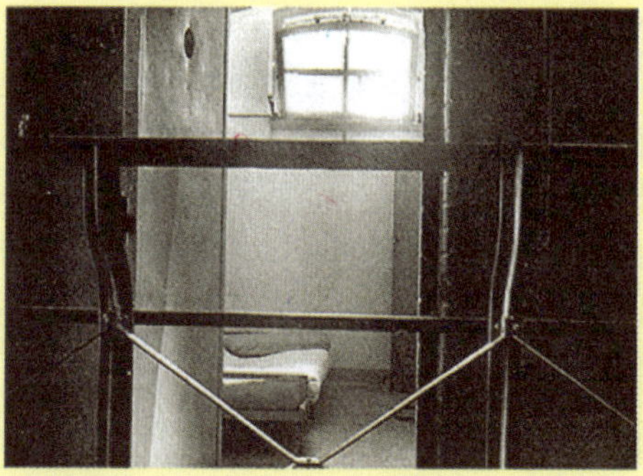

A Secret Code

den mir vorgeschriebenen zu ersinnen trachtete. Ich warf in Gedanken die juristischen Studien weg und widmete mich allein den Sprachen, den Alterthümern, der Geschichte und allem, was daraus hervorquillt.

Zwar machte mir jederzeit die poetische Nachbildung dessen, was ich an mir selbst, an andern und an der Natur gewahr geworden, das größte Vergnügen. Ich that es mit immer wachsender Leichtigkeit, weil es aus Instinct geschah und keine Kritik mich irre gemacht hatte; und wenn ich auch meinen Productionen nicht recht traute, so konnte ich sie wohl als fehlerhaft, aber nicht als ganz verwerflich ansehen. Ward mir dieses oder jenes daran getadelt, so blieb es doch im Stillen meine Ueberzeugung, daß es nach und nach immer besser werden müßte, und daß ich wohl einmal neben Hagedorn, Gellert und andern solchen Männern mit Ehre dürfte genannt werden. Aber eine solche Bestimmung allein schien mir allzu leer und

Bonhoeffer used this code to communicate with his family while he was in prison . By reading the underlined letters from the back, various messages could be spelled out.

THE FINAL PLOT AGAINST HITLER

July 20th, 1944, marked a tragic day for the German Resistance. On that day one last, unsuccessful attempt was made on Hitler's life.

The Allied armies were closing in on Germany from both the east and west. Hitler summoned his High Command to his secret military headquarters in what is now Poland, in order to discuss a counterattack. During the conference, Colonel Claus von Stauffenberg arrived. He was a wounded officer from the African campaign. He brought with him reports which Hitler had requested. He had these in a briefcase – together with a time bomb. Von Stauffenberg, another key figure in the German Resistance, had volunteered to carry the bomb into Hitler's bunker. When he entered, the Fuhrer looked up from the map table but continued explaining his plan to his officers. Von Stauffenberg hesitated, then placed the briefcase under the table close by the Fuhrer's feet. "It must be done," he thought to himself, "for this man is the Evil One himself."

The bomb was silently ticking in the briefcase. Von Stauffenberg excused himself to go to the bathroom but instead, walked away from the bunker and into a waiting car.

"What's this?" asked Hitler, irritated as he kicked the briefcase.

"Von Stauffenberg's reports, I think," replied an officer. He moved the briefcase to the back of the room.

Von Stauffenberg drove away, hurrying to catch a plane back to Berlin. He

looked at his watch, then at the bunker behind him. Now!

The building exploded into a thousand pieces. The colonel was convinced they had finally assassinated Hitler. But when he arrived in Berlin later that day, Hitler's police were waiting for him. They arrested Von Stauffenberg and immediately shot him through the head, together with the other key con-

spirators. Four high-ranking officers were killed in the bunker, but Hitler had survived. Now the Fuhrer shut down all communication with the outside world. He vowed revenge and sent his blood-stained uniform to his mistress with the triumphant words, "This is proof that Providence protects me and that we no longer have to fear our enemies." He believed that God had miraculously saved him. The next day, when Benito Mussolini, the Italian premier, visited him, Hitler fumed, "I'll crush and destroy the criminals who have dared to oppose themselves to Providence and me!"

During the next two months, the Nazi People's Court in Berlin arrested and tried 7,000 officers and civilians. Five thousand of them – some of the brightest minds in Germany – were executed in reprisal for the plot of July 20th.

GOETHE'S
WERKE
MUSIÓ

NO WAY BACK

Even though Bonhoeffer was not directly involved in the July 20th assassination attempt, the Gestapo did find materials linking him with the conspirators. Friends outside the prison, helped by his personal guard who had come to admire his prisoner, were already planning Bonhoeffer's escape to Sweden. But when he heard that his own brother Klaus had also been arrested, he decided to abandon his escape plan. He would not risk the lives of others in order to ensure his own safety. Instead, he sat down and wrote a poem about the prophet Jonah who offered his life for the sake of his fellow men. Three days later Bonhoeffer was transferred from Tegel to the dark cellar of the main Gestapo prison on Prinz Albrechtstrasse in Berlin.

Maria von Wedemeyer, Bonhoeffer's fiancee

A Love Story

Bonhoeffer first met Maria von Wedemeyer–Weller at the Finkenwalde seminary in 1937. At the time, she was thirteen, he was 31. Five years later, the year before Bonhoeffer was imprisoned in Tegel, Maria's father was killed on the eastern front. When Bonhoeffer visited his widow, he and Maria fell in love. They were engaged in the winter of 1943 – despite Maria's mother's request that they did not see each other for a year. Less than three months later, Bonhoeffer was arrested, and the engagement was publicly announced.

Bonhoeffer looked forward to the wedding. For him, marriage meant faith in the mercy of God and an affirmation of the world's future. "And I do not mean the kind of faith which flees the world," he wrote Maria, "but the one that endures the world and which loves and remains true to the world in spite of all the suffering which it contains for us. Our marriage shall be a yes to God's earth!"

Maria and Dietrich were never married. After the war Maria married twice and became an engineer in the United States. She died in 1977.

A MESSAGE TESTED

At the Gestapo security prison Bonhoeffer was denied his former privileges of receiving visitors and books and of being able to write letters regularly. He never saw his beloved Maria again, but he was allowed to write her one final Christmas letter.

He did, at least, have the company of Maria's cousin Fabian, who had also been committed to the Gestapo prison. During an airraid, while the soldiers moved the prisoners to a cement shelter, the two men had a chance to discuss their interrogators.

"Do they use torture?" asked Fabian.

"Yes, they are brutal and disgusting," answered Bonhoeffer.

Fabian watched Bonhoeffer closely. He saw how kind and polite he was to everyone – even to the guards. He seemed confident and hopeful, trusting in God's goodness, even though the Gestapo had threatened to arrest Maria and his parents if he did not reveal his past activities and the names of his fellow conspirators. But Bonhoeffer refused to betray them.

After the war, when Bonhoeffer was dead and Fabian had been released, he returned to the ruins of his former home. Fabian wrote, "At first I saw nothing but rubble. Anything that the bombs had spared had been stolen. Only one book lay undamaged among the bricks and mortar: Dietrich Bonhoeffer's 'Cost of Discipleship.'"

More than any other work by Bonhoeffer, this book would become his special gift to the world. His last days at Buchenwald and Flossenburg were only a confirmation of its message.

The Last Letter to Maria

On December 17, 1944, Bonhoeffer wrote his last letter to Maria. The letter is his final written message to the world. After this letter Maria made several attempts to see her beloved Dietrich. She even traveled on foot across Germany in the hope of finding him in one of Hitler's concentration camps. But she never found him. In fact, she did not even learn about his death until July, when a memorial service held by Bishop Bell was aired by the BBC in England.

Altogether, Dietrich wrote his fiancee thirty-eight letters from prison. Some of them were smuggled out. The letters have not yet become public, since at Maria's request they are stored under lock and key at Harvard University and will not be opened until the year 2002.

However, an excerpt from that Christmas letter has become public:

"These will be quiet days in our homes. But I have had the experience over and over again that the quieter it is around me, the clearer do I feel the connection to you. It is as though in solitude the soul develops senses which we hardly know in everyday life. Therefore I have not felt lonely or abandoned for one moment. You, the parents, all of you, the friends and students of mine at the front, all are constantly present to me. Your prayers and good thoughts, words from the Bible, discussions long past, pieces of music, and books – they all gain life and reality as never before . . . . Therefore you must not think that I am unhappy. What is happiness and unhappiness? It depends so little on the circumstances; it depends really only on that which happens inside a person. I am grateful every day that I have you, and that makes me happy."

CELL NUMBER ONE AT BUCHENWALD

In February 1945, when the Gestapo prison in Berlin was destroyed by an air raid, Bonhoeffer was transported for further interrogation to the infamous concentration camp at Buchenwald. The guards had orders to keep him healthy since he was an important prisoner still witholding information. He was confined to cell number one – a dark and damp cell in an air-raid shelter outside the actual camp. One of the prisoners who survived the war, Captain Payne Best of the British Secret Service, was imprisoned across the corridor from Bonhoeffer. Although the two men could not see each other because of the wall, they could communicate, and became good friends.

"Bonhoeffer was all humility and sweetness," Best wrote later. "He always seemed to diffuse an atmosphere of happiness, of joy in every smallest event in life, and of deep gratitude for the mere fact of being alive . . . . He was one of the very few men I ever met to whom his God was real and ever close to him."

On Easter Day they could hear American guns booming in the distance. The Allies were on their way.

From the eastern front, the Russians were also advancing. It was a lovely spring day, and it would be only a matter of weeks before the war was over. The prisoners were cheerful and even joked with the guards as they were hauled away from Buchenwald to safer quarters.

The heavy truck pulled up at a farmhouse, and the prisoners were fed milk and rye bread before being transported on to the county jail in Regensburg. Friday morning they were back in the truck, this time going west toward Schonberg where they were locked inside a school. The sun was shining. Birds were singing in the trees. The beautiful valley stretched out below the windows. They felt confident they were on their way to freedom.

A SOLIDARITY SERVICE

One of Bonhoeffer's fellow prisoners was a Russian air force officer, Wasiliew Kokorin. Kokorin was teaching Bonhoeffer Russian. Bonhoeffer shared his books and tobacco with Kokorin. He also shared the Gospel of Jesus Christ with the young Russian communist. Kokorin was impressed by this man's sincere and honest faith.

The next morning was the first Sunday after Easter. Payne Best plugged in his electric razor and everyone took turns around the mirror.

"Pastor Bonhoeffer," said Best, "why don't you conduct a worship service and preach to us?"

"I don't think so," answered Bonhoeffer. "Kokorin is an atheist. He

may not want to be part of that. Solidarity between us is more important than a religious service."

"Yes, Comrade Bonhoeffer," Kokorin joined in, "solidarity is more important than religion. So I think we should all have a worship service together."

The text for the day was, "With His wounds we are healed." Bonhoeffer looked at the faces in front of him, so full of pain and suffering, yet with hope that freedom was near. Then he cleared his throat and firmly said:

"Behold the man sentenced by God, the figure of grief and pain. That is how the Reconciler of the world appears. The guilt of mankind has fallen upon Him. It casts Him into shame and death before God's judgment seat. This is the great price which God pays for reconciliation with the world. Only by God's executing judgment upon Himself can there be peace between Him and the world and between man and man. But the secret of this judgment, of this passion and death, is the love of God for the world and for man. What befell Christ befalls every man in Him. It is only as one who is sentenced by God that man can live before God. Only the crucified man is at peace with God. It is in the figure of the Crucified that man recognizes and discovers Himself. To be taken up by God, to be executed on the cross and reconciled, that is the reality of manhood."

APPLICATION OF A THEOLOGY

Bonhoeffer had hardly finished his sermon when the door was pushed open and two Gestapo officers in civilian clothes walked in.

"Prisoner Bonhoeffer, take your things and follow us," they ordered.

Everyone in the room was shocked. This could mean only one thing. Bonhoeffer remained relaxed and composed. Quickly he scribbled down his name and address in a book and handed it to one of his fellow prisoners. Then he turned to Payne Best and said,

"Tell Bishop Bell in England that this is the end for me – but it's also the beginning of life!"

On that Low Sunday of April 9th, 1945 – less than a month before General Patton's Allied armies closed in and overthrew the Nazi regime, Bonhoeffer was taken to the notorious concentration camp at Flossenburg. Several of his friends from the Resistance were already there, being

tried and executed – by special order of the High Command. The final testimony of Bonhoeffer's faith and courage was given by a camp doctor who would never quite understand that what he witnessed at the scaffold, was the costly application of a man's theology.

"In the almost fifty years that I worked as a doctor," he testified, "I have hardly ever seen a man die so entirely submissive to the will of God."

That same morning, April 9th 1945, Hans von Dohnanyi was executed at Sachsenhausen concentration camp; and two weeks later, Klaus Bonhoeffer and a brother-in-law were killed for their role in the conspiracy.

On April 20th, eleven days after Bonhoeffer's death, the American soldiers moved in and liberated the survivors at Flossenburg concentration camp.

Dietrich Bonhoeffer's body was never found. But the costly message he died for has since spread throughout the world.

Main Events in Bonhoeffer's Life

1906 4. Feb.	Born in Breslau.
1912	The family moves to Berlin.
1914	World War I begins.
1918	Kaiser Wilhelm II abdicates
1919	Treaty of Versailles.
1920	Decides to study theology.
1923	Begins studies at the University of Tubingen.
1927	Defends doctoral thesis.
1928	The Great Depression Curate in Barcelona, Spain.
1929	Lecturer at the University of Berlin.
1930	Studies at Union Theological Seminary in New York.
1931	Appointed youth secretary of the World Alliance. Teaches con-fir-
1932	mation class in Berlin.
1933	Von Hindenburg appoints Hitler prime minister. Bonhoeffer's radio broadcast. The Aryan Clause. Pastor in London.
1934	Hitler becomes presi¬dent. The Barmen Declaration. World peace speech at Fano.
1935	The Finkenwalde seminary opened.
1936	Declared an "enemy of the State." Expelled from the university.
1937	Resigns as youth secretary from World Alliance. Niemöller arrested. Finkenwalde closed by the Gestapo.
1938	Pastors ordered to pledge allegiance to Hitler. Contacts the German Resistance. Writes Life Together. Sabine and her Jewish husband escape to Switzerland. Crystal Night.
1939	Germany invades Czecholovakia and Poland. England and France declare war on Germany. Bonhoeffer's second trip to the U.S. Agent in the Abwehr.
1940	Prohibited from public speaking.
1941	The Soviet Union and the U.S. join the Allies.
1942	Hitler steps up extermination of Jewish people.
1943	Engagement to Maria. Arrested and
1944	imprisoned at Tegel. Allied landing in Normandy. Assassination attempt against Hitler. Bonhoeffer moved to Gestapo prison on Prinz
1945	Albrechtstrasse. Moved to Buchenwald and Schonberg. Hanged at Flossenbürg concentration camp, April 9.

Martin Luther King

THE PASTOR WHO HAD A DARING DREAM

1929 —1968

Great men and women are not in need of our praise.
We are the ones in need of getting to know them.

By Sharon Jones

Illustrations by Andrea Jula

IT WASN'T SUPPOSED TO END THIS WAY

On the evening of April 3, 1968, it was difficult to push through the crowd that had gathered in Memphis to hear Martin Luther King, Jr. Once on the podium, King looked out over all eager faces. Then he bowed his head and thanked God for being chosen to lead the march later that week. He added a few words about their objectives. Then the tone of his speech changed unexpectedly.

"Some began to talk about the threats that were out, of what would happen to me," he intoned, "but it really doesn't matter to me now, because I've been to the mountain top and I've seen

the Promised Land. I may not get there with you, but I want you to know, tonight that we as a people will get to the Promised Land! So I'm happy tonight. I'm not worried about anything! I'm not fearing any man! Mine eyes have seen the glory of the coming of the Lord!"

The audience leapt to its feet, shouting, clapping, and cheering. But Dr. King's friends knew something was strangely different. He never concentrated so much of a speech on himself. They thought, "What's wrong with him? He is working much too hard. After the march, Dr. King needs a long rest."

That night Dr. King and his friend, Rev. Abernathy, were driven to the Lorraine Motel on Mulberry Street. Dr. King would occupy room 306 on the second floor. His room had a balcony from which he could see the parking lot and pool, and from which he could communicate with his staff who occupied the rooms around his. Their presence served as a convenience as well as added security against violence. The plainclothes officers whose job it was to protect him, relaxed.

The next day, following meetings and strategy sessions, King and Abernathy had lunch in the motel, rested, and then began to dress for dinner. King stepped out onto the balcony to give last-minute instructions to his staff about the upcoming meeting. Rev. Abernathy stood in the balcony doorway to the rear. Then it happened.

A single gun shot was heard. Friends stared in disbelief as both Dr. King and Rev. Abernathy hit the floor. Time froze. Abernathy saw the figure sprawled beside him and hoped Dr. King had simply fallen to the floor in order to avoid the danger. But the position of King's body told a different, much more horrifying story.

Abernathy noticed that a bullet had hit King in the neck with such velocity that it knocked him flat on his back. On the balcony floor lay the man on whom all their hopes for continued victories over racial injustice had been pinned. The unbelievable fact slowly began to sink in. Dr. Martin Luther King, Jr. had just been assassinated.

WHAT'S IN A NAME?

A violent end was the farthest thing from the minds of Alberta Christine and Mike King, Sr. on January 15, 1929 when Mike Jr. was born to them. Their 15-month-old daughter had recently survived a severe illness and the young family was still growing. Only eighteen months later, Alfred Daniel (A.D.) was born. Still, Mike Sr. was working hard as assistant pastor at the prominent Ebenezer Baptist Church, doing his best to carve out a comfortable existence for his family. Family was important.

Since birth certificates were not commonly issued to black sharecropper families, Mike Sr. had never had one. His father insisted that he was originally named Martin Luther, after two of his father's brothers. "Names are important," Grandpa King would say. "They carry on the legacy of family. Names are especially important in black families. We live in a society which allows us to have little else

than family to be proud of." So, as Mike Sr. stood by his father's deathbed with 4-year-old Mike Jr., he had promised to take out the necessary legal papers. Soon after his father's death, Mike Sr. officially became Martin Luther King, Sr. and his son became Martin Luther King, Jr.

When the Depression of the thirties hit, the family had an important opportunity to put into action what was being preached. One night the children overheard their father telling a group from the church, "Do unto others as you would have them do unto you. This Depression has hit everybody hard. There are very few jobs for white people, so you know the Negro is having even worse luck. Let's use the church as a storehouse. Everyone can bring what they have–potatoes, tomatoes, carrots, blankets, diapers, anything. Then, whoever needs something can simply exchange what they have for what they need."

The children got excited. Not remembering that they were supposed to be asleep in bed, they ran down the stairs and into the middle of the meeting, blurting out ideas they had for toys and clothes they could give away, The room grew silent. Rev. King approached the children and said sternly, "Aren't you supposed to be in bed? It's obvious that you have been eavesdropping."

The children froze. Then Martin Jr. spoke up. "We couldn't help overhearing. You always taught us to do whatever we could to help. That's the Bible way."

Daddy King's stern expression suddenly changed to one of pride as he pulled Martin close to him. "Did you hear the eagerness of these three children?" He looked straight into Martin's eyes. "Son," he said, "God has given you your heart to help others. There will come a day when you'll have your chance to make a real difference." Somehow, Martin knew his father was right.

SOMETHING CHANGES

As a child, Martin learned things quickly and, thanks to his mother's early teaching at home, was advanced when he entered first grade. Martin was already thinking of books as untiring teachers with amazing amounts of knowledge in them. When he secured a job as a paper boy delivering the Atlanta Journal, Martin started buying his own books.

There was so much to know, but there were some things Martin found hard to understand. One day, when he went over to a friend's house to play, the friend's mother stopped Martin at the door of her home. "Martin," she said, "I'm afraid you can't come into the

The King Children

The three King children had very different personalities. Christine, the oldest, seemed determined to follow in the footsteps of her mother and grandmother and pursue a teaching career. She was always eager to learn. The boys, Martin and A.D., were being groomed by their father and grandfather to keep up the family tradition and become ministers. A.D., the youngest, was boisterous and stubborn, but his father could see these traits being shaped into the qualities needed to be a fiery Baptist preacher. M.L., as Martin was called as a child, was a deep thinker with an inquisitive mind. Early in life he displayed great speaking skills and he also had a fine singing voice. His family knew that he would be a natural for the pulpit of Ebenezer Baptist Church.

Left: Martin's birthplace in Atlanta, Georgia. Right: The King family 1939. Back row: Martin's mother, father and grandmother. Front row: A.D., Christine and M.L.K.

AMERICA

house and play with Arthur anymore. Goodbye."

Martin just stood there as the screen door slammed shut. What had he done? As hot tears filled his eyes, he rushed on home.

His mother was busy squeezing lemons to make her famous homemade lemonade when Martin appeared at the screen door. She noticed right away that something was terribly wrong. Taking both of his shoulders in her hands and kneeling down beside him, she asked, "Martin, what happened? What has upset you so?"

For a moment or two, Martin could only stare at her as the tears burned his eyes and streamed over his cheeks. Finally he shouted, "Why Momma, why? Arthur is my best friend. Every day we ride our bikes or play ball. I've always been good around his house. What did I do? Why did they say I can't go there anymore? Why Momma, why?"

Martin's mother hugged and rocked him for a long time. She knew very well what was wrong. But how could she tell her sensitive, innocent seven-year-old child that he had reached the age when some thought the races should be separated? Once you reached a certain age, white people simply did not associate with black people as friends and equals.

"Martin," his mother began, "many things in this world are done that shouldn't be done. Separating people from their friends because of the color of their skin is one of them."

The puzzled look would not leave Martin's face. Alberta King looked him straight in the eye. Her tone was gentle yet determined. "Now you listen to me," she said. "People who try to make you feel like you are less of a person just don't know the truth. The truth is, everyone is the same, equal, in God's eyes. And God's opinion is the only opinion that matters. You did nothing wrong. It is this system of separation that is wrong. You're as good as anyone else."

With that, his mother went back to squeezing the lemonade, but now she was humming "We Shall Overcome."

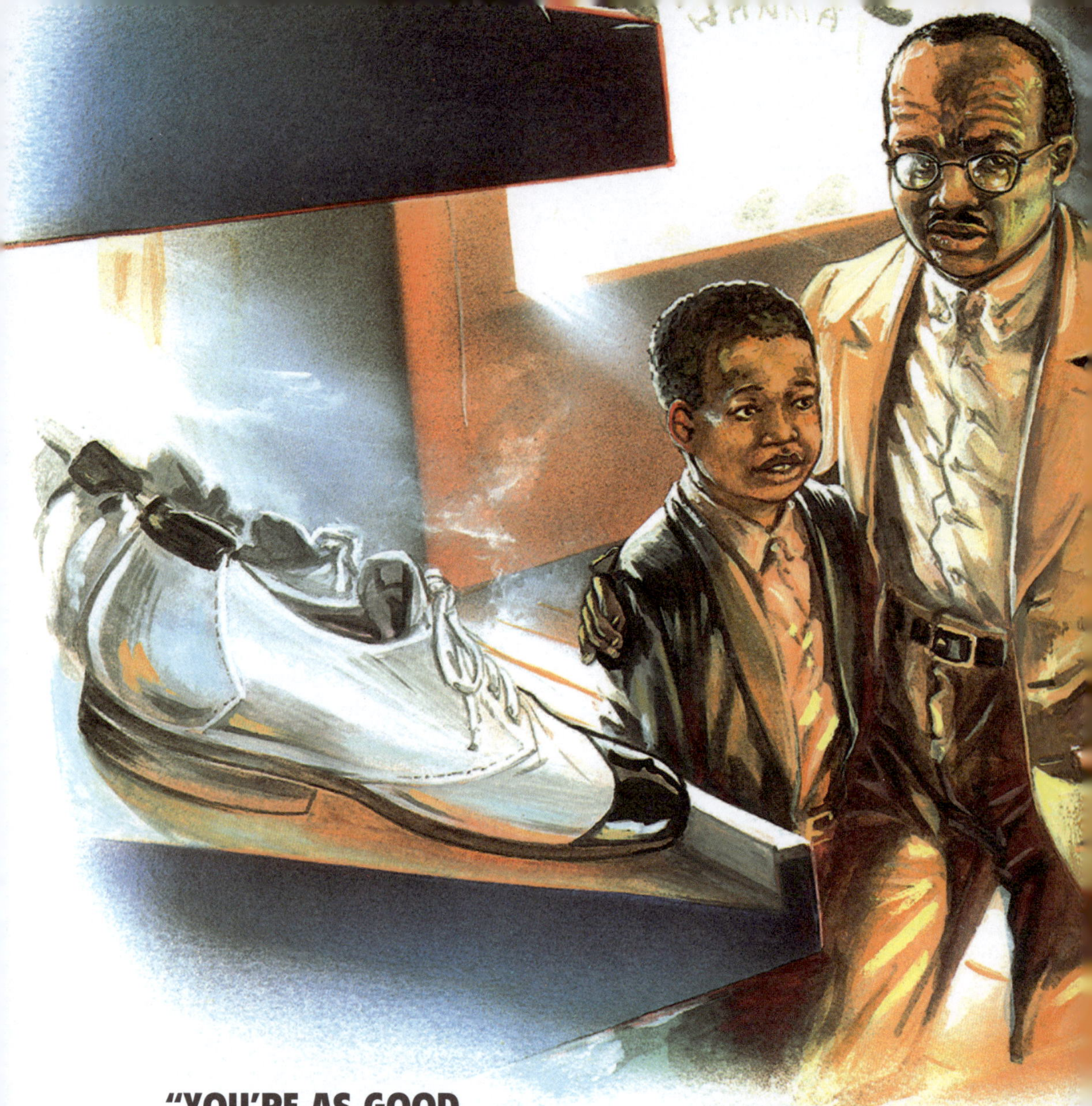

"YOU'RE AS GOOD AS ANYONE ELSE"

Since the abolition of slavery, the Southern states had come up with a system in which blacks and whites lived under different rules. Martin was familiar with separate entrances to stores, separate seating in movie theaters, separate elevators and staircases in public buildings, and water fountains marked "Whites Only" or "Colored Only."

Martin's parents were determined to raise their children with a sense of dignity no matter how they were treated by others. Blacks were expected to bow their heads and slouch their shoulders in public, but Martin saw his father always walking tall and proud through the streets of Atlanta. One time when he went shopping with his father, Martin saw a pair of shoes that he wanted in the store window. He and his father entered the store through the front entrance.

A clerk ran up to them shouting, "If you want something, come in through the back of the store like the other niggers do." "Nigger" was a very degrading word white people used to insult black people.

Martin's father had stood firm and looked the man straight in the eye. "If you cannot sell us these shoes here in the front of the store " he said, "we will take our money elsewhere." Then Martin felt his dad's strong hand on his shoulder as they left the store, by the front door.

Martin looked up and saw the sad look in his father's eyes. "Some people think they are better than others simply because of the color of their skin. They have thought this for a long time and have convinced themselves that this is true." The sad look turned to one of proud determination. "Son, don't you ever believe that any one person is better than any other person. Especially

son, remember that you are just as good as anyone else."

They were both silent as they got into the car to go home, but their thoughts were disturbed when a police officer stopped them. When the officer walked up to the car, he motioned for Martin's father to roll down his window. "Listen, boy," the officer began. Before he could finish his statement, Martin's father interrupted him. Pointing at Martin, he faced the officer and said, "That is a boy, I am a man."

Martin never forgot that lesson. He decided then and there that he would work with his father to put an end to the terrible system of racial separation.

Above: Martin's father preaching at Ebenezer Baptist Church. Right: Crozer Theological Seminary in Pennsylvania where Martin studied to become a pastor.

IT'S DIFFERENT UP NORTH

Martin entered college when he was just fifteen years old. During his sophomore year, his parents allowed him and his brother A.D. to work one summer in the tobacco fields up north in Connecticut. The plentiful work, good pay, and curiosity about the North drove many Southern young people to the area. Although the work was hard, the bosses tended to be fair. The most amazing thing to Martin was experiencing whites, blacks and immigrants sweating side by side as equals. They strung young plants together, picked the large tobacco leaves together, and carried the full lathes to the shed rafters together.

One weekend, he and A.D. decided to relax by going to the movies. After they paid for their tickets, the usher

Martin's Schooling

Martin's mother, Alberta King, taught her children at home until they entered first grade. Between the ages of 5 and 11, Martin attended public school and was at the top of his class every year. When he was eleven, he was enrolled in a school for exceptionally bright children. He loved this school and advanced at an even faster rate. Unfortunately, the school closed two years later. In those days, black children and white children were not allowed to attend school together, so Martin had to transfer to the all-black high school near his home. By this time, he was three years ahead of his classmates. After just a couple of years of high school, Martin was accepted as a freshman at Morehouse College. He was only fifteen years old.

Martin graduated from Morehouse College when he was nineteen. There was still much more that he wanted to learn. He attended two more schools and graduated with his master's degree from Crozer Theological Seminary and obtained his doctorate from Boston College.

directed them to their seats. "A.D., does something seem strange to you?" Martin asked as they eased into their seats.

"Yeah Martin," A.D. replied. "I think that usher sat us in the wrong section. These seats don't feel like 'Colored Section' seats. Look! These seats are clean with full cushions and no exposed springs " They both laughed.

At the end of that summer, Martin and A.D. left to go back to Atlanta as two changed young men. On the train headed home they reminisced about the back-breaking work they had endured, the friends they had made and money they had earned Mostly, though, they talked about the phenomenon of racial equality. Then something happened.

As they approached the Atlanta city limits, the conductor came up to

Martin, A.D., and the other black passengers. "You boys are going to have to move to the back of the dining car now."

The other black people did as they were told, but Martin sat paralyzed in his seat. He was surprised at his anger. It was as if now that equality was being snatched away from him, it felt even better than he had realized.

The conductor stood over Martin and began to shout, "What's the matter, boy? I don't want any trouble out of you. Now move to the back!"

Martin's feet felt like lead as he dragged himself to the back of the car. He and his friends said nothing as the conductor pulled a screen to separate them from the white passengers. Martin thought, "Only ten minutes ago we were passengers just like everybody else. How can our presence be so offensive now, that others can't even see us?"

CHOOSING THE MINISTRY AS A CAREER

Morehouse College was a place to study in preparation for the ministry. Martin wanted a college education, but he didn't want to spend his life behind a pulpit. His father was now senior pastor of Ebenezer and both he and A.D. were feeling the pressure to follow in their father's footsteps. Martin loved the Church, but he disagreed with the strict standards of behavior he was expected to uphold and he realized these standards would become even stricter if he entered the ministry. During his early college years, he found himself often bragging about how he intended to be free of these rules as an adult.

"Going to another dance tonight, Martin?" asked Philip, his roommate. Philip laughed as he casually leaned against the door frame, chomping on an apple. "You're going to dance holes in your shoes."

"Yeah, I can hear my father now. 'Good Baptists don't dance to the devil music. It destroys your brain and corrupts your soul.'" Martin smiled as he straightened his tie. "But seriously, all that hand-waving, foot-stomping, and yelling 'Amen' isn't going to free the Negro from segregation. In the Bible, God helped people in their real-life situations. If He's the same God, He'll do the same for us just because He loves us, not because we obey a bunch of man-made rules."

Martin loved his social life, but he loved God more. He prayed often about what God wanted him to do with his

life. By the spring of his senior year at Morehouse, Martin reached a decision. Through his classes and from listening to mentors like Dr. Benjamin Mays, Martin knew that God wanted him to reach blacks with the Bible's message as it related to their present problems. He also realized that the Church was the

strongest institution that the white power structure did not control. At church, blacks were free to talk, cry, rejoice, and complain about anything.

So, even though the Church was strongly traditional, Martin knew he would become a minister. Changes in accepted traditions came about slowly.

So since no one would listen to his words if his actions upset them, he decided to renounce dating and dancing. He was afraid his bachelor days would stretch far into the future, but he was wrong.

LOVE ARRIVES

When Martin graduated from Crozer Theological Seminary with his master's degree, his friends and family expected him to come home and marry a local girl. Characteristically, Martin had other ideas. As it turned out, Martin moved to Massachusetts and entered Boston College's doctoral program.

There he met a girl from Marion, Alabama. Martin fell in love with Coretta Scott from the first moment he saw her. They spent long hours studying in the library together, where Martin became more and more convinced that she was as intelligent, serious, and ambitious as she was beautiful. Coretta was in Boston studying performing arts at the New England Conservatory of Music. As the months went by and their relationship grew more serious, they both became concerned about her plans for becoming a professional singer. How could they ever combine the careers of a Baptist minister with that of a traveling concert musician? On the day Martin's parents were due to visit him in Boston and meet Coretta, he was extremely nervous.

When the doorbell rang, Coretta took hold of Martin's hand and said, "Remember, if we're to be together, it will work out." Coretta always knew just what to say to calm him. Martin realized that Coretta was the stabilizing voice he would need in his life. He loved her so much.

A they opened the door together, they heard, "Anybody home? What's wrong with these Northerners? It sure is

rude to keep company waiting on the front step so long." Martin's father let out a strong, hearty laugh.

Once everyone was inside, Martin introduced his parents to Coretta. They talked about their families, their classes, and ultimately, future career goals. Martin's parents could see the tender hand touches and glances exchanged between Martin and Coretta. It was obvious to them that the relationship had already become serious. Martin and his mother soon excused themselves and went to the kitchen. Coretta shifted nervously in her seat.

Martin's father was very direct with Coretta. "Young woman, a career on the concert stage is hardly appropriate for a young woman seeing a young man from a strict Baptist upbringing and background. I believe you and M.L. are just experiencing a little infatuation that probably won't last out the school term. You would be better suited for someone within your own profession. Besides, M.L. has dated daughters of some fine, solid Atlanta families, people who have much more to offer him."

Coretta stood up. Her eyes flashed with anger, but she was determined to control her emotions, speak her mind, and still be respectful to Martin's father. "I clearly understand the sacrifice I am being asked to make," she said. "I would probably have to abandon my plans to travel and perform. My life would be totally different as a Southern pastor's wife, a mother, and a member of a tight-knit church community. Through it all, though, I know I will have plenty to offer to Martin."

Martin's father had never been spoken to this way before, especially not by a woman. When Martin and Mrs. King entered the room again, the older man rose slowly to his feet. Everyone could feel the tension as he looked directly at Coretta and said, "Martin, I'm not exactly certain what God has planned for you, but whatever it is, you will need a wife with spunk and heart. Coretta is just that kind of girl. Besides, when you come home to Ebenezer, your mother could use some help in the music department."

On June 18, 1953, Martin and Coretta were pronounced man and wife on the lawn of her parents' home in Marion, Alabama.

MOVE TO MONTGOMERY

On a cold January morning in 1954, Martin and Coretta stood across the street looking at their first church, the Dexter Avenue Baptist Church. Martin lost no time in making changes. He had plans for getting the congregation to recruit new members from among the poorer people of the city. This last suggestion was not very popular, though.

"Dr. King, we've worked hard for years here at Dexter Avenue to try and raise the sights of our people. When we have fellowship with others of the same social status as ourselves, it is easier to run business meetings and get things done." When an elder from his church said this to him during a meeting, Martin could not believe his ears.

He looked around the room at his board of elders. He was shocked. "Gentlemen, in the midst of this heinous racial separation between whites

and Negroes in the South, I never thought I would find a greater evil. But I have. How can you possibly accept, in any form or fashion, the separation of Negroes from ourselves – and worse yet, separation along lines of class?

"We are all in the same boat. The well-dressed, college-educated Negro and the unshaven, uneducated Negro are both considered 'niggers' by white society. We cannot believe in our money. We must believe in ourselves as Men. We cannot afford to stoop to the level of our white brothers who have labeled us as less than men. How dare we do the same thing to our black brothers, just because we have bigger bank accounts?"

Under the leadership of Dr. King, Dexter Avenue Baptist Church began to change. They didn't know when or how, but they could feel that something big was about to happen.

THE BEGINNING OF A MOVEMENT

Rosa Parks was a faithful member of Dexter Avenue Baptist Church. Little did she know she would be the catalyst of the biggest change the South had seen since the abolition of slavery – the breakdown of the segregation system. On an ordinary day in December, 1955, Rosa left her job as seamstress in a downtown department store and got on her bus to go home. But as the bus filled up, the driver looked back and noticed that a few white passengers had nowhere to sit. He stopped the bus and asked the blacks in the first seats behind the white section to relinquish their seats. Mrs. Parks was one of them, but she refused to move.

"No, I don't think I should have to give up my seat," she said. The bus driver asked her again, and then called the police. A patrol car soon arrived and an

officer escorted Mrs. Parks off the bus and to jail.

The black citizens of Montgomery were used to this "Jim Crow" system of laws in the South. Jim Crow laws were the ones which among other things, forced blacks to sit at the backs of buses, wait for trains in separate areas, use different and substandard restrooms, and watch movies in isolated sections of the theaters. Blacks were not allowed to vote in general elections or eat at lunch counters. In addition, black children were not allowed to attend the same schools as white children. Rosa Parks knew these laws, but on this particular day, she did not accept them. Instead she thought about young Dr. King's sermons on the need for change in their thinking, so she challenged the rules she judged to be unfair.

When the black population of Montgomery heard about the incident they felt angry enough to do something

about all the injustices they were suffering. There were 48,000 blacks in the city. It was their money which kept the bus lines in business. So the city's black activists decided to organize a boycott of the city buses. At the quickly assembled meeting, Martin Luther King, Jr. was voted the head of the newly formed organization that would run the boycott – the Montgomery Improvement Association (M.I.A.).

Leaflets were quickly printed and distributed which stated, "Don't ride the bus on Monday, December 5." When Monday morning came, Martin and Coretta watched anxiously for the first bus to pass their home. Coretta noticed it first. "Look, Martin," she exclaimed, "it's empty." And so were all the others. All day long and for the weeks and months to come, the blacks of the city stayed off of the buses. The M.I.A. had organized car pools and black-run taxi companies to take people back and forth to work. Many people walked and some even used horses and buggies.

White employers threatened to fire their black employees and black taxi drivers were penalized. On Monday, January 30, 1956, about two months into the boycott, the King house was bombed. A crowd gathered and a riot threatened to break out, but Dr. King quieted the crowd. "God is with this movement. We must answer violence with nonviolence, aggression with peacefulness." With tears and nodding heads, the crowd went home.

By the winter of 1956 the Montgomery bus line was bankrupt. The Supreme Court finally declared segregated buses unconstitutional. It had taken more than a year, but the blacks had won their first victory over segregation in the South, nonviolently. A movement had begun.

STOPPED
STAY

VIOLENCE AGAINST THE NONVIOLENT MOVEMENT

The first black passengers who returned to the Montgomery buses and sat wherever they wanted, met with vicious assaults from the whites. Some were called nasty names, while others were hit in the face or pushed around by white passengers. This was the repayment for their year-long struggle. The tension could be keenly felt on buses all over the city. But the black population of Montgomery had discovered the power of nonviolence. Their reactions to these attacks were proof of their growing inner strength.

One of the members of Dr. King's church told him, "You would have been proud of Deacon Wilson. He looked the man straight in the face with his good eye as the injured one began to swell shut. They say it was silent on the bus for a good ten seconds. Then the deacon calmly took his seat – at the front of the bus, directly opposite his attacker, opened his morning paper, and began to read."

At some point, Coretta said to Martin, "This nonviolent approach is not easy. Look at all that has happened just this morning. How long will we be able to just stand and take the punishment? How long will we have to struggle against others who insist on keeping us down?"

Martin answered, "My dear, we will stand for what is right as long as it takes. They may knock us down, but we'll keep getting up. They may arrest us, but we'll keep speaking out. They may try to kill us, but the next generation will be there to carry on the struggle. You cannot kill the truth."

He had expressed these same sentiments in sermons and speeches many

times before. News of the bus boycott's success and Dr. King's amazing leadership traveled like wildfire across the country. Dr. King began to travel, spreading the message of nonviolent resistance and the Civil Rights Movement.

Late in the summer of 1958, Martin's first book, Stride Toward Freedom was published. He was invited to New York for an autograph session. He was surprised to hear the crowd outside booing him, even though he knew that Northern blacks were not as patient with the nonviolent message as their Southern counterparts.

Back home in Montgomery, Coretta received a distressing call from a hospital in New York. "Your husband has just arrived. He was attacked by a deranged woman at the autograph session."

"Is he all right? Please, is he alive?" Coretta's voice trembled.

"Oh yes, ma'am. But the stab wound was made by a letter opener that is still in his chest, so we must operate." The delicate operation lasted several hours. The tip of the letter opener had been so close to his heart that if Martin had coughed, it could have meant his death.

While Martin was recovering, he and Coretta noticed a change in the way the Northerners were now willing to accept him. The quiet manner in which he had handled this crisis had proven his method to them. He was now being compared to Gandhi. He and Coretta decided to travel to India so they could find out more about the nonviolent movement going on there.

India's Caste System and Segregation in America's South

In India during the first half of this century there was a strict system of social separation known as the caste system. People were divided into groups so that the very rich were considered better than those with less money. They were allowed many more privileges. For example, thousands of India's lowest caste, known as the Untouchables, starved to death every year, whereas the higher castes had an overabundance of food. The caste system was supported and endorsed by the government of India.

Mahatma Gandhi was a man who dreamed of a truly united India, Muslims living in peace with Hindus and Christians, free from the unfair caste system. He felt that the people who were being hurt the most should do something about the way they were being treated. He had preached that nonviolent resistance against the injustices of the caste system could bring about a change. By resisting the government's unjust laws without violence, many changes were made in India.

Dr. King saw a parallel between the caste system in India and the Jim Crow system of the South. He believed that if nonviolent resistance could work to break down the caste system in India, it could work to break down segregation in the South.

Left: Sit-in demonstrators harrassed by angry white youths in North Carolina, 1960. Above: MLK and wife Coretta lead march in Selma, Alabama, March 1965.

INJUSTICE REMAINS

When Dr. King returned from India, he felt more strongly than ever that nonviolent resistance was the best possible means of bringing about social change. In 1960, he and his family returned to Atlanta where he assisted his father in the pulpit of Ebenezer Baptist Church. With renewed vigor, he spoke at church services and rallies all over the country. As president of the Southern Christian Leadership Council (SCLC), he continued to direct the staging of bus boycotts in cities throughout the South. Yes, the message of the need for social equality had caught on, but the tone of the movement began to change. Young people, both blacks and whites, were beginning to force confrontation by directly disobeying unjust laws through actions such as sit-ins and the "Freedom Rides." This drew violence from those who disagreed with racial equality.

The day finally came when Martin

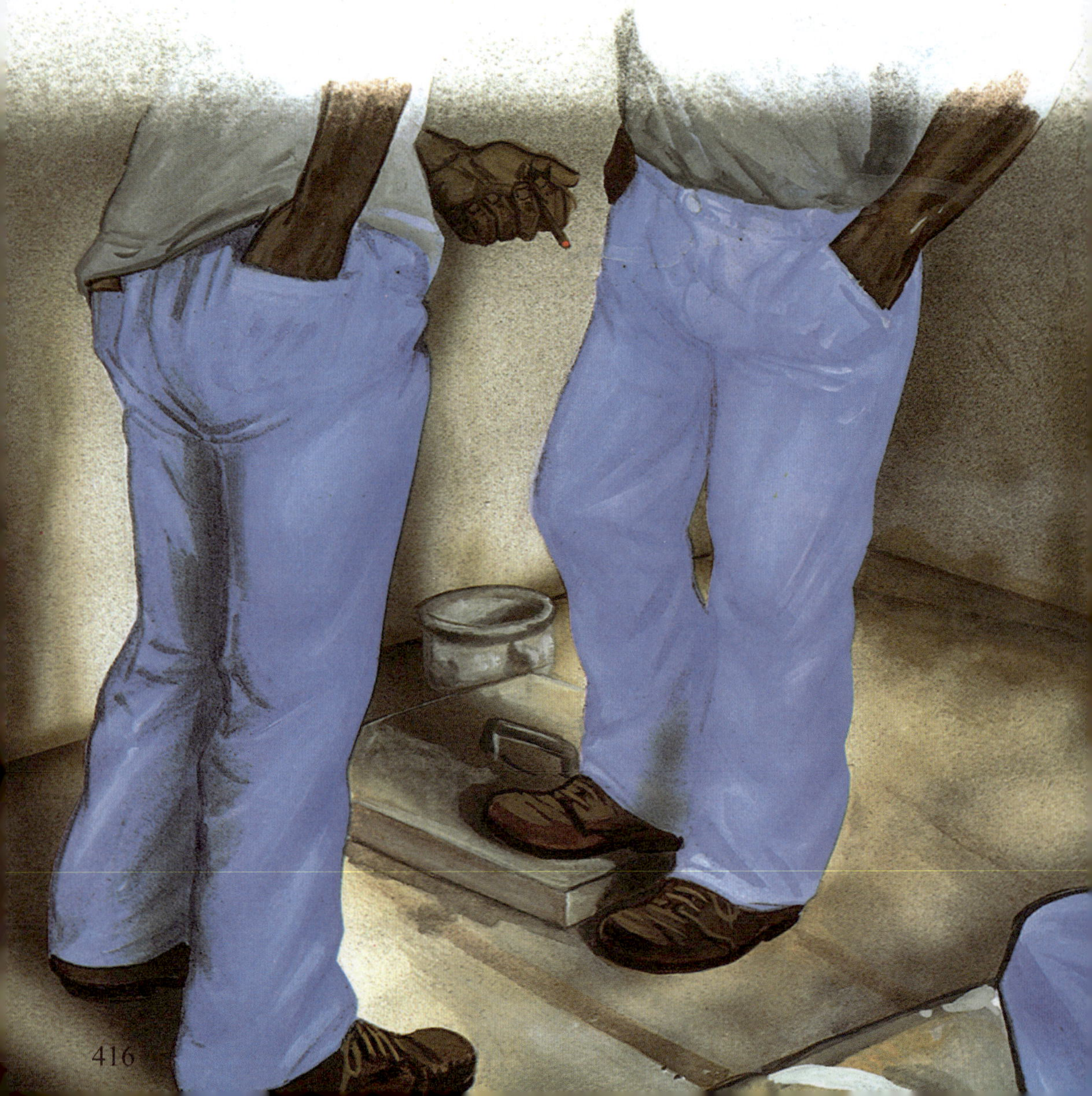

was arrested and thrown into jail. Martin's father found the phone number of the judge and called him right away. "Judge Mitchell, this is Reverend Martin King, Sr. I understand that you have seen my son this evening."

"Why Dr. King, it seems your son didn't transfer his driver's license from Alabama to Georgia. Shame, shame."

"Surely, you cannot expect to hold and convict him on something as insignificant as a traffic charge."

"I've sentenced your precious son to four months at hard labor. Maybe some time in chains will teach him his place."

News of Dr. King's arrest traveled fast. His father contacted a prominent Atlanta attorney who had political connections and soon the White House also knew what was going on. President Eisenhower and Vice-President Nixon thought it over, but decided they should not get involved. It was a state problem.

Coretta was extremely upset about the turn of events. She knew how her husband hated isolation. Besides, he

The Freedom Rides

The year was 1961. The purpose of the Freedom Rides was the desegregation of interstate buses. Martin Luther King, Jr. was the chairman of the SNCC, the group organizing these rides. White and black passengers would ride on Greyhound and Trailways buses, then get off them at stations and make a point of mixing and using the same dining room and restroom facilities.

The first Freedom Riders left Washington, D.C. and planned to travel through Virginia, North Carolina, South Carolina, Georgia, Alabama, and Mississippi. Everything went fine at first, but the deeper into the South the buses went, the more violent the white reaction grew. In Rock Hill, South Carolina, and Anniston and Birmingham, Alabama, mobs savagely beat the passengers trying to get off the buses.

Despite the opposition, change did come about because of the Freedom Rides. In November 1961, the Interstate Commerce Commission ruled against segregation on all interstate vehicles and in public facilities.

would worry about how all this was affecting her. She was pregnant with their third child. Then, just when everything seemed so hopeless, she received an unexpected call from John F. Kennedy, the senator from Massachusetts. "Mrs. King," she could hear his Boston accent clearly, "I want to express my extreme concern over the imprisonment of your husband. I am alarmed over the clear violation of law that has taken place in this case. My brother Robert, has considerable influence with Judge Mitchell. He is contacting the judge and I am sure a change is forthcoming. Our prayers are with you."

Judge Mitchell's telephone rang again. "This is Robert Kennedy." The judge's eyes grew big. "Why hasn't bail been granted in the King case? No serious crime is involved. Washington is very interested in how you are handling things there." In no time at all papers were signed ordering Dr. King's release for the very next day.

The political friends Dr. King had in John and Robert Kennedy solidified his position as national leader of the Civil Rights Movement. Martin realized that fewer than five per cent of the American black population (22 million) were actively participating in the movement. So, after John F. Kennedy was elected president of the United States, Dr. King decided it was time to take the Civil Rights Movement to all of America in a big way.

Letter From a Birmingham Jail

Martin Luther King, Jr. was arrested many times for disobeying unjust laws. One time he was arrested in Birmingham, Alabama for leading a march that had been forbidden by a court injunction. Birmingham was known as the meanest city in the South, but segregation was just as wrong there as in any other Southern city. Dr. King was thrown into solitary confinement in a cell with no mattress, pillow or blanket and subjected to extremely abusive language by his jailers. He was held from Good Friday, April 12, 1963 until Easter Sunday, April 14, without being allowed to make any calls or have any visitors.

His wife Coretta, got very worried so she called President Kennedy for help. Robert Kennedy returned her call because the President was out, but he assured her that her husband was all right. The next day, the President himself called her to say that he had talked personally with officials in Birmingham. He assured her that she would soon receive a call from her husband.

Dr. King wondered why the guards changed and suddenly became so polite. When they allowed him to call his wife, he found out that she had requested and received help directly from President Kennedy. He asked her to let everyone know that the president was watching Birmingham. Then he set about to put his time to good use.

While in jail, he wrote a 6,400-word essay that has become known as the famous "Letter from Birmingham Jail." The following is an excerpt from that letter:

"One may well ask, 'How can you advocate breaking some laws and obeying others?' The answer lies in the fact that there are two types of laws: just and unjust. I would be the first to advocate obeying just laws. One has not only a legal, but a moral responsibility to obey just laws. Conversely, one has a moral responsibility to disobey unjust laws. . . . Oppressed people cannot remain oppressed forever. The urge for freedom will eventually come. This is what happened to the American Negro. Something within has reminded him of his birthright of freedom; something without has reminded him that he can gain it."

"I HAVE A DREAM"

By 1963, Martin and Coretta had four children, Yolanda Denise, Martin III, Dexter Scott, and Bernice. The couple taught their children to love Jesus just as their parents had taught them. In light of the life they led as the family of Martin Luther King, Jr., they had more than their share of opportunities to put the truth of the Bible to the test.

One night Martin could see there was something bothering his oldest son, Martin III. When he asked the boy what was the matter, tears began to flow down little Martin's cheeks. He blurted his answer in a way that shocked everyone around the table. "I don't understand! You tell Negroes not to fight back. But I've seen the mobs and the police on T.V. They beat the Freedom Riders and turn fire hoses full force on peaceful marchers. How can I bless those people? They hate us. And it looks like they'll never change."

Dr. King stayed calm. He understood his son's frustration. He had felt the same when he was a boy. "Times are changing, son. It takes time, but little by little, our persistence upon that which is right and true, is breaking down the walls of separation. Things are better for me than they were for my father. I'm involved in this struggle because I want America to be an even better place for you. Hating our enemies makes us just like them. God knew what He was talking about. Blessing our enemies beats them with a weapon stronger than any other – love. Do you understand now, son?"

Martin III ran around the table to hug his father. That night, Dr. King was preparing his speech to be delivered at the long-planned "March on Washington." He may have had conversations with his children like the one above in mind when he wrote the following section of his famous "I Have a Dream" speech:

"I have a dream my four little children will one day live in a nation where they will not be judged by the color of their skin, but by the content of their character. I have a dream today! . . . And when we allow freedom to ring, when we let it ring from every village and hamlet, from every state and city, we will be able to speed up that day when all of God's children – black men and white men, Jews and Gentiles, Protestants and Catholics – will be able to join hands and to sing in the words of the old Negro spiritual, 'Free at last, free at last; thank God Almighty, we're free at last.'"

The March on Washington

Back in 1941 A. Philip Randolph had had a vision of a massive, nonviolent, dignified parade marching through the nation's capital in favor of civil rights. That parade never materialized, but on August 28, 1963, nearly 250,000 people – all of different ethnic backgrounds, ages, and occupations – marched from the Washington Monument to the Lincoln Memorial in order to "arouse the conscience of the nation over the economic plight of the Negro."

It was a hot summer afternoon and the heat was taking its toll on the gigantic crowd. At around 3 p.m., everyone stood listening to the beautiful contralto voice of gospel singer Mahalia Jackson. After she sang "I've Been 'Buked and I've Been Scorned," the crowd turned its attention to 74-year-old A. Philip Randolph. He introduced Dr. Martin Luther King, Jr. as "the moral leader of the nation."

The speech Dr. King delivered on that day was not very long, but what it lacked in length it made up for in power. Although Dr. King's dream would not be fully realized for many years, history will never be able to forget the movement or the man who stated so eloquently, "I have a dream today!"

The "I Have a Dream Speech."

Significant Court and Congressional Acts

Important Dates

1956
U.S. District and Supreme Court rule that segregation on city bus lines is unconstitutional.

1960 Civil Rights Act calls for:
1. Penalties for obstructing school desegregation orders.
2. Preservation of voting records.
3. Strengthening civil rights act of 1957.

1964 Civil Rights Act calls for:
1. Equal access to public accommodations.
2. Desegregation of public facilities and schools.
3. Equal employment.
4. Nondiscrimination in federally assisted programs.

1965
Voting Rights Act authorizes federal examiners to register black voters at the state level.

1966
Civil Rights Bill bans racial discrimination in the sale and/or rental of housing.

1968
Civil Rights Act places a federal ban on housing discrimination

President Lyndon B. Johnson signs Civil Rights Act, July 2, 1964. Luther King, Jr. is standing behind the president.

THE NOBEL PEACE PRIZE

The March on Washington was an overwhelming success. It alerted the entire nation to the plight of blacks in the South, and to the unjust laws and attitudes against blacks all over the country. The wheels of the legislative process were turning to get a sweeping Civil Rights Bill passed and added to the Constitution of the United States.

Then the hopes of the movement were temporarily dashed on November 22, 1963 – just three short months after the March on Washington – when President John F. Kennedy was killed by an assassin's bullet. The movement had lost a staunch ally, but Dr. King continued leading the struggle and his efforts

did not go unnoticed.

The telephone rang at the residence of Reverend King, Sr. "Hi, Dad. It's Martin." Father and son always enjoyed talking to each other. "I've been thinking. You need a vacation."

"Do I?" answered Martin's father. "And where do you propose that I go?"

"I think you and Mom would enjoy seeing Oslo, Norway."

"We don't know anybody in Oslo, Norway. Why would we want to go there? M.L., what are you up to?"

"Well, Dad, I just thought you might like to attend the ceremony where they hand out the Nobel Peace Prize. They tell me that's where I have to go to pick it up."

There was a pause on the other end of the line.

"Dad, are you still there?" Dr. King asked.

"Son, I'm so glad I lived to see this moment. I'm so proud of you."

"I knew you would be, Dad. This award is just as much yours as it is mine. You taught me how to have the dream. Will you go? Tell Christine and A.D. The children will stay home, but I want the rest of my family with me."

So on December 10, 1964, Dr. Martin Luther King, Jr. received the Nobel Peace Prize for his efforts towards racial peace and unity.

Notable American Nobel Prize Laureates

1906 Theodore Roosevelt (honored for bringing Russo-Japanese war to an end).
1919 Woodrow Wilson (establishment of League of Nations).
1925 Charles Dawes (helped readmit Germany into European fraternity; healing after the war).
1931 Nicholas Murray Butler (fighting to make the world safe for democracy).
1946 John R. Mott (organized Christian Student Union and Intercollegiate Young Men's Christian Association (YMCA)).
1950 Ralph J. Bunche (negotiation between Israel and four Arab neighbors).
1962 Linus Carl Pauling (work against atomic warfare).
1964 Martin Luther King, Jr. (fight for Civil Rights for American blacks).

THE LAST FOUR, HARD YEARS

When they returned from Oslo, Coretta said to Martin, "You know Martin, the Nobel Peace Prize is the most significant recognition you have received for your work. Things might get easier for us now. After all, the whole world knows about the movement now."

But it was not to be. The next four years were as full of turmoil as they were triumphs. Events seemed to unfold so rapidly that it was hard to keep up with them.

February 21, 1965: Just two months after Dr. King received the Nobel Peace Prize, a prominent black leader, Malcolm X, was shot and killed.

March 7, 1965: Two weeks after Malcolm X's assassination, a situation that had been brewing in Selma, Alabama came to a head. The Student Nonviolent Coordinating Committee (SNCC) had been making progress in registering black voters, but police had been called in with guard dogs to force marchers and their children away from the steps of the capitol building.

August 6, 1965: The Voting Rights Bill was signed into law.

August 11, 1965: The Watts section of Los Angeles, California, erupted in riots. Martin said to Coretta that night, "I was afraid it would come to this. Once a people have learned to see injustice for what it really is, they can tolerate it only so long. Racial hatred is breaking this country apart. Will the country have to be literally burned to the ground before it can be rebuilt into somewhere worthwhile to live?"

Summer 1966: Riots were breaking out in various cities across America. The movement was being met with stringent opposition, especially in all-white neighborhoods. Dr. King still felt the nonviolent approach could win out over the violence exploding all around him. He took on the Chicago slum problem by moving into a slum apartment to publicize the plight of blacks in urban centers around the country.

By 1967, Dr. King was speaking out against the war in Vietnam. His nonviolent stand was not something he checked at the border, and this cost him the support of the administration under President Lyndon Johnson.

April 1968: The sanitation workers in Memphis, Tennessee, went on strike because of low pay and other unfair conditions. Most of the sanitation workers in the city were black, and since the city was ignoring their demands, they called on Dr. King. Despite his heavy schedule, he felt the need to answer their call. It was the last aid he would ever give.

LOOKING BACK - LOOKING AHEAD

In his book Daddy King, Reverend King, Sr. remembers April 4, 1968: "We went upstairs to my study and I turned on the radio. The newscaster had a final, somber bulletin: Martin Luther King, Jr. had been shot to death while standing on a balcony at the Lorraine Motel in Memphis. I turned to Bunch (Mrs. King, Sr.). Neither of us could say anything. Suddenly, in a few seconds of radio time, it was over. My first son, whose birth had brought me such joy that I jumped up in the hall outside the

room where he was born and touched the ceiling – the child, the scholar, the preacher, the boy singing and smiling, the son – all of it was gone."

Dr. Benjamin Mays had challenged and taught the young Martin Luther King, Jr. while he was a student at Morehouse. He remembers Martin's intensity. He stayed in contact with Martin throughout his life and recalls:

"Segregation went unchallenged until 1955. King went to Montgomery to relax and finish his Ph.D. dissertation. One week after he mailed it in, Rosa Parks sat down in the front of the bus. King was destined to lead a great movement. He once said, 'You are God's children and every man from a bass black to a treble white is significant on God's keyboard.' Martin devoted his life to bringing about the recognition of the significance of the American Negro. . . . It's the teachings of Jesus; right there in the New Testament. . . . We've preached it and talked about it for a long time. But it was talk and no action. He made it walk on the ground."

And walk they did.

Significant Marches, Boycotts, Campaigns and Movements

The Montgomery Bus Boycott. Began December 5, 1955 and lasted over a year.

Prayer Pilgrimage in Washington 1957.

Interracial Youth March 1958. Dramatized support for school integration.

Student sit-ins 1960. Student Nonviolent Coordinating Committee (SNCC) staged protests across the South.

Freedom Rides. Began May 4, 1961 for the purpose of desegregating interstate buses and terminals.

Birmingham Movement 1963. Dr. King jailed; wrote "Letter from Birmingham Jail."

The Children's Crusade 1963.

March on Washington 1963. Dr. King delivered famous "I Have a Dream" speech.

St. Augustine campaign 1964. Focused on the issue of states' rights.

Mississippi Freedom Summer 1964. Students focused on lack of opportunities and justice in Deep South states.

Selma Campaign 1965. Voter registration drive.

Bloody Sunday 1965. Turning point when many from all races joined Freedom Movement.

March from Selma to Montgomery 1965.

Chicago Movement 1966. Called attention to conditions in city ghettos.

Poor People's March 1967. Highlighted need for jobs and freedom among black and white poor people.

Memphis 1968. Striking sanitation workers needed help.

On Monday, April 8, 1968, the nonviolent march that Dr. King had planned was held as scheduled with Coretta Scott King, the slain leader's wife, walking in her husband's place. The next day, hundreds of thousands of mourners followed Dr. King's body as it was carried through the streets of Atlanta on a mule-drawn farm wagon. Mrs. King

chose to honor him in this way because he had represented the simple, common people during his life.

The bullet fired from the rifle of James Earl Ray may have ended the life of Dr. Martin Luther King, Jr., but it could not snuff out his dream. Thousands of people continued the struggle to ensure that blacks continued to receive their rights. Hundreds of schools, buildings, streets, and parks across America were renamed in his honor. And although it took eighteen years, on January 15, 1986, Dr. King's birthday was declared a national holiday – America's first official national holiday in honor of a black American. Dr. Martin Luther King, Jr., a great man, a great American, a great Christian.

Main Events in Luther King's Life

1929 MLK born January 15.

1944 MLK enters Morehouse College, age 15.

1948 MLK ordained a Baptist minister.

1951 MLK graduates from Crozer.

1953 MLK marries Coretta Scott, June 18.

1954 MLK installed as pastor of Dexter Avenue Baptist Church.

1955 MLK gets his Ph.D. in systematic theology from Boston University.

1955 Yolanda King born Nov. 17.

1955 Rosa Parks arrested for violating Montgomery's bus segregation ordinance, Dec. 1.

1955 Montgomery Bus Boycott begins, Dec. 5.

1956 Federal and Supreme courts rule bus segregation is unconstitutional.

1957 SCLC formed, Feb. 14.

1957 MLK III born, Oct. 23.

1958 MLK's 'Stride Toward Freedom' published, Sept. 17.

1958 MLK stabbed in Harlem, Dec. 19.

1959 MLK's trip to India.

1960 MLK becomes co-pastor at Ebenezer Baptist Church, Jan.

1961 Dexter King born, Jan. 30.

1961 Freedom Rides bagin, Mar.

1963 Bernice King born, Mar.28.

1963 MLK writes "Letter from a Birmingham Jail."

1963 March on Washington; "I Have a Dream" speech, Aug. 28.

1964 MLK awarded Nobel Peace Prize in Oslo, Dec. 10.

1965 MLK leads Selma-to-Montgomery march, urges marchers to turn back, Mar. 9.

1965 Voting Rights Bill signed into law, Aug. 6.

1966 MLK moves into a slum apartment in Chicago.

1967 MLK first denounces Vietnam War.

1968 MLK leads a demonstration in Memphis that turns violent, Mar. 28.

1968 MLK's `Mountaintop' speech in Memphis, Apr. 3.

1968 MLK assassinated in Memphis, Apr. 4.

1968 MLK's funeral, Apr. 9.

1986 Dr. King's birthday officially celebrated as a national holiday (first holiday in US to honor a Black American).

Saint Augustine

BISHOP OF HIPPO
FATHER OF THE CHURCH

354 —430

Great men and women are not in need of our praise.
We are the ones in need of getting to know them.

By Ben Alex

Illustrations by Giuseppe Rava

OUTSKIRTS OF AN EMPIRE

The white houses shone in the morning sun. The town of Tagaste, nestled on a plateau between three cone-shaped mountain peaks under the soft blue sky of northern Africa, was waking up to another busy market day. Farmers and merchants with loaded donkeys and wagons were already crowding the country roads, eager to find good spots for their booths and merchandise.

The year was 368 A.D. Tagaste (modern-day Souk Ahras in Algeria) was part of the great Roman empire that stretched from Rome across most of Europe and Asia Minor, extending through Syria and what was then Palestine, into Africa.

Located on the outskirts of the empire, Tagaste could enjoy the best of both worlds: the natural abundance and political independence of Mediterranean Africa, and the protection, pleasures and rich culture belonging to a Roman province. The city market was crowded with cattle from the mountain regions. There was wheat, wine and olives from the surrounding hills and plains, vegetables from the irrigated fields, fruit from plentiful orchards, and dates from the Saharan regions to the south. The streets were paved in mosaic tiles and decorated with marble statues of gods, emperors, famous poets and philosophers. There were Roman baths, fountains, and aqueducts. There was even a modern theater, a library and a forum. Tagaste was a beautiful and prosperous city.

Idyllic scenes from the Roman Empire (4th-5th century mosaic).

Pax Romana and t

Augustine was born in Tagaste in 354 A.D. At that time the Roman empire with its more than sixty million people was in decline. The empire was struggling to hold onto its power and faced a severe leadership crisis. The original empire had been split into eastern and western sections. There were many different emperors in a short period of time (in the year 307 A.D. alone there were six different emperors). The Senate had partly lost its power to army generals. The population was groaning under the pressure of increased taxes and barbarians were threatening to invade an empire too large for all its borders to be patrolled (over two-and-a-half million square miles).

When the Roman empire was strongest, it was one of the greatest civilizations the world had ever seen. The empire recognized the right of holding

Christian Church

property, and its juridical system and ideals of justice were unparalleled in history. The Romans also had superb systems of health and education, including universities. The empire consisted of thriving industries and cities, a vast network of roads, as well as sewage, irrigation, and heating systems. Trees were planted by the millions, and vast areas of land were cultivated. In addition to all of this, the Roman empire also contributed its Latin language and scientific and philosophical knowledge to the world.

In 312 A.D., Emperor Constantine the Great renounced pagan Roman religions by declaring the Christian faith the official state religion. Constantine soon incorporated the formerly struggling and persecuted Church into the State organization and increased the power of the bishops. But as the Church grew outwardly in power and popularity, it became weaker inwardly due to strife, schisms and heresies (Manichaeism, Donatism and Arianism). Only through bishop synods like the Councils of Antioch and Nicaea (325 A.D.), Constantinople (381 A.D.), Ephesus (431 A.D.) and Chalcedon (451 A.D.) did the Church survive, and the constitution and dogmatic foundation of the Church become established.

Augustine, more than any other individual, helped define the Christian faith within the Church as it is outlined in the New Testament.

Augustine teaches his new-found faith to friends and disciples.

MONICA AND PATRICIUS

Located just outside Tagaste, along the paved road between Hippo Regius and Cirta, was the family farm of Patricius Herculus, Augustine's father. The house itself was simple, built of uncut stones piled on top of each other. Irrigation ditches crisscrossed the surrounding groves and wheat fields. Patricius was a **possessor mediocris** – owner of a small amount of land and a few slaves – and even though he was a descendent of the Berbers who had lived here long before the Romans invaded and turned Numidia into a Roman province, he had recently been granted Roman citizenship with the right to wear the Roman toga instead of the short tunic worn by slaves and common people. He was proud to be a free Roman citizen, and wanted to be just like his wealthy neighbor Romanianus, who lived in the marble palace on the hill above his fields.

But Patricius was not wealthy. Neither was he popular like Romanianus, who was always greeted with reverence by people whenever they passed him in his curtained litter or whenever he took his seat in the theater or at the games. In addition to tending his farm, Patricius was also responsible for the collection of the **annones** – the tax money collected by the government to pay its officials and mercenary armies. Tax collectors like Patricius were generally disliked – especially during the harsh rule of Emperor Constantius II.

Patricius and his wife Monica were as different as night and day. Not only was Monica nearly twenty-five years younger than her husband – she was also a committed Christian. She wanted to give their three children a strict Christian upbringing, and she hoped her faith would eventually rub off on her husband, who still preferred to worship the pagan gods.

Monica was a good and able wife, though, and Patricius admired her. She loved the children, especially Aurelius Augustinus, their fourteen-year-old son who was very intelligent. Augustinus' teacher in Tagaste had recommended he continue his studies in nearby Madaura. Now Augustinus was home on his first free weekend, and Monica was determined to feed him well.

MONICA'S PRAYERS

"Tell us about school, son!" said Patricius at the breakfast table.

"It's very good, sir," answered Augustine as he gulped down his mother's homemade bread. "I really enjoy my new teachers. They're not tyrants or 'executioners' like the grammarians here in Tagaste. They treat us with respect and don't beat us, even when we play jokes on them."

"I certainly hope you and your friend Licentius behave," interrupted Monica harshly. "If it weren't for Licentius' father, you wouldn't be able to continue school at all."

Licentius was the son of their wealthy neighbor, Romanianus. Romanianus had early on discovered Augustine's superior intelligence. He hoped it would be to his own son's advantage if the boys studied together, so Romanianus had offered to help pay for Augustine's education. That way the boys could room together and Licentius might learn more.

"Oh Monica, they're young," grinned Patricius. "Don't you be too hard on them."

"And don't you make excuses, Patricius!" retorted Monica. Then she turned to Augustine and added softly, "I'm so worried sometimes that you'll get in some kind of trouble. Madaura is such a corrupt city with all kinds of parties and orgies. I pray to God every day that He would protect you from the pleasures of the world and lead you to the door of the Church."

The Ladder of Education

Relief showing a school scene from the 4th century

Augustine's brilliant mind and ability to speak eloquently were discovered and nurtured early on by his teacher in Madaura. There he eagerly studied both the Latin and Greek authors and playwrights in the four classic disciplines: **lectio** (reading aloud, the art of diction), **ennaratio** (interpretation and the meaning of the text), **emendatio** (evaluation of the text, grammar and literary style), and **judicium** (overall critique and conclusion). Augustine quickly excelled, and by the time he was sixteen he was so far ahead of his teacher that he embarrassed him with the questions he asked. It was time to move on to higher studies in Carthage, the closest to a full Roman education anyone could get in Africa. Augustine was extremely talented. He had the makings of a philosopher and rhetorician (public speaker) and might well become a successful lawyer, teacher or politician, or even rise to become a senator! But first he had to climb the ladder of education.

A teacher in Madaura once explained the educational system this way, "The first work is done by the teacher who begins to polish the roughness of the boy's mind. Then comes the grammarian who lays down a groundwork in various subjects. Finally it is the turn of the rhetorician who places in his hand the weapon of eloquence." Augustine had long surpassed his teacher in Tagaste and his grammarian in Madaura. Now it was time to learn the rhetorics of Carthage.

The elderly Augustine writing **The City of God**

STOLEN PEARS

Augustine was a lively teenager with dark, curly hair and quick black eyes. He was not so willing to be influenced by his mother's fervent prayers. On the same evening after his mother had warned him at breakfast, Augustine was heading off with a group of loud, noisy boys, when they spotted a pear tree on a neighbor's property.

"Let's see how many pears we can steal without being caught!" joked Augustine.

"Yuk," said Licentius, as he threw a pear into the nearby pigsty, "these pears taste bad."

"Let's steal them anyway," continued Augustine. "It's fun!"

In no time at all the boys had stripped the tree of its fruit and were hauling the pears away to the pigsty. There they began to throw them at the pigs. The pigs kicked and squealed. The boys grinned and kept throwing until there were no more pears. Then they took off and disappeared down the road, looking for more trouble.

"MISTRESS OF THE SEA"

Augustine was sixteen when he arrived in Carthage, ready for his greatest adventure yet. Carthage was the capital of the Punic province. It was called the "Queen of North Africa," the "Mistress of the Sea," and was almost as splendid and worldly as the great cities of Alexandria, Byzantium and Antioch, and Rome, of course. From Carthage it was only a night's journey by ship to the great city of Rome, just beyond the Mediterranean sea. Augustine hoped that some day he could set across the ocean and seek his fortune in the city of the gods. But first he wanted to discover the pleasures and opportunities of an education in Carthage.

It was a busy city with chariot races and gladiatorial fights in the amphitheater, comedies, tragedies and operas being played at the theater, poetry competitions, parties, carnivals and all those perfumed women in the streets. For a provincial boy like Augustine, Carthage had much to offer.

More than anything else, however, Augustine pursued the pleasures of learning. Two years after he had arrived in Carthage, Augustine had already made a name for himself. Besides studying dialectics, music, geometry, mathematics, law and the rhetorics outlined by the great Latin writer Cicero, he was also gathering a crowd of eager student followers around him. The questions they were seeking to answer formed the basis of philosophy: What is the meaning of life? Why do we suffer misfortune and pain? Where does evil come from? What is truth? Augustine, not sure of the answers himself, was searching for wisdom along with his students. "O Truth, Truth," he recalled later, "how intimately did even the very marrow of my mind sigh for you!"

BAD COMPANY

In Tagaste, Monica continued to pray for her son. She was worried that Augustine's appetite for life could get him into serious trouble. She had heard a rumor that he had joined a gang of young people who called themselves the "Wreckers." She had also learned that he had moved in with his pregnant girlfriend, the daughter of a former slave. Monica hoped that her favorite son would eventually come to his senses and turn away from his reckless life. Yet the letter which her neighbor, Augustine's patron Romanianus, had received from him that morning had given her reason for serious concern. In the letter Augustine had claimed finally to have found the answer he had been seeking – not in the Christian faith, but in a strange sect called Manichaeism. Monica spread out the letter on the table and read:

"I'm in great debt to my fellow students who introduced me to the Truth. All my questions have suddenly fallen in place, like pieces in a difficult puzzle. I read the Old Testament, but to me it seemed like nothing but cruel stories about a primitive God made up by humans with a questionable morality. I was also drawn to astrology, the relation between the position of the stars

and our life on earth. Yet it was the teachings of the Manicheans that gave me solid answers and started me on the course I now must take. I have already with some success been able to publicly refute some eloquent Christian preachers here. I feel encouraged, for even though I may not be able to reach the state of perfection in this short life, I feel confident I shall succeed in a later one."

Monica was devastated. Had she known it would be another nine years until Augustine would give up his strange ideas, she might have felt discouraged and bitter. But instead, as she bent over the letter and prayed for her favorite son, she felt hopeful he would soon join the Church and give his heart to Christ.

A BISHOP'S ADVICE

Three years later Augustine had become a master of rhetorics and obtained the title of professor in Carthage, when he suddenly decided to return to Tagaste. Monica was thrilled. Maybe this would mark her son's spiritual homecoming as well! She recalled how only two years earlier her poor Patricius had given up his pagan beliefs and been baptized to Christ minutes before he died. Now perhaps it was Augustine's turn!

But Monica was to be deeply disappointed, for not only did Augustine bring with him his uneducated mistress and their two-year-old son Adeodatus, he also carried with him his Manichaean heresy, and he was eager to win followers in his own hometown. Romanianus had already been won over. Monica refused to have anything to do with her son and went to her bishop to ask him to talk to Augustine.

"Leave him alone," advised the bishop. "All you can do is pray. I myself was once misguided by the Manichaeans, but I came to my senses by reading the Holy Scriptures. Augustine will come around, too."

"Please go visit him, Father," pleaded Monica.

"No," insisted the bishop, "your son

Young Augustine's "New Age" Religion

Manes (216–276 A.D.), the founder of the Manichaean sect, was a former Christian slave in Persia who claimed to have found the "Truth" by mixing ancient Eastern religions with Christianity. According to Manes, the universe is the battleground of two eternal kingdoms: the good kingdom of light and the evil kingdom of darkness. The earth and all material things are occupied by evil forces, and the purpose of living is to free ourselves from the bondage of evil by fighting the powers of darkness.

Only the Elected Ones, the holy men who lived according to Manes' strict teachings, can survive the battle in which Evil eventually is destroyed, together with all material things. An Elect must give up everything he has, including family, and live in poverty and humility without any desire for food or sexual and other pleasures. He must do nothing to survive since the body is considered a miserable part of the realm of Evil. All he can do is accept the food and physical protection of other people. Since life is considered a battle between Good and Evil, and mankind a platform for Evil, the human race must cease reproduction in order to speed up the victory of Good over Evil. When finally the earth and all material things are destroyed by fire, the disciples of Manes will emerge purified

will be won through your prayers and tears!"

"Then I shall weep," said Monica determined, "even if it be over his dead body!"

Augustine's Flirt With Astrology

Astrologers believe that human life is affected by the same energies which cause the sun, moon, and planets to move in their orbits. They believe they can tell a person's personality and future by calculating the exact position of the stars and planets at the moment the person was born and then interpret the person's birth map.

In Augustine's time, astrology was considered a "science," and it appealed greatly to Augustine's inquisitive and rebellious mind during the years when he was still searching for scientific truth beyond the Christian faith. He eagerly consulted astrologers and fortune-tellers. Later, in his Confessions, he recalls, "These impostors, whom they designate astrologers, I consulted without hesitation, because they used no sacrifices and invoked the aid of no spirit for their divination."

"If astrology were true," he later argues, "why don't twins then have the same destiny? Why is it that many strangers are more like them than they are like each other, despite the fact that they were conceived at the same moment and separated at birth only by a few minutes?"

Some of Augustine's friends at Carthage eventually talked him out of his "bondage of astrology." As he grew older he became convinced that man's destiny was not determined by the stars; it is shaped by the Lord of history – the Creator of both men and stars.

and with everlasting life.

Manichaeism was considered a heresy (false belief) by the early Church fathers because of its exclusive doctrines, and its denial of Christ's atoning death and resurrection. The Manichaeans started their own churches and elected their own bishops and priests.

Augustine, with his careless lifestyle, was not a great candidate for election. But the Manichaean sect also welcomed less-devoted followers – sympathizers, or "Hearers." As a Hearer, Augustine promoted Manichaeism through his public-speaking ministry. He won many disciples, among them his protector Romanianus and his close friends Licentius and Alypius, all of whom he later would have to convert back to Christianity.

Old Manichaean painting

MONICA'S DREAM

It did not take long for Augustine to settle in Tagaste with his girlfriend and little Adeodatus. Romanianus arranged for him to teach grammar, and Manichaeism on the side. The eloquent professor soon attracted a group of young people who became his ardent admirers and held him up as their role model. But Monica continued to weep bitterly for her educated son.

One night, Monica woke up from a vivid dream. She had dreamt that she was standing on a "wooden rule" when a splendid young man came walking towards her, smiling.

"Why are you weeping?" asked the young man.

"I'm weeping for my lost son," she explained.

"Be at rest," continued the man, "and notice the place around you. Where you are, your son will be also."

As Monica looked up in her dream, she saw Augustine standing on the wooden ruler beside her. Then she woke up and thanked God for the dream. It could only mean that someday Augustine would be converted to the Christian faith.

The next day she arranged to meet with her son in the street. She told him eagerly about her dream. But Augustine only smiled at her and said, "Mother, it's obvious that your dream means you'll become a Manichaean!"

"No," cried Monica, "the man in the dream told me that where I was you would be! And I'm a Christian, not a Manichaean!"

Without replying, Augustine turned around and disappeared in the crowd.

A FRIEND'S DEATH

A few days later, Augustine was sitting at the deathbed of an old friend whom he had recently converted to the Manichaean faith. They had often joked about the simple Christians who believed in stories and fables; they had even mocked the Church.

Now the friend had fallen into a coma, and a priest had been summoned. Augustine could not believe his own eyes when the priest proceeded to baptize the dying young man. Without his friend even knowing about it, this priest was dragging him right into the

arms of the very Church he so disdained!

Augustine's friend recovered miraculously. Several hours later, though, when Augustine joked about the baptism, his friend sat up in bed and stared at him with a horrified look. He looked almost as if he were facing an enemy, and exclaimed, "This is no laughing matter! My baptism was real!"

Augustine was shaken. And two weeks later, when the friend suddenly did die, the arrogant Manichaean was shaken even more. Augustine began to reexamine his attitude and beliefs.

FAUSTUS FAILS TO GIVE AN ANSWER

Tagaste was too far from Carthage for an aspiring professor of rhetorics, and too close to Monica. After a few months, twenty-two-year-old Augustine decided to return with his family to Carthage to teach, and to think about his future.

Monica followed after him – impatiently waiting for her son to become a Christian and give up his girlfriend. In Monica's view, a plain girl like Modesta would only hinder a man like Augustine.

Augustine set up a "word shop" in the African capital, but he grew more and more restless and disillusioned because he felt he was cheapening his profession by selling "tricks," rather than truth. Besides, his Manichaean faith was slowly unraveling, and it became even more uncertain when the prominent Manichaean bishop Faustus arrived in Carthage.

Augustine had been looking forward to meeting the charming and eloquent bishop. He had some pressing questions that demanded real answers, and he thought Faustus must be the man to ask. But Faustus proved to be uninformed about the subjects in which Augustine had expected him to be an expert. Augustine went home disappointed, his faith severely weakened. "The keen interest which I had had in Manichaean doctrines," said Augustine later, "was checked by this experience. Unwittingly and without intent, Faustus who had been a deadly snare to many, now began to release me from the trap."

ROADS TO ROME

Augustine needed a change. A professorship in the eternal city of Rome on the other side of the Mediterranean seemed like a good idea. Rome paid its professors more money, and the students there were said to be quieter and better behaved than the reckless youth of Carthage who "come blustering into the lecture room like a gang of maniacs and upset the orderly arrangements which the master has made in advance in the interest of his pupils."

Also, Augustine needed to be free of his domineering mother who watched his spiritual development with hyena-like tenacity.

One memorable evening in 383 A.D., Augustine packed a few belongings and kissed Modesta and Adeodatus goodbye.

"I'll send for you as soon as I'm settled in Rome," he promised. Then he headed for the waiting ship.

But Monica got wind of her son's plans and hurried to the port.

"Please come back," she cried. "Don't leave your old mother alone! But if you must go – take me with you!"

"Mother, I'm not going anywhere," lied Augustine. "I'm here to say goodbye to a friend who's going away. But there's no wind, and I'm not going home until I've seen him off. You go and spend the night at the shrine of Cyprian the Martyr. I'll see you in the morning."

While Monica was asleep and dreaming, the wind blew and filled the sails. The ship shot forward, and the shore disappeared from sight.

Augustine was finally free to pursue a career on his own.

AUGUSTINE'S BIG CHANCE

Rome, with its million-and-a-quarter inhabitants, was a city of cruel contrasts. Even though it was no longer the residence of the emperor and his imperial court, it still retained its former glory: the capitol with its white marble stairs, the forum with its columns and gilded bronze statue of Augustus, the first emperor, the magnificent colosseum with its circus games, the three thousand palaces of the wealthy upper class. Augustine could see it all from the miserable **insulae** in the African quarter where he lived: a crowded slum area of six-story apartment buildings with no heating or running water. This was both a fire trap and breeding ground for malaria and other diseases.

It was a hard year for Augustine. He was often sick and discouraged, and he missed Modesta and Adeodatus. His students may not have been as difficult as the students in Carthage, but they

did continuously transfer to new teachers in order to avoid paying their tuition. Augustine had practically no money at all.

Then came the opportunity he had been waiting for. A friend introduced him to Symmachus, the influential prefect of Rome. Symmachus had been a governor of Africa and was sympathetic to Africans. His cousin Ambrose was bishop of Milan, the city in northern Italy which housed the imperial court. Symmachus did not agree with his cousin's Christian faith, so when a new professor of rhetoric was to be appointed in Milan, a position similar to that of spokesman for the emperor, Symmachus recommended Augustine. He knew that the young Manichaean would be an unpleasant challenge to Ambrose's authority.

Augustine was appointed to the post. Immediately after getting the job, he sent for Modesta and twelve-year-old Adeodatus.

KNOCKING AT THE DOOR

Bishop Ambrose was not only a skilled administrator and politician, he was also a humble believer and a great preacher. After being installed in his new office, Augustine went to hear him preach – and was astonished at the bishop's discourse, especially the way he explained the spiritual meaning of the same Old Testament texts Augustine had earlier mocked.

Augustine grew troubled. Ambrose's preaching and manner delivered the final blow to his Manichaean faith. When he came home he wrote in his journal, "Great hope is born in me, because I have found that the doctrines of the Catholic faith are not what I thought them to be."

The following spring, when the shipping traffic on the Mediterranean reopened, Monica arrived in Milan with her eldest son Navigius, her two nephews Rusticus and Lastidianus, and Nebridius, an old friend of Augustine. They all moved in with Augustine. Monica was eager to send Modesta away and take over the household.

Perhaps it was Monica's influence, perhaps it was Ambrose's exemplary life, or maybe it was his own conscience. In any case, Augustine allowed Modesta to be sent away, after almost fifteen years of their being together. "The woman with whom I had been living," he later wrote, "was torn from my side as an obstacle to my marriage and

Bishop Ambrose

Ambrose, former prefect of northern Italy and administrator of the Roman State, was a man of great authority and courage. When he first came to Milan, commissioned to keep the peace during an episcopal election, he had no ambitions of a career in the Church. But the people of Milan chose him as their bishop, and Ambrose was baptized, ordained as a priest and consecrated bishop, all within a week. However, the imperial court still made use of him as their ambassador in negotiations with other countries.

But Ambrose was his own man, and he was not afraid to confront the government when necessary. Once, when Emperor Theodosius had massacred 7,000 people in Thessalonika as punishment for defiance of an imperial decree, Ambrose refused the emperor admission to his church when he came to receive Communion. And when Empress Justina, who favored the Arian sect, demanded two church buildings for the Arians in Milan, Ambrose refused to give in and barricaded himself and his congregation against the imperial guard inside the church. The empress and her young son, Emperor Valentinian had not expected such strong opposition from the Milanese bishop, and they eventually withdrew their troops. At this occasion, Valentinian remarked that Ambrose's power was nearly equal to his own.

Contemporary mosaic of Saint Ambrose

Ambrose's influence and authority left a great impression on Augustine. He saw embodied in the Milanese bishop the same power struggle between state and Church which he later discussed at great length in his twenty-two-volume work on the city of man and the City of God, a concept that was to influence church policy for the next thousand years.

Ambrose also composed hymns and music for the Church. He is considered the founder of Latin hymnody and rhyming stanzas for congregational singing.

this was a blow that crushed my heart to bleeding, because I loved her dearly. She went back to Africa, vowing never to give herself to any other man, and left with me the son whom she had borne me."

A marriage was arranged, probably by Monica, with a twelve-year-old daughter of a notable Milanese, upper-class family. But since girls were not allowed to marry until their fourteenth birthdays, Augustine had to wait. In the meantime he took another concubine. "I was impatient at the delay of two years which had to pass before the girl whom I had asked to marry became my wife," he confessed later, "and because I was more a slave of lust than a true lover of marriage, I took another mistress."

PLATO

A DETOUR THROUGH PLATO

Technically, Augustine was still a Manichean, primarily because he had not yet found anything else to replace it. But his quest for truth took him beyond the simple answers of Manichaeism. Then a new friend, Manlius Theodorus, a former proconsul at Carthage who had retired to his palace outside Milan, introduced Augustine to the ideas of the great Greek philosopher Plato. Plato's thoughts had recently been revived through a new translation by his interpreter, a Greek philosopher in Egypt called Plotinus. Augustine devoured Plato and Plotinus' writings. It was like entering a world in which he began to understand God and himself in a brand new way.

One day, when he was visiting with Ambrose and Simplicianus, the bishop's chief counselor, he remarked that he had discovered Plato and Plotinus' philosophy.

"Congratulations," answered Simplicianus, "those Platonist philosophers really knew God and His Word!"

Platonism, or what is today called Neoplatonism, became a stepping stone to God's Truth for the future father of the Church. He began to lose interest in a worldly career and dreamt of founding a retreat like the Egyptian monk St. Anthony, "a life of quiet, apart from the crowd," where he and his close friends could discuss faith and philosophy undisturbed. Besides, his health did not suit his profession. He was often sick and also suffered from asthma attacks which left his voice hoarse and weak.

"How about a quiet Christian convent?" suggested Monica. "I'll handle the household."

"No, Mother," answered Augustine, "just because I no longer believe in Manichaeism doesn't mean I've become a Christian."

"Someday you will be," Monica went on. "Before I depart this life I'll see you a faithful Catholic!"

A CHANGED MAN

Finally Monica's stubborn faith paid off. One beautiful autumn day, when Augustine and a close friend had been reading in the Epistles of Paul, Augustine laid the book on the table and sighed. He felt discouraged. "What's the matter with me, Alypius? I feel guilty and troubled. I wish I wasn't so obsessed with earthly pleasures. I

wish I could live a disciplined life like you. Here I am, waiting to be married, and yet I can't abstain from the pleasures of the flesh!" Then he went outside and lay down under a fig tree. For the first time in his life he was troubled enough to seriously cry out to God.

"Oh Lord," he wept, "how long will You be angry with me? Why not put an end to my uncleanness this very hour?"

As he was praying, he heard the voice of a child from a nearby house. "**Tolle lege**, take up and read," chanted the voice in Latin. The words were often sang by the children's choir at Ambrose's church.

Augustine recognized this as the voice of God. He hurried into the house, opened the Epistles of Paul to his letter to the Romans and read, "Let us behave decently, as in the daytime, not in orgies or drunkenness, not in sexual immorality and debauchery, not in dissension and jealousy. Rather, clothe yourselves with the Lord Jesus Christ, and do not think about how to gratify the desires of the sinful nature."

Suddenly a light went on in the philosopher's mind, and "all the darkness of doubt was dispelled." He realized he had been obsessed with his own sins instead of trusting in God's grace. That same moment he received Christ as his Savior. Alypius did too, and the two friends went into the house to tell Monica what had happened.

"Thank You, thank You, God!" she cried and leapt for joy. Monica's dream for her son had finally come true. Later,

Augustine expressed it this way: "God, You converted me to Yourself, so that I no longer desired a wife or placed any hope in this world but stood firmly upon the rule of faith, where You had shown me to her in a dream so many years before."

THE REFUGE AT CASSICIACUM

That same year Augustine resigned from his professorship. Then he went away to a friend's summer residence in Cassiciacum, by Lake Como under the snow-covered Alps. He needed time to rest and regain his health, and to get grounded in his Christian faith. Some of his close friends had come with him.

It was a dream come true for Augustine. For years he had been longing for a quiet community of friends with plenty of opportunity for leisure and philosophical discussions. Cassiciacum with its luxurious baths, mosaic floors and vine-covered pergolas was the perfect place.

Augustine loved the company of his friends. First there was Alypius, his closest friend and former student at Tagaste and Carthage. He had resigned his position as lawyer in Milan. Then there was his friend Nebridius, his cousins Rusticus and Lastidianus, and his students Trygetius and Licentius, the son of Romanianus; and of course his broth-

er Navigius, his son Adeodatus, now almost a teenager, and Monica who supervised the entire household. "She took care of us," Augustine wrote later, "as though she had been mother to us all, and she served us as though she had been daughter to all of us."

In the fresh winter air at Cassiciacum, Augustine began to write about his newfound faith, and he was not afraid to admit his struggles in doing so. "I began at last to serve You, God, with my pen," he noted. "The books I wrote are evidence of this, although the old air can still be sensed in them." Nevertheless, he sent the books to Romanianus in Africa in the hope that his protector would welcome the Christian faith as heartily as he had accepted Manichaeism earlier. Out of the Cassiciacum days grew a whole body of thought that was to shape the thinking of the medieval Church. The refuge in the Alps became a turning point, not only for Augustine and his friends, but also for the entire Christian Church.

THE JOURNEY HOME

The following spring Augustine was ready for baptism. He had prepared himself thoroughly through prayer and study, and by renouncing Satan and all his pleasures and mindful schemes. Augustine knew what he was doing in this. He had been blinded in his search for Truth for too long. "O Beauty so ancient and so new," he wrote, "too late have I loved You! Behold You were within me, while I was outside: it was there that I sought You, and, a deformed creature, rushed headlong upon those things of beauty which You have made. You were with me, but I was not with You. They kept me far from You, those fair things which, if they were not in You, would not exist at all."

On April 24, 387 A.D., the night before Easter Sunday, the future father of the Church was baptized in Milan by Bishop Ambrose, together with Alypius and Adeodatus. Afterwards they intended to go home to Tagaste to resume what they had started at Cassiciacum.

Their plan was to go to Ostia, the port of Rome, and board a ship for Carthage. But there were political upheavals in Italy, and they could see the journey would be too dangerous. Besides, Monica fell ill, so the travelers were forced to spend the winter in Ostia.

One evening Augustine and Monica were talking by the window that overlooked a garden on the Tiber.

"How happy I am, my son," said Monica faintly, "although I'm facing death."

"You'll be all right, Mother," said Augustine tenderly.

"Yes," answered Monica, "but first I must die. I must forget those things that are behind and stretch forward to those that are before. And I can do this with joy, for God heard my prayers for you."

"I love you, Mother," whispered Augustine.

At that tender moment, mother and son felt totally united in their faith. It was as if they were lifted beyond earthly things until they soared before the throne of God.

Nine days later Monica was dead. Augustine and his companions continued their journey home without her and arrived in Tagaste to what they assumed would be a quiet and happy life of prayer and contemplation.

FORCED INTO THE PRIESTHOOD

But tragedy struck again, and through his losses, Augustine was forced into a life of service that he had never even imagined.

First, his dear friend Nebridius died. Then, at the age of only eighteen, his son Adeodatus passed away. Within only a few years, Augustine had lost his father, Modesta, his mother, and his beloved son. With his family now gone, he was more eager than ever to set up a retreat for his extended family – his friends and fellow philosophers. But instead of studying Plato, Cicero and other classic writers, they would dedicate themselves to the study of Holy Scripture. "I came as a young man to this city," he later wrote. "I was looking for a place to set up a monastery, to live with my 'brethren.' I had given up all hope in this world."

But Augustine's plans were disrupted. The great leader's talents were needed in the troubled African Church. One

day old Valerius, the bishop of Hippo Regius on the coast, invited Augustine to come and discuss his latest book. When Augustine arrived at the Basilica of Peace in Hippo, Valerius had gathered his congregation and began to preach on the need for priests. Whether the crafty bishop had arranged this beforehand or not is unknown, but someone in the congregation recognized the famous speaker from Italy and exclaimed, "It's Augustine!" Soon everyone began to shout, "Augustine – a priest!"

It was not uncommon in the Early Church that people were forced into the priesthood. Ambrose himself had become bishop by popular acclaim, against his own will. Now Augustine was grabbed and pushed forward by the excited crowd until he stood in front of the aging bishop. Then he bowed his head and burst into tears because he did not feel worthy to be a priest, he who had earlier mocked the Church and all its priests.

AUGUSTINE VERSUS FORTUNATUS

For the next forty years, until his death in 430 A.D., Augustine lived a busy life in Hippo. Soon after his ordination as a priest, Valerius handed over most of his duties to Augustine, including preaching the sermons in church.

"To have a priest preach is against our custom," protested some of the other African bishops. "Only bishops can preach the Word of God." But Valerius insisted on giving this responsibility to Augustine, and people flocked to the Basilica of Peace to hear his sermons. And during a bishop synod in Hippo, Valerius further demonstrated his confidence in his new priest by appointing him as main speaker. Augustine chose to carefully go over the creed and teach the Church what it believed.

On another occasion, Augustine took part in a public debate with Fortunatus, a famous Manichaean teacher. The Hippo congregation had begged their eloquent priest to confront the Manichaean heresy head on. Fortunatus accepted the challenge, and the day and place were set: August 28, 392 A.D., in the hall of Sosius' public bathhouse. Referees were appointed and a curious crowd of Catholics, Manichaeans and pagans filled the hall. Augustine and Fortunatus faced each other like two boxers in a ring.

"When I was a Manichaean," began Augustine gently, "I believed Manichaeism was the truth. But now I realize it's an error. Tell me now, Fortunatus, do you think I'm wrong in this opinion? I want to hear your points."

The debate lasted for two days.

Heresies Augustine Battled Against

In the African Church there were four major controversies that threatened to divide the Catholic Church: Manichaeism which dealt with the nature of God; Arianism which dealt with the nature of Christ; Pelagianism which dealt with the nature of man; and Donatism which dealt with the nature of the Church. During his thirty years as bishop of Hippo, Augustine spent a majority of his time preaching and writing against these heresies.

Manichaeism

As a young man Augustine was a devoted follower of this sect. For details about its major doctrines, see page 446.

Arianism

The Arian controversy broke out in Egypt between Arius and his bishop during a disagreement over the theology of the Church father Origen. Arius and his followers insisted that Jesus the Son is not equal to God the Father, but subordinate. The Arian interpretation stated that Jesus should no longer be considered eternal and true God like God the Father, but that he was subject to change. Bishop Alexander opposed this since Arius' interpretation undermined the sure ground for salvation through Jesus.

Emperor Constantine called a council in Nicaea in 325 A.D., attended by over 300 bishops. The council agreed that Jesus is both true God and true man, and Arius and his followers were banished by imperial decree. Anyone who refused to deliver up Arius' books was sentenced to death.

After Constantine's death in 337 A.D., the Arian controversy flared up again. The Nicene verdict was reversed in favor of the Arians who prevailed until 381 A.D., when the Council of Constantinople finally ratified the decisions of Nicaea and reaffirmed the original creed.

Pelagianism

The Pelagian controversy helped Augustine develop his doctrine of grace. Pelagius, the founder of the movement, was a

Celtic monk who visited Rome in 400 A.D. Shocked by the Christian capital's moral decay, Pelagius began to preach the necessity for righteousness and moral virtue. The Christians in Rome responded enthusiastically, and Pelagius became a latter-day prophet whose message spread all over the Christian world.

Pelagius rejected the idea of original sin. Adam and Eve's sin in the garden of Eden, he claimed, was their own sin and not fatal for the rest of mankind. True, we sin, admitted Pelagius, but it is a matter of individual choice, and we are responsible for our own sins. The consequence of this reasoning was that we are not really in need of God's grace as long as we act responsibly and do the will of God.

Pelagius was excommunicated in 417 A.D. and the Pelagian heresy was officially condemned at the Council of Ephesus in 431 A.D., only one year after Augustine's death.

Donatism

The Donatist movement was more political than doctrinal. Since the beginning of the fourth century the Donatists (named after their bishop) had excluded themselves from the Catholic Church because they felt that the Catholic bishops had compromised the true Christian faith and betrayed the martyrs during the persecution by Emperor Diocletian (303–305 A.D.). They had a large following, especially among wealthy landowners, and in many cities there were more Donatist churches than Catholic. Ironically, the Donatists, especially the most fanatical who were called Circumcellions, would stop at nothing to harass the Catholics. They only accepted them after they were rebaptized into the "pure" Donatist church. Many Catholic leaders were brutally tortured and murdered by Donatists. Augustine himself would have been killed once, had he not avoided their ambush by taking a wrong road.

The controversy was finally settled in 410 A.D. when Emperor Honorius summoned the Catholic and Donatist bishops to Carthage. Only seven bishops from each side were allowed to speak. Augustine kept silent until the concluding moment. When he spoke, he landed the final verbal blow against the Donatists. The verdict was given: The Donatists were declared misbelievers and their churches ordered closed down.

Augustine systematically attacked Fortunatus until the noted Manichaean felt so humiliated that he had to leave the city, never to return again. Augustine had not only dealt a polemic knockout, but also the death blow to Manichaeism. The Catholics had won a victory that gave them great gains in the city. Augustine became the undisputed defender and spokesman for the Catholic faith.

Three years later, Augustine was consecrated co-bishop with Valerius. This happened despite the fact that it violated the Council of Nicaea to appoint a new bishop before the retirement of the preceding one. But Augustine's theological genius and moral leadership was recognized by everyone, even by his Donatist enemies who flocked to hear him preach, and the Catholic Church desperately needed him in its battle against the heresies threatening to split the Church. When Valerius died the following year, Augustine succeeded him as bishop of Hippo.

The oldest portrait of Augustine (6th century).

Books by Augustine

Augustine wrote more than 230 books in which he explores and defines the nature of God, Christ and man. Each book came precisely at the right moment, meeting a particular need in the Church. Augustine also wrote numerous letters and epistles, of which over two hundred have survived. Possidius, his biographer, says that Augustine dictated so many books and letters that even the most studious reader would not be able to cover them all in a single lifetime!

In his writings Augustine laid the foundations of the doctrines of God's omnipotence, of grace, and of original sin. Whenever he wanted to examine a topic he always turned to Holy Scripture to find out what it had to say. Augustine was a walking Bible encyclopedia, and in his writings he quoted the Bible 42,816 times.

A Christian at thirty-three, a priest at thirty-six, and a bishop at forty-one, the former heretic was on his way to becoming the final authority and teacher. From Hippo he spoke to the entire Christian world. "I came to this city," he humbly recalled later, "to see a friend whom I thought I could win over to God's service and who might perhaps enter our monastery. I felt quite safe since a bishop (Valerius) was in occupation of the see. But I was caught and made a priest, and once that step had been taken I was made a bishop."

Augustine at meditation. Painting by Botticelli.

A Prayer by Augustine

At some point Augustine realized it was crucial to hammer out a biblical doctrine on the Trinity, the relationship between God the Father, God the Son, and God the Holy Spirit, in order to answer the heresies of Manichaeism and Arianism. It is mainly because of Augustine's thorough work in this area (which he published in the seven-volume **On the Trinity**) that the Church has been able to understand and maintain its teaching on the nature of God. Augustine ends his work with this beautiful prayer:

"O Lord my God, my one hope, listen to me, do not let me give up seeking You for weariness, let me eagerly seek Your face always.

"Give me the strength to seek, since You have let Yourself be found, and have given us the hope of finding You more and more. You have before You my strength and my weakness; preserve the one, heal the other. You have before You my knowledge and my ignorance; receive me as I enter the door You have opened to me, open to me as I knock at the door You have closed to me. May I remember You, understand You, love You. Increase in me these three things, until you change me to perfection."

"THE BARBARIANS ARE COMING!"

Largely due to Augustine, the Catholic Church survived its enemies from within. But as the fifth century began, an even more dangerous enemy threatened to invade not only the Church, but also the empire itself.

The Romans called the Goths barbarians. The Goths fought their way into Rome, then robbed and looted the city. Now the barbarians were perched at Gibraltar in southern Spain, ready to invade Africa.

"The barbarians are coming!" warned the many refugees from Italy who were arriving in Hippo. Augustine's hometown was one of the few fortified cities in Africa.

Augustine was horrified because he foresaw the collapse of the empire and the Catholic Church. He feared that the

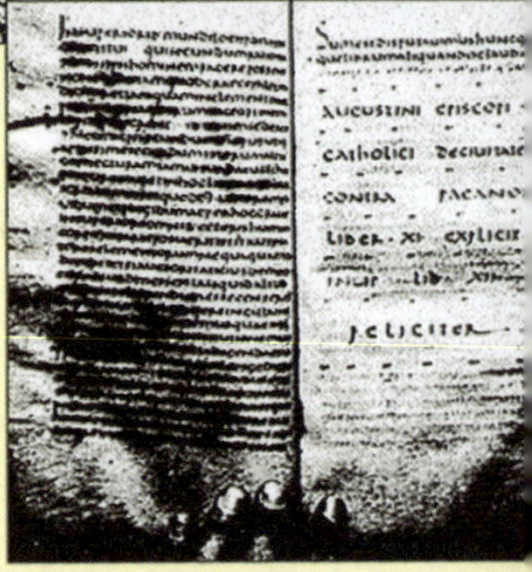

Above: A medieval artist's interpretation of the two cities (1489).
Right: The oldest known manuscript of The City of God (5th century).

world would be led back into barbarism, heresy and pagan religions. Yet he conscientiously carried out his clerical duties and set up a refugee camp for the exiles that were flooding in.

"Do not forget," he told his congregation, "that in every suffering man we must see Christ. How can we see a man dying of cold in exile? As for ourselves, we must not lose hope. I hear you say, 'The end of the world has come!' But your real life cannot be taken from you by the barbarians. Man's true lot is not to weep but to build for tomorrow."

That night, the aging bishop sat down at his desk, took a blank piece of paper and wrote across the top the title of a new book he intended to write: **The City of God.**

The City of Man and the City of God

It took Augustine more than ten years to write this twenty-two volume masterpiece. More than anything else Augustine had written so far, this work introduced a new way of thinking which the Church was badly in need of. **The City of God** would give birth to the Christian Middle Ages when knowledge, science, art and philosophy became subordinated to faith.

It was written in response to a specific historical situation: The Roman civilization had been overrun by barbarians and the Christians craved a new sense of belonging despite the pagan culture around them. Many Romans outside the Church blamed Christianity for Rome's fall. Had the empire kept its pagan religion, they claimed, Rome would have survived. Augustine answered the charges with a fresh theology of history in his **The City of God**.

The book covers an amazing range of topics, but the basic idea is the contrast between the eternal city of God (God's people down through the ages) and the city of man (the world). "These two cities," says Augustine, "were made by two loves: the earthly city by the love of self unto the contempt of God, and the heavenly city by the love of God unto the contempt of self." Since the days of Cain, who was the spiritual founder of the worldly city, and Abel, founder of the heavenly city, a rivalry has existed between the two cities. Cain murdered his brother, and since then the descendants of Cain have been out to destroy the city of God. After Noah, when the peoples were scattered all over the world, the city of man developed into the ancient civilizations in the East, then into the Greek and Roman cultures which unified the nations under common laws and ways of thinking, thus preparing the world for the coming of Christ. For now the two cities are "inextricably mixed," but at the last judgment they will be separated and clearly seen as Jerusalem and Babylon. The city of man will perish in damnation; the city of God will live on in final happiness under Christ. "Let us beg for that faith," concludes Augustine, "that hope, and that charity which are the mark of the Christian. No one will be lost who has faith and hope, no one can think he is abandoned who has faith in Jesus, since He lives within his heart. We need nothing more than faith, hope, and charity to be enlightened as to the meaning of human history. Man acts; God guides."

Bishop Augustine, painted by El Greco

Confessions
Augustine's Autobiography

Shortly after he became bishop of Hippo, Augustine wrote his most acclaimed book, Confessions. Despite Augustine's popularity, he was still being criticized by his enemies for things in his past and his former involvements with astrology and Manichaeism. Therefore he decided to put his response down on paper, in the form of a prayer to God.

Confessions is still a best-seller, a classic devotional, the first "modern" autobiography loaded with deep spiritual insights and sharp understanding of the human mind. In many ways **Confessions** is a forerunner of modern psychoanalysis. It is one man's quest for God, and in this quest we may find our own. Much of what is written in this book about Augustine's life is taken from his **Confessions**, including the pear-tree story (page 8) which Augustine used to illustrate the depraved nature of man's heart.

One of the most popular passages from **Confessions** states, "Man wants to praise You, man who is only a small portion of what You have created and who goes about carrying with him his own mortality, the evidence of his own sin and evidence that You resist the proud. Yet still man, this small portion of creation, wants to praise You. You stimulate him to take pleasure in praising You, because You have made us for Yourself, and our hearts are restless until they find their rest in You."

FEEDING THE FLOCK

As the barbarian enemy became an ever-greater threat, the old bishop gathered his congregation once and sometimes twice a day to teach them from his cathedra, the bishop's throne. Outside the door men and women who had come from far away would crowd around to hear about Augustine's God.

"I see in what crowds you've come today," he began. Then he added with a wry smile, "And you see how I'm perspiring!"

The people laughed and hooted. Then their beloved bishop spoke inti-

mately about the grace of God, and then about peace and charity.

"Now repeat after me, 'Charity from a pure heart.'"

"Charity from a pure heart!" repeated the congregation.

"Louder! I can't hear you."

"Charity from a pure heart!" they shouted.

"Good. What time is it? My goodness, I've been speaking for over two hours! I can tell by the smell in here that I've definitely preached too long. Besides, I can hear some stomachs rumbling. Go now, my dear brothers and sisters, and restore your strength. Then come back for more spiritual food! There will be another sermon tomorrow, so come with hungry maws and devout hearts. And if there are fewer people tomorrow, so much the better. Then I can give this hoarse voice of mine a well-deserved rest!"

Then the tired bishop would return to the monastery, followed by his devoted monks. He wanted to write down the sermon he had just preached, then maybe even start on a new book idea about Christian doctrine. But he would leave the door open, for he was seldom too tired or busy to help a person in need.

EMPTYING THE SEA

By the time Augustine was in his seventies, he was crippled by rheumatism and could no longer preach. He spent most of his time in his monk's cell where he was dictating his final principal work, **On Christian Doctrine.**

One day he took a walk on the beach at Hippo with his friends when they came across a little boy who was digging a hole in the sand with a cockle-shell.

"What is the boy doing?" asked Augustine.

"He's trying to empty the sea by pouring water into the hole," came the reply.

The elderly bishop stopped and watched the boy. "Impossible!" he smiled.

The boy looked up at Augustine. The bishop thought he looked like an

angel in disguise. Then the boy said, "No more impossible, Augustine, than for your limited mind to understand the mysteries of God."

The brilliant bishop knew that the boy was right. He had learned to submit his intelligence to faith – just like the child whose singing had once led him to the Word of God.

Augustine asked his friends to leave him alone in his cell during the last few days of his life. "A Christian should never leave this life without a thorough examination of his conscience," he had often said. Now it was his turn. Methodically the old man reviewed his past, moment for moment. Were his past sins too much for God? No, God had nailed every one of them to the cross of Jesus. Were his merits too many? No, Jesus had carried them, too. His brilliant mind, his many books and kind deeds, the model church and the monasteries he had established, nothing could separate him from the grace of God!

On August 28, 430 A.D., in the third year of the Vandal siege of Hippo, the dying bishop was surrounded by his friend Alypius and two other bishops. They were singing canticles. Augustine joined in for a while. Then his feeble voice died away like a burned-down candle.

Augustine died in the middle of a song.

Shortly afterwards, when the Vandals stormed the city and pillaged its treasures, it was nothing short of a miracle that the bishop's writings were not destroyed and burned.

At present, the Roman empire is gone. The old Hippo is gone. The Vandals are gone. But most of Augustine's writings remain, as well as the Church he was committed to serve.

Food for Thought

Augustine had a remarkable talent for making up paradoxes and juxtapositions from which truth could spring forth. Here are some examples from his writings:

"On His cross, Jesus healed your wounds by making them His own."

"The Son of God became a son of man so that through Him, sons of men might become the sons of God."

"It was pride that caused the fall of Lucifer and Adam. If you should ask me what are the ways to God, I would tell you that the first is humility, the second is humility, and the third is still humility. Not that there are no other precepts to give, but if humility does not precede all that we do, our efforts are fruitless."

"He who refrains from sin out of fear of chastisement is an enemy of justice."

"You think you are doing God a service when you love Him. Be not deceived. In loving God you are the one who draws the benefit."

"To live the truth is better than preaching it. Be a listener. When we are among the listeners we remain humble; when we preach, it is hard to keep a little vanity from slipping into our hearts."

5th century copy of a letter by Augustine

"Satan has no power to force us to do what is contrary to our will. He only tries to use persuasion."

"Fear no enemy than yourself. Conquer yourself and you have conquered the world."

"Our hearts are restless until they find their rest in You."

Main Events in Augustine's Life

354	13 Nov.	Born at Tagaste.
364		Separation of the two Roman empires.
365-366		School at Madaura.
370	Autumn	Studies at Carthage.
371	Autumn	Takes girlfriend in Tagaste.
372	Summer	Birth of Adeodatus.
373		Gets involved with Manichaeism.
375		Returns to Tagaste to teach rhetoric.
376		Dying friend is baptized.
381		The Council of Constantinople completes the Nicene Creed and condemns heretics.
383		Professor at Rome.
384		Professor at Milan.
385		Appointed public orator at Milan.
386		Discovers Neoplatonic philosophy. Studies Epistles of Paul. Conversion in garden. Resigns post. Retreat at Cassiciacum.
387	24 April	Baptized by Ambrose. Leaves Milan. Monica dies at Ostia.
388		Departure for Africa. Retreat at Tagaste.
389		Death of Adeodatus.
391		Ordained priest at Hippo. Monastic life.
392		Debate with Fortunatus.
396		Becomes bishop of Hippo.
397		Death of Ambrose.
401-404		Councils at Carthage.
403-412		The Donatist controversy.
410		Rome sacked by the Goths.
412-421		The Pelagian controversy.
413-426		Writes The City of God and On the Trinity.
429		The Vandals invade North Africa.
430		The Vandals besiege Hippo.
	28 August	Augustine dies at Hippo.

BOOK RESOURCES

St. Augustine, by Jacques Chabannes (Doubleday & Company, 1962).

Augustine, by Henry Chadwick (Oxford University Press, 1986).

Augustine: His Life and Thought, by Warren Thomas Smith (John Knox Press, 1980).

Saint Augustine and His Influence Through the Ages, by Henri Marrou (Harper and Brothers, 1957).

Early Christianity, by Roland H. Bainton (Van Nostrand Company, 1960).

Christian History, Issue 15, 1987: St. Augustine.